SAGE was founded in 1965 by Sara Miller McCune to support the dissemination of usable knowledge by publishing innovative and high-quality research and teaching content. Today, we publish over 900 journals, including those of more than 400 learned societies, more than 800 new books per year, and a growing range of library products including archives, data, case studies, reports, and video. SAGE remains majority-owned by our founder, and after Sara's lifetime will become owned by a charitrust that secures our continued independence.

Los Angeles | London | New Delhi | Singapore | Washington DC | Melbourne

GOVERNANCE AND MANAGEMENT OF HIGHER EDUCATION IN INDIA

India Higher Education Report

Higher education in India has experienced substantial transformation in recent decades. The expansion and massification of the sector is a major change, and it is posing challenges to several aspects of higher education development in India. The challenges relate to equity and inclusion, teaching–learning and quality, reliance on public resources and the privatization process, employability of university graduates, and managing and expanding a diversified system.

The India Higher Education Report (IHER) is a series started in 2015 by the Centre for Policy Research in Higher Education (CPRHE) of the National University of Educational Planning and Administration. The IHER series is envisaged to provide a holistic picture of higher education by highlighting various aspects and dimensions of growth and development in the sector. It brings out a collection of scholarly articles written by those engaged with research, policy and planning in the area of higher education.

The first IHER 2015 was comprehensive and touched on all aspects of higher education. Its subsequent issues focused on important issues such as equity, teaching–learning and quality, and financing, and the current volume focuses on governance and management. One of the success points of the series is the centre's capacity to mobilize eminent scholars to contribute to each of the volume in the series. IHER is an annual publication and serves as a good reference document for researchers and policymakers in India.

The volume on equity (IHER 2016) examined issues related to expansion of higher education; economic, social, regional and gender inequalities and their implications for education; student diversity and discrimination and the changing roles of the state; market; and private sector in a period of massification of the sector. The volume also addressed topics on learning outcomes and employment and employ-ability of higher education graduates.

The volume on teaching–learning and quality (IHER 2017) evaluated the Indian higher education system in terms of teaching, learning and quality and presented a comprehensive analysis of reforms in these domains.

The volume on financing (IHER 2018) discussed various aspects of financing in higher education in India, focusing on public and private financing and student financing in India.

The current volume (IHER 2019) examines issues of governance at the macro and institutional levels. It focuses on the role of the state and the market, regulation at the national and state levels, and accountability measures. It also looks at institutional issues of autonomy, affiliation, teacher recruitment and managing quality and excellence.

INDIA HIGHER EDUCATION REPORT

GOVERNANCE AND MANAGEMENT OF HIGHER EDUCATION IN INDIA

Edited by

N.V. Varghese • Garima Malik

Los Angeles | London | New Delhi
Singapore | Washington DC | Melbourne

First published in 2020 by

SAGE Publications India Pvt Ltd
BI/I-I Mohan Cooperative Industrial Area
Mathura Road, New Delhi 110 044, India
www.sagepub.in

SAGE Publications Inc
2455 Teller Road
Thousand Oaks, California 91320, USA

SAGE Publications Ltd
I Oliver's Yard, 55 City Road
London ECIY ISP, United Kingdom

SAGE Publications Asia-Pacific Pte Ltd
18 Cross Street #10-10/11/12
China Square Central
Singapore 048423

**National Institute of Educational
Planning and Administration
(NIEPA)**
17-B, Sri Aurobindo Marg
Opposite Adchini
New Delhi–110016

Published by Vivek Mehra for SAGE Publications India Pvt Ltd. Typeset in 10.5/13 pt Bembo by Zaza Eunice, Hosur, Tamil Nadu, India.

Library of Congress Cataloging-in-Publication Data

Names: Varghese, N.V., editor. | Malik, Garima, editor.
Title: Governance and management of higher education in India/Edited by
   N.V. Varghese, Garima Malik.
Description: New Delhi, India; Thousand Oaks: SAGE Publications India Pvt
   Ltd, 2020. | Includes bibliographical references and index.
Identifiers: LCCN 2020008436 (print) | LCCN 2020008437 (ebook) | ISBN
   9789353883188 (hardback) | ISBN 9789353883195 (epub) | ISBN
   9789353883201 (ebook)
Subjects: LCSH: Universities and colleges—India—Administration. | Higher
   education and state—India.
Classification: LCC LB2341.8.14 G673 2020 (print) | LCC LB2341.8.14
   (ebook) | DDC 378.1/010954—dc23
LC record available at https://lccn.loc.gov/2020008436
LC ebook record available at https://lccn.loc.gov/2020008437

ISBN: 978-93-5388-318-8 (HB)

SAGE Team: Rajesh Dey, Syed Husain Naqvi and Rajinder Kaur

Contents

List of Figures   xi
List of Tables   xiii
List of Abbreviations   xv
Preface   xxi
Acknowledgements   xxv

Chapter 1   Governance of Higher Education in India:
               An Introduction
               N.V. Varghese and Garima Malik   1

Part I: Governance and Management: Macro Issues

Chapter 2   State, Market and Governance
               of Higher Education
               Kuldeep Mathur   25
Chapter 3   Regulation of Higher Education in India
               Furqan Qamar   44
Chapter 4   The State Councils of
               Higher Education:
               A Case for Strengthening
               Intermediary Agencies
               I. Ramabrahmam and
               G. Umamaheswararao   71
Chapter 5   Accountability Measures to
               Improve Governance
               M. Anandakrishnan   87

Part II: Governance and Management: Institutional Issues

Chapter 6	Governance and Management of Affiliated Colleges *Mohd Muzammil*	111
Chapter 7	Management of Autonomous Colleges: A Movement from Academic Colonialism to Freedom and Democratization of Higher Education *G. D. Sharma*	131
Chapter 8	Governance and Autonomy: A Study of Central and State Universities *Garima Malik*	152
Chapter 9	Governance and Management of Higher Education at the Institutional Level: Reality, Concerns and Transmutation *Rakesh Raman*	174
Chapter 10	Managing Transition from 'State' to 'Central' University in the University of Allahabad: Issues and Challenges *Rajen Harshe*	200

Part III: Managing Quality at the Institutional Level

Chapter 11	Managing Quality and Excellence: Conceptual and Institutional Factors *Supriya Chaudhuri*	221
Chapter 12	Managing Quality and Excellence at the Institutional Level: A Study of Bharathiar University *Narayanan Annalakshmi, Rajalakshmi Bhavana and Bhuvana Esther*	247
Chapter 13	The Political Economy of Governance in Higher Education: Temporary Teachers Phenomenon *Sudhanshu Bhushan*	276

Chapter 14   Leveraging Technology to Solve the
              Pentagon Puzzle of Higher Education
              in India
              Pankaj Mittal   296
Chapter 15   Managing Student Diversity in Indian
              Higher Education Institutions:
              Achieving Academic Integration and
              Social Inclusion
              Nidhi S. Sabharwal   315

About the Editors and Contributors   345
Index   348

List of Figures

7.1   Growth of Autonomous Colleges over the Period
      1979–1985 to 2012–2018   146

9.1   Evolution of Governance and Management System   178
9.2   Faculty Perception of Its Participation
      in Decision-Making   187
9.3   Proportion of Faculty Believing That It Has 'No
      or Only Partial Autonomy in Academic,
      Financial and Administrative Matters'   189

15.1 Institutional Integration Approach:
      Five Constructs Influencing Students' Experiences   319
15.2 Mean of Marks Scored across Social Groups   327

List of Tables

3.1 Number of and Enrolment in Various
     Types of HEIs in India   48

4.1 Composition of the State Councils of
     Higher Education   79

5.1 Total Strength of Management Council/Syndicate   102

7.1 The Difference between University and
     Autonomous College   143
7.2 Distribution of Autonomous Colleges by States, 2018   144
7.3 Growth of Autonomous Colleges over the Period
     1979–1985 to 2012–2018—All India   145
7.4 Growth of Autonomous Colleges during 1979–1985 to
     2012–2018, by States   147

8.1 Governing Bodies in Sample Universities   164
8.2 Governing Bodies in Sample Colleges   165

9.1 Criteria for Effective Governance and Management   186
9.2 Percentage of Faculty Having Either No or
     Very Little Say in Deciding Teaching Processes   188
9.3 Extent to Which the Important Objective Criteria
     Are Heavily Valued in Promotions   190
9.4 Percentage of Teachers Who Felt That the System
     of Evaluation and Reward Is Either Not Developed or
     Is Underdeveloped   192

11.1 Grade Break Up of Institutions Accredited
     (As on 16 August 2018)   233

11.2 Times Higher Education Criteria   236

13.1 Position of Teachers during 2015–2016 to
     2017–2018   281
13.2 Number of Guest Lecturers in Arts and
     Science Colleges   287
13.3 Status of Teachers in Sample Colleges and
     Departments of Kashmir University   290
13.4 Different Nomenclatures and Remuneration of
     Temporary Teachers of J&K State   291

List of Abbreviations

AICTE	All India Council for Technical Education
AIIMS	All India Institutes of Medical Sciences
AISHE	All India Survey of Higher Education
AIU	Association of Indian Universities
API	Academic Performance Indicator
ARPIT	Annual Refresher Programme in Teaching
ARWU	Academic Ranking of World Universities
ASIHSS	Assistance for Strengthening of Infrastructure for Humanities and Social Sciences
ASIST	Assistance for Strengthening of Infrastructure for Science and Technology
ATC	Advanced Technology Cell
AUSU	Allahabad University Students Union
BCI	Bar Council of India
BHU	Banaras Hindu University
BU	Bharathiar University
CABE	Central Advisory Board of Education
CAS	Career Advancement Scheme
CCCC	Community College Consultancy Centre
CCH	Central Council of Homeopathy
CCI	Commissionerate of Collegiate Education
CCIM	Central Council of Indian Medicine
CETs	Common Entrance Tests
CoA	Council of Architecture
CPEPA	Centre with Potential for Excellence in Particular Areas
CPRHE	Centre for Policy Research in Higher Education
CSEs	Civil Services Examinations
CSIR	Council of Scientific and Industrial Research

CSS	Centrally Sponsored Scheme
CUs	Central Universities
DAE	Department of Atomic Energy
DCE	Directorate of Collegiate Education
DCI	Dental Council of India
DEB	Distance Education Bureau
DEC	Distance Education Council
DHEO	District Higher Education Officer
DOST	Degree Online Services Telangana
DPI	Directorate of Public Instruction
DST	Department of Science and Technology
DTH	Direct-to-Home
DUs	Deemed Universities
EC	Executive Council
EEC	Empowered Experts Committee
EFA	Education For All
EQUAM-BI	Enhancing Quality Assurance Management and Benchmarking Strategies in Indian Universities
FDP	Faculty Development Programme
GER	Gross Enrolment Ratio
GIAN	Global Initiative for Academic Networks
GoI	Government of India
HECI	Higher Education Commission of India
HEERA	Higher Education Empowerment Regulation Agency
HEFA	Higher Education Financing Agency
HEIs	Higher Education Institutions
ICAR	Indian Council for Agricultural Research
ICT	Information and Communications technology
IGNOU	Indira Gandhi National Open University
IIITs	Indian Institutes of Information Technology
IISER	Indian Institute of Science Education and Research
IIT	Indian Institute of Technology
INC	Indian Nursing Council
INIs	Institutes of National Importance

INQAAHE	International Network for Quality Assurance Agencies in Higher Education
IoEs	Institutions of Eminence
IQAC	Internal Quality Assurance Cell
IRAHE	Independent Regulatory Authority in Higher Education
ISLs	Institutes under State Legislature
IT	Isabella Thoburn
JNU	Jawaharlal Nehru University
KCG	Knowledge Consortium of Gujarat
KGMC	King George's Medical College
LEAP	Leadership for Academicians Programme
LTC	Leave travel concession
MCI	Medical Council of India
MHRD	Ministry of Human Resource Development
MIS	Management information system
MLNMC	Motilal Nehru Medical College
MOOCs	Massive open online courses
MoUs	Memoranda of understanding
MP	Member of Parliament
NAAC	National Assessment and Accreditation Council
NAPS	National Apprenticeship Promotion Scheme
NBA	National Board of Accreditation
NCERT	National Council of Educational Research and Training
NCHER	National Commission for Higher Education and Research
NCS	National Career Service
NCTE	National Council for Teacher Education
NET	National Eligibility Test
NGO	Non-governmental organization
NIEPA	National Institute of Educational Planning and Administration
NIPER	National Institute of Pharmaceutical Education and Research
NIRF	National Institutional Ranking Framework

NIT	National Institute of Technology
NKC	National Knowledge Commission
NMEICT	National Mission on Education through Information and Communication Technology
NOC	No Objection Certificate
NPE	National Policy on Education
NPM	New Public Management
NSS	National Service Scheme
NUIs	Non-university Institutions
OBCs	Other Backward Classes
OECD	Organisation for Economic Co-operation and Development
OER	Open educational resource
PCI	Pharmacy Council of India
PFSUs	Public-funded state universities
PG	Postgraduate
PPC	Policy Planning Committee
PPP	Public–private partnerships
QS	Quacquarelli Symonds
RCI	Rehabilitation Council of India
RHED	Regional Higher Education Director
RHEO	Regional Higher Education Officers
RISE	Revitalising Infrastructure and Systems in Higher Education
RMSA	Rashtriya Madhyamik Shiksha Abhiyan
RTI	Right to Information
RU	Rajasthan University
RUSA	Rashtriya Uchchatar Shiksha Abhiyan
SAAC	State Assessment and Accreditation Council
SAIs	Stand-alone institutes
SAP	Special Assistance Programme
SBPU	Savitribai Phule Pune University
SFCs	Self-financed colleges
SFPUs	Self-financed private state universities
SCHE	State Council of Higher Education
SHECs	State Higher Education Councils

SPAs	Schools of Planning and Architecture
SRNH	Swaroop Rani Nehru Hospital
SWAYAM	Study Webs of Active Learning for Young Aspiring Minds
SYLFF	Sasakawa Young Leaders Fellowship Fund
THE	Times Higher Education
TRB	Teachers Recruitment Board
UB	University of Barcelona
UG	Undergraduate
UGC	University Grants Commission
ULIs	University-level institutions
UNESCO	United Nations Educational, Scientific and Cultural Organization
UoA	University of Allahabad
UoH	University of Hyderabad
UoR	University of Rajasthan
UP	Uttar Pradesh
UPE	University with Potential for Excellence
UT	Union territory
VCI	Veterinary Council of India
VCs	Vice Chancellors

Preface

Governance is concerned with structures and processes of decision-making. Empirical evidence shows a positive association between effective governance and improved institutional performance. The governance of universities differs from that of private corporations and public sector organizations. Unlike other institutions, universities are concerned with the generation and transmission of knowledge. It is difficult to measure the quantity of knowledge produced and the quality of knowledge transmitted by higher education institutions. This makes it difficult to have objectively verifiable criteria to assess the efficiency of institutional performance and effectiveness of governance of institutions of higher education.

Universities have been known to have followed a collegial model of governance when they remained peripheral to the economic activities of the state. The state became active in the affairs of the universities when higher education institutions became central to the strategy of development, especially in the post–Second World War period. Universities became more aligned to the national strategies for developing human capital for economic development. Most universities in the world were established as public institutions with state funding. These changes led to a move from collegial models of governance to state-controlled models of governance in higher education, and it worked well when the state was financially sound and politically committed to finance higher education development.

The fiscal crisis of the 1980s combined with the policies followed during the structural adjustment regime reduced the financial capacity and commitment of the state to finance an expanding sector of higher education. The institutions relied on managerial approaches to direct institutional functioning under the framework of New Public

Management (NPM). Many governments embraced market principles of operation in public higher education institutions and promoted private sector operations in the sector. Governance structure and processes at both system and institutional levels were highly influenced by market forces. While the reforms became market friendly, markets did not always become people friendly, resulting in inequalities in access to and success in higher education.

The state enjoyed a near monopoly in the provision of higher education in India during the post-independence period. The state funding was accompanied by a good degree of autonomy in the functioning of universities since they were seen as self-governing institutions. India established intermediary bodies such as the University Grants Commission (UGC) and the All India Council for Technical Education (AICTE) to regulate the higher education sector. India has a multiplicity of regulatory bodies reflecting the nature of involvement of different ministries in the provision of higher education.

The state-funded and state-controlled model of governance did not last long when the capacity of the state to meet the increasing social demand for higher education declined drastically in the 1980s. This led to the proliferation of private colleges in the last decades of the 20th century and fast expansion of private universities in the early decades of the 21st century.

The public institutions became starved of funds, and they adopted reform measures to save cost, share cost and generate income at the institutional levels. The nature of governance structure and practices in the public institutions underwent changes whereby they became more autonomous in their functioning and less reliant on the government for funding. The government introduced a new idea of performance-based graded autonomy in institutions of higher education. Under the new framework, for purposes of granting autonomy, the institutions were divided into three categories based on their scores in institutional accreditation and position/rank in the national rankings. Category I institutions enjoy full autonomy, while category II institutions are mostly autonomous, unlike category III institutions which are subject to strict regulations and more control by the government.

The India Higher Education Report (IHER) Series initiated by the Centre for Policy Research in Higher Education (CPRHE) of the National University of Educational Planning and Administration provides an in-depth analysis of some of the critical dimensions of higher education in India, with contributions from eminent scholars, engaged in research, policy and planning in the area of higher education. The first report—IHER 2015—provided a comprehensive account of the higher education developments in India. The second report—IHER 2016—focused on issues related to equity and diversity in higher education. The third report—IHER 2017—focused on issues related to teaching–learning and quality in higher education. The fourth report—IHER 2018—focused on the financing of higher education in India.

IHER 2019 is the fifth in the series, and it focuses on governance of higher education in India. This volume also succeeded in attracting eminent scholars engaged in research and institutional heads. We are grateful to the authors of various chapters for their valuable contributions. I take this opportunity to place on record my deep appreciation of my faculty colleague at CPRHE/National Institute of Educational Planning and Administration (NIEPA) Dr Garima Malik for her sustained efforts and contribution to lead the process and all other members of the centre for their support in preparing this report.

N.V. Varghese
Vice Chancellor, NIEPA

Acknowledgements

CPRHE published the first issue in the India Higher Education Report (IHER 2015) series. We are happy to present the fifth in the series IHER 2019 titled 'Governance and Management of Higher Education in India'. It discusses various aspects of governance and management in higher education in India, focusing on the role of state, market and various regulatory structures as well as leadership and autonomy. This volume, like the previous ones, is the outcome of support received from various intellectuals and institutions and the efforts put in by CPRHE.

The volume includes chapters by some of the leading academics and policymakers in higher education. They not only contributed the chapters but also contributed substantially to shape the current volume through their extensive comments on chapters by others. We gratefully acknowledge the valuable contribution of all the authors.

We are grateful to the Registrar, NIEPA, Professor Kumar Suresh, and his team for their support in facilitating the publication process and procedures. We also thank Dr Pramod Rawat and his colleagues in the NIEPA publication department for their help at different stages.

We thank Mr Rajesh Dey, Mr Syed Husain Naqvi and the entire team at SAGE in the processing of the document for publication.

We are also grateful to all colleagues at CPRHE, including Professor Mona Khare, Dr Nidhi S. Sabharwal, Dr Jinusha Panigrahi, Dr Anupam Pachauri, Dr Malish C. M. and Dr Sayantan Mandal, for their continuous support and several rounds of comments.

Ms Chetna Chawla extended her help in preparing the final manuscript. Ms Anjali Arora, Mr Mayank Rajput and Ms Monica Joshi extended all logistics support to organize peer review meetings and contacting the authors. We gratefully acknowledge their support in preparing this volume.

N.V. Varghese
Garima Malik

Chapter 1

Governance of Higher Education in India

An Introduction

N.V. Varghese and Garima Malik

INTRODUCTION

Governance is concerned with structures and processes of decision-making to ensure improved performance and accountability of organizations. Governance at the national level involves actors such as political leadership, regulatory bodies and senior administrators. At the institutional level, governing bodies play a major role in providing guidance to institutional leaders to translate their vision into operational practice. The governing bodies help institutions set targets, prioritize allocation and re-allocation of human and financial resources, put in place accountability procedures and ensure enhanced outcomes.

The focus on governance is a newfound passion; it follows from an understanding that governance matters and makes a difference in the functioning of systems and performance of institutions. The empirical evidence shows that there exists a strong causal relationship between good governance of public institutions and development outcomes (Kaufman et al. 1999, Mulyadi et al. 2012). This evidence points to an added advantage and an urgency to focus on the effective governance and management of public institutions.

The governance of public institutions is complex primarily due to the multiplicity of actors involved in decision-making. The governance of public institutions involves engaging in complex relationships between those with primary accountability/responsibilities (Parliament and ministers), others who are engaged in the administration of the sector programmes and institutional leaders who are directly engaged with managing institutions. The governance of private sector organization is different from this pattern primarily since the role of the actors external to the institution is minimal and accountability to public bodies is limited. Further, in many private organizations, there is a widely accepted criterion of profits and profitability to measure good governance and institutional effectiveness.

University governance varies from the principles of governance practised in public sector institutions and private organizations. Universities stand for preserving the existing knowledge, generating new knowledge and transmitting the intellectual inheritance to the next generation. It is believed that an effective institutional governance help universities enhance their gains in each of these functions. However, it is very difficult to quantify the success made by universities in each of these attributes and equally difficult to produce empirical evidence to establish a link between good governance and their success in these domains.

Unlike the private sector, profitability is not considered to be an index of success of public universities. Unlike in many private and public sector undertakings, the outputs of the higher education system are vaguely defined, and quality of the product varies substantially. It is difficult to quantify the higher education product and equally difficult to specify uniformity in the quality of the products. These characteristics contributed to the evolution of vaguely defined governance structures in the universities.

Given the traditional role the universities played and vaguely defined outcomes of higher education institutions, a collegial model of governance evolved in the sector. Over a period of time and more recently due to the emphasis on the notion of value for money in the context of increasing financial constraints, the traditional collegial models of decision-making in the universities gave way to managerial approaches to direct and streamline institutional functioning under the framework of New Public Management (NPM). As the higher education context has changed, the nature, content and delivery modes of study programmes changed and stakeholders pressurized universities to transform their orientation and functions within the framework of market principles of operation. This chapter attempts to provide a brief overview of the changing orientations in the governance and management of higher education institutions globally and in India.

CHANGING MODELS OF GOVERNANCE IN HIGHER EDUCATION

Traditionally, the governance and institutional decision-making process in the universities were collegial and consensus based, and the interactions were informal. The institutional leader was elected from among the university's scholars. The professoriate welcomed this model of governance since it provided academic freedom for intellectual discourses of varying viewpoints. The freedom enjoyed by the professoriate encouraged a spirit of curiosity and tolerance to differing ideological orientations. When universities remained small entities and peripheral to the core economic activities, the collegial model and informal institutional interactions worked fairly well. The institutional mission to preserve knowledge, generate knowledge and transmit knowledge was neither monitored nor questioned. Any attempt to introduce accountability measures to manage activities and monitor performance was considered as an attack on academic freedom (Saint 2009).

This informal nature of intra-institutional relations underwent changes when government became more active in intervening in the affairs of the universities. The state played a dominant role in the post–Second World War reconstruction period in Europe. The role of universities changed, and they became active agents of change in the strategy of development. This model played an important role in designing and facilitating development in the developing countries during the post-independent period. Higher education institutions were relied on for overcoming the constraints imposed by severe shortage of qualified human resources to plan and promote development. The role of universities changed from institutions for intellectual discourses to producing human resources to promote economic and social development. In many instances, universities became core elements in the development strategies of the government (Chandra 2017).

Following the state-led model of development, universities were established in most countries as public institutions to develop national capacities to manage the economy. The state encouragement and funding were forthcoming and helped universities to expand their spheres of influence in the debates on strategies of development and their role in human capital formation to promote economic growth. The universities in turn aligned their research and teaching activities with the areas of national priority. In many instances, the national political leaders and heads of states became heads of the governing bodies in the public universities. The ministries of education played a proactive role in the appointment of the head of higher education institutions (vice chancellors/rectors).

The state enjoyed near monopoly in higher education development. Some governments viewed public universities as extensions of the public service and felt that the governments of the day should have an important say in organizing the services rendered by public universities. The increased government intervention in the affairs of the academic institutions led to a 'state control' model of higher education governance and management (Neave and van Vught 1994). State intervention was increasingly seen in the financing, managing and appointment of institutional heads. In other words, public financing and state control characterized higher education governance in many regions of the world (Varghese 2009).

The state-controlled model of higher education development had its inherent limitations. Higher education as an extension of state structure worked well when the sector remained elite and access was limited. However, the state-sponsored model acted as a constraint for the sector to expand, especially since the fiscal crisis of the 1980s which eroded the capacity of the state to finance an expanding higher education sector

(Altbach 1989). The policies followed during the structural adjustment regime in the 1980s further helped marginalize the higher education sector in public resource allocation processes. The social demand for higher education and the resultant pressure to expand the system questioned the state-controlled model of expansion of higher education. The success of education for all (EFA) programmes further increased the pressure on the system to expand.

The inability of the state to respond to the increasing social demand for higher education resulted in the privatization of the existing public institutions or opening the sector for the private sector to establish institutions or both (Varghese 2009). Privatization measures reduced state control of public institutions even when their ownership remained with the state. The private sector, on the other hand, does not rely on state funding support and represented an alternative to the state-supported model of higher education development. Public universities became more autonomous since they liberated themselves from government funding. Autonomy permitted institutions to set priorities, evolve strategies, develop study programmes and courses, recruit staff, diversify funding sources and decide on internal resource allocation criteria (Salmi 2007).

These changes redefined the relationship between the state and institutions of higher education and impacted the governance and management of institutions of higher education (Varghese 2014). The globalization processes further reinforced the market forces in higher education decision-making. The new governance models emerged in the market framework of NPM. The NPM opened the doors for market-friendly reforms and managerialism as an approach to govern and manage higher education institutions. The governance paradigm that evolved from the NPM perspectives emphasized less bureaucracy, devolved management, public–private partnerships, the development of quasi-markets and the inclusion of a range of different stakeholders (Olssen 2002, Varghese and Martin 2014).

All these changes produced a fundamental shift in the way public institutions are defined and the way delivery of public services are designed. Further, the underlying ethos of higher education as a spirit of curiosity and tolerance of differing views disappeared. Many professional for-profit organizations have entered for personal gain introducing unscrupulous practices that seem to exploit the students and the community (Mathur 2020). Some of the seemingly corrupt activities especially in student admissions and staff recruitments became acceptable practices under the market led governance regime.

Unlike public institutions, private corporations and entities are established to produce profits and are assessed on the basis of the profits they produce. The profits are expressed in measurable monetary terms. Therefore, it is easy to evaluate the success and failure of private institutions based on the profit they produce. In the absence of reliable measures to compare public and private sector entities, the profit-based assessments, very often, led to conclusions that show the inefficiency of the public institutions and efficiency of the private corporate entities. Such understanding leads to reforms to introduce corporate governance structures in public higher education institutions.

Corporate governance generally refers to the processes by which organizations are directed, controlled and held to account (IFAC 2001). There are two aspects of corporate governance: conformance and performance (Tricker 1984). Conformance consists of monitoring and supervising executive performance and maintaining accountability. Performance consists of strategy formulation and policymaking. In the private sector, more emphasis is given to conformance aspect and institutional performance in matters related to governance.

Fielden (2007) attempted to sketch the evolution of institutional governance models ranging from control to autonomy as follows: (a) state control model, (b) semi-autonomous model, (c) semi-independent model and (d) independent model. The state control and semi-autonomous model can be an agency of the government, a state-owned corporation or a statutory body. The semi-independent and independent model can be a statutory body, charity, or profit or non-profit corporation with no government participation and control linked to national strategies and related only to public funding. Fielden (2007) argued that the international trend seems to favour the increasing autonomy and corporatization of public institutions by making them independent and self-governing organizations.

Accountability in public sector governance requires established missions and goals and the widespread use of performance indicators and performance management systems, as well as enhanced forms of monitoring and reporting systems to hold the organization and its workers accountable for maximum efficiency. These key principles and arrangements have become institutionalized and now form the core of good governance in transforming public sector organizations in global contexts.

These changes fitted very well because as university systems became large and complex, governments found it impossible to directly manage and control individual institutions. The new governance model ensured redistribution responsibility, accountability, and decision-making power among external and internal stakeholders. It seems the conflicting situation is characterized by institutional governance for academic research versus research commercialization mission dominated by profit maximization and corporate principles of governance (Narayan et al. 2012).

The reforms initiated for institutional survival needed decisions to be taken at the institutional level and it implied a marked shift in governance and management of higher education institutions. The shift in the locus of decision-making from ministries of education to institutions of higher education marked the beginning of an end to the state-controlled model of higher education governance and development. Some authors consider this change as a change to a stage of steering from distance or state supervision model and the 'rise of the evaluative state' (Neave 1988).

Some others consider this as a state of increased reliance on the self-regulative capacities of the universities (Kivisto 2005). The institutions of higher education became increasingly autonomous in their functioning. The institutional autonomy included academic and administrative and financial matters. However, autonomy at this stage was without state funding. The collegial model of governance was found to be less relevant since most decisions were bound more by resources constraints than by academic considerations (Austin and Jones 2016, Bush 2003). The bureaucratic models of governance and management were found to be rule-bound and less reliable to face the emerging situation. Market and managerialism became the new global mantras and formed the basis for new governance structures and processes of decision-making in higher education.

EVOLUTION OF GOVERNANCE STRUCTURES IN HIGHER EDUCATION IN INDIA

The governance of higher education in India followed the global trends. The first universities were established in India in 1857 when the country was under the colonial rule. The functions of these universities were administrative in nature until the first decade of the 20th century. Teaching and academic interactions took place in colleges. There existed no regulatory bodies until the 1930s to provide overall guidance for governing institutions of higher education.

The post-independence period saw an increased focus on higher education more as an extension of self-reliance policy and the sector received priority in policies for human resource development. The first commission on education was on higher education and was established immediately after independence. The recommendations of the Radhakrishnan Commission (MoE 1950) laid the foundations of higher education development and establishment of regulatory bodies in higher education in India.

Indian policy on higher education development relied on promotion of public universities and institutions. Many of the private institutions were taken over by the government during the post-independence period. The state enjoyed a near monopoly in the provision of higher education in the 1950s and 1960s. The government played an important role in planning, funding and managing higher education institutions. It was a stage of state-sponsored development of higher education. However, the state funding did not imply absence of autonomy to higher education institutions in India.

The universities in India enjoyed considerable degree of academic freedom, and it was believed that academic freedom is essential to maintain and improve quality of teaching and research. This was a stage of aligning academic priorities with national compulsions of producing human resources for self-reliance in development. The harmonious coexistence between state priorities and institutional autonomy with liberal funding support defined the governance of higher education at this stage.

The trends in the 1970s disturbed the then existing harmony between the state and the higher education sector. The expanding social demand for higher education and a relative decline in the public funding created social tensions especially among the youth population. The emergence of private higher education institutions was in response to these changes. The decades of the 1970s and 1980s saw proliferation of private higher education institutions in India. The private sector emerged initially as a government-supported sector receiving grants-in-aid from the centre and state governments.

Some of the institutions of higher education experimented with introduction of self-financing courses as a strategy for diversification of sources of funding to compensate for the loss of state funding. Many institutions found that the experiment was successful and households were willing to invest in education of their children provided the institution provides study programmes which are employment friendly. Many private unaided higher education institutions especially in the domains of professional and technical education came up in the southern states of India. Given the high cost of education, these 'capitation fee colleges' provided an opportunity for children from well to do families with low academic scores.

The next stage in the development of private higher education was the emergence of private universities with authority to award degrees. The private universities were established in India from the first decade of this century. At present, a majority of higher education institutions and a larger share of enrolment in higher education in India are in the private higher education institutions.

These changes have dramatically reduced the direct control exercised by the state. The declining public funding reduced the authority enjoyed by the government in matters related to governance and management of public institutions of higher education. The public institutions were starved of funds and were compelled to mobilize their own resources from non-traditional sources. The introduction of cost saving, cost sharing and income-generating activities in institutions of higher education necessitated decisions to be taken at the institutional level. These changes helped shifts in governance structures from a state-controlled model to a state supervised model whereby institutions became more autonomous in their functioning. The state interventions became more of regulatory and supervisory in nature.

It can be argued that the privatization of public institutions reduced state control on the governance and management of public higher education institutions. The public institutions became more autonomous and diversified their sources of funding. In many instances, a reduction in student subsidies, an introduction/increase in student fees and income-generating activities such as self-financing courses and programmes are measures adopted to overcome severe resource paucity experienced by higher education institutions. It seems that the centrally funded institutions are less severely affected by resource constraints than state-funded higher education institutions.

The emergence and expansion of private higher education institutions influenced the governance and management of higher education at the macro level. Most of the private institutions established at this point of time were mostly professional and technical colleges which were popularly known as capitation fee colleges. Most of the capitation fee colleges were located in the states of Andhra Pradesh, Karnataka, Maharashtra and Tamil Nadu. Their primary motivation was to generate profit. There were several court cases related to student admissions, and very often the court orders were putting brakes on the unsatisfied thirst for excessive profits by them. These court orders acted as a good regulatory basis for their operations. While many felt that there is a need for more regulations on the private sector institutions, the managers of the private sector institutions felt that there were too many regulations on their functioning.

GOVERNANCE STRUCTURES AT THE SYSTEM LEVEL

Higher education governance in India needs to be analysed at three levels: (a) relationship between the government and higher education institutions, (b) relationship between and participation of different stakeholders within an institution and (c) relationship between universities and their affiliated colleges.

Although education is a joint responsibility of centre and state governments after the constitutional amendment of 1976, India followed a decentralized model of governance and management and regulatory arrangement at the school level and centralized model of regulation in higher education. India established regulatory bodies and buffer institutions to mediate between the government and institutions of higher education. There were regulations related to granting of permission to open and operate an institution, to decide on the intake of students and introduction of courses and to ensure equity and social justice. The central bodies enjoyed the authority to intervene in these areas (Varghese and Malik 2016).

The first regulatory body in higher education in India was the Medical Council of India (MCI) established in 1934. The MCI had the authority to lay down norms and standards, and recognize or derecognize courses and institutions. The regulatory bodies in higher education established after independence were based on the recommendations of the Radhakrishnan Commission, 1948 (MoE 1950) and include the University Grants Commission (UGC) and All India Council for Technical Education (AICTE). While the UGC is responsible for universities and general higher education, the AICTE is responsible for technical education institutions in the country. The UGC, established in 1953, became a statutory body by the Parliament 'for coordination and determination of standards in universities' in 1956. Although it is a recommendatory body, it is influential in all major decision-making in higher education.

The Ministry of Human Resource Development (MHRD) along with the regulatory bodies plays an important role in the governance of higher education at the system level in India. Unfortunately, India has a number of regulatory bodies in higher education. The multiplicity of regulatory bodies is a reflection of the involvement of several ministries in providing higher education. Most of the ministries have their own regulatory bodies at the national level.

At the state level, the ministry of education or higher education wherever it exists and Directorate of Higher Education are important players in the governance of higher education. Following the National Policy on Education (NPE) in 1986 and UGC guidelines of 1988, several state governments established State Higher Education Councils (SHECs). The SHECs are entrusted with planning and coordination, academic, advisory and administrative functions. Although only few SHECs were established in the 1990s, their number has increased in the current decade since it became mandatory to transfer funds under the newly initiated sponsored scheme Rashtriya Uchchatar Shiksha Abhiyan (RUSA) to rejuvenate higher education in India.

GOVERNANCE STRUCTURES AT THE INSTITUTIONAL LEVEL

The institutional diversity in higher education surprises many. To start with, universities had more of administrative functions and authority to award degrees. Teaching used to take place in colleges. The public universities in India are funded by the central or state governments. A majority of the public universities are in the state sector. India has a large number of affiliating colleges. Most of the central universities are not affiliating institutions with notable exceptions of Banaras Hindu University and Delhi University.

Universities are more autonomous, and they focus more on research and teaching at graduate and postgraduate levels while the colleges are more of teaching institutions mostly at the undergraduate level and are subjected to more regulations even in academic matters. Universities are responsible for developing curriculum and syllabus for study programmes which are offered in the colleges. The colleges have the authority only to transact curriculum developed by the universities except in autonomous colleges.

The vice chancellor is the chief executive in the university administration. The governance structure at the university level consists of bodies such as senate/syndicate, executive council/governing body and academic council. Some of the universities have courts. The senate is responsible mainly for financial and budgetary estimations and appropriations. The executive council or the governing body is the executive body of the university and is responsible for all management and administrative matters. The academic council is responsible mainly for study programmes and research in the university.

The composition of the senate in affiliating state universities includes the principals of affiliated colleges, making the number too large for discussions and decision-making. The syndicate wields powers and has more political clout than other bodies. The state governments put their nominees into the syndicate and at times a majority of the members may be directly or indirectly connected to the government. These factors influence the decision-making process at the institutional level and at times there is a domination by the syndicate on other bodies influencing their proceedings (Qamar 2016).

Thus, very often the syndicate in many affiliating universities is dominated by elected members and non-academics. This has important implications for how the university is run. In some universities, the ex-officio members of the syndicate include four directors: collegiate education, medical education, technical education and three secretaries from education, health and law. This leads to a large concentration of power in the syndicate, thus compromising the independence of the academic council and other statutory bodies.

The governance structure at the college level consists of government nominees, and the others are university nominees whose names are approved by the government: the principal, teachers from the university and from the college. The governing body of the colleges meets once/ twice in a year in order to discuss various issues and aspects related to the development of the college and its academic standards. As discussed earlier, the teachers in the government colleges are appointed by the public service commission and their accountability more is to the state-level administration than to the head of the institution.

INSTITUTIONAL AUTONOMY AND ACCOUNTABILITY

The degree of autonomy reflects the nature of relationship between government and higher education institutions, governance structures and level of participation in decision-making define the extent of decentralization at the institutional level and the delineation of domains of decision-making indicate the nature of relationship between universities and their affiliated colleges.

The relationship between universities and the government revolves around the issues of autonomy and accountability. The state and universities are constantly engaged in redefining their mutual relationship, with the state introducing more and more accountability measures, on the one hand, and universities demanding more autonomy, on the other hand. Universities in India were seen as autonomous entities from the very beginning. Committees and commissions in India, starting with the Radhakrishnan Commission of 1948, emphasized on the importance of universities to be self-governing organizations and free them from interference by the government.

The subsequent commission (Kothari Commission report of 1966) also underlined the importance of institutional autonomy (GOI 1966). So also the UGC Committee on university governance in 1968. The Gnanam committee report asked for greater autonomy of universities from the government and participation of teachers and students in managing the universities (UGC 1990). The government appointed a Central Advisory Board of Education (CABE) Committee on university autonomy (MHRD 2005), which also upheld the importance of autonomy for institutions of higher education. The committees in the recent period too argued for increased institutional autonomy.

University autonomy can be either substantive or procedural. Substantive autonomy gives institutions authority to take decisions and operate with regard to their own goals and programme matters. However, procedural autonomy implies freedom regarding administrative and financial matters. Substantive autonomy includes the freedom to design the curriculum, evolve research priorities and determine student admission policies and staff recruitment criteria and criteria for the awarding of degrees. Procedural autonomy involves the freedom to prepare and administer budget and financial administration, appoint non-academic staff, and procure and enter into a contract with others outside the institution (Raza 2009, Varghese and Malik 2019). The actual exercise of autonomy depends on the governance structure and management practices at the institutional level.

Academic autonomy is the freedom to decide academic issues such as curriculum, instructional material, pedagogy and methods of student evaluation. Universities in India enjoy considerable degree of freedom on academic matters to decide on curriculum, instructional material, pedagogy and methods of student evaluation. The colleges affiliated to universities, on the other hand, enjoy limited freedom on academic matters since most of the academic decisions are taken by the university.

The teachers in the universities of India are not civil servants. They are university employees and hence the institutions enjoy freedom and authority to recruit teachers following the guidelines provided by the UGC regarding the qualifications, salary and service conditions. The government colleges do not enjoy the autonomy to recruit teachers. The teachers in the government colleges are appointed by the public service commissions through either a written test or interview or both. They are appointed to the system and can be transferred from one institution to another. Many appear for the common competitive test to qualify for the teaching positions. They are posted to different institutions. These teachers are part of the state civil services and they are governed by the rules and regulations applicable for the state civil service (Malik 2017).

Universities, in general, enjoy limited autonomy in matters pertaining to administrative and financial issues. The resource allocation criteria and the rules governing financial management give limited scope for deviations from the established norms. Higher education institutions are starved of funds and are compelled to mobilize their own resources since the allocations may not meet even the salary expenditure of the employees. However, the government has initiated measures to give more autonomy to well-performing institutions.

The new initiative is to introduce graded autonomy in institutions of higher education based on their performance. The NITI Ayog (GOI 2017) in its agenda for development released in 2017 and with the approval of UGC introduced the notion of graded autonomy to institutions of higher education. For purposes of granting autonomy, the institutions will be divided into three categories. Universities either accredited by National Assessment and Accreditation Council (NAAC) with a score of at least 3.5 or ranked in the top 50 institutions of the National Institutions Ranking Framework (NIRF) for two consecutive years will be under 'category 1'; universities which have been accredited by NAAC with a score between 3.01 and 3.49 or ranked between 51 and 100 in the NIRF ranking will be under category 2 and all other institutions will be under category 3.

Category 1 institutions will have the autonomy to start a new course, department and school without UGC's approval. They will also be exempt from UGC's regular inspections and can collaborate with foreign educational institutions without the regulator's permission. Their performance will be reviewed based on self-reporting. The category 2 universities will be exempt from UGC's regular inspections but will need the UGC's permission to sign MoUs with foreign universities. Their performance will be reviewed by a peer group. The category 3 will be the most regulated universities with limited autonomy.

The new financing arrangements help the universities be free from dependence upon the government for finds. The Higher Education Financing Agency (HEFA) would provide financial assistance to centrally aided institutes for promotion of world-class infrastructure. It would provide the much-needed funds for premier institutions such as IITs, NITs and IIMs. It is expected that HEFA would finance the civil and lab infrastructure projects through a 10-year loan, and the principal portion of the loan will be repaid through the 'internal accruals' of the institutions.

The chapters in the book deal with different aspects related to the governance of higher education in India.

THE IHER 2019

The *India Higher Education Report 2019* focuses on the governance and management challenges of an expanding system of higher education in India. The volume has three thematic sections and the first four chapters examine macro issues of governance, the next five chapters look at institutional issues and the final five chapters discuss issues relating to managing quality at the institutional level.

Macro Issues of Governance

Kuldeep Mathur in Chapter 2, titled 'State, Market and Governance of Higher Education', focuses on how the stance of the state has shifted from being a welfare state to that guided by neoliberal policies. Educational reforms are also located in this neoliberal framework.

The next two chapters look at regulatory structures at the national and state levels. Furqan Qamar in Chapter 3, titled 'Regulation of Higher Education in India', examines the role of regulatory bodies and the context in which they came into existence, maps their deficiencies and assesses if there is a possibility for an alternative framework for improving quality. Chapter 4, by I. Ramabrahmam and G. Umamaheswararao, titled 'The State Councils of Higher Education: A Case for Strengthening Intermediary Agencies', examines the regulatory bodies at the state level and discusses the mandate and functioning of State Councils of Higher Education and Directorate of Collegiate Education.

Accountability in the form of academic, social and legislative and the role of quality assurance agencies to ensure accountability is captured by Chapter 5 on 'Accountability Measures to Improve Governance' by M. Anandakrishnan. The dimension of countering political interference while being accountable, and the vague accountability norms of private institutes are also highlighted in this chapter.

Governance and Management at the Institutional Level

Governance and management of higher education institutions is a serious concern. The next section focuses on Institutional Issues of Governance and Management.

Chapter 6, titled 'Governance and Management of Affiliated Colleges', by Mohd Muzammil looks at academic monitoring of colleges for improvement in view of a large number of colleges at the district level. Chapter 7 by G. D. Sharma, titled 'Management of Autonomous Colleges: A Movement from Academic Colonialism to Freedom and Democratization of Higher Education', deals with autonomy and accountability issues of autonomous colleges and governance and management with reference to the relationship of the autonomous colleges with the state government and university. The management of academic resources at the college-level and academic management of practice of teaching is examined in detail.

Chapters 8 and 9 focus on governance and autonomy and governance at the institutional level, highlighting case studies, respectively. Chapter 8, titled 'Governance and Autonomy: A Study of Central and State Universities', by Garima Malik deals with the theoretical dimension of autonomy and the shift from the state-controlled to state-supervised model, while also highlighting empirical studies of central and state universities bringing out differences in academic, administrative and financial autonomy. While accepting that there cannot be one single ideal structure of governance, Chapter 9, titled 'Governance and Management of Higher Education at the Institutional Level: Reality, Concerns and Transmutation', by Rakesh Raman looks at the best practices in some selected institutions.

The final chapter in this section, Chapter 10, titled 'Managing Transition from 'State' to 'Central' University in the University of Allahabad: Issues and Challenges:' by Rajen Harshe, focuses on some real challenges being faced in the transition from a state to a central university with regard to both undue interference in the running of the university and student politicization.

Managing Quality at the Institutional Level

The third and final section focuses on managing quality at the institutional level. Chapter 11, titled 'Managing Quality and Excellence: Conceptual and Institutional Factors', by Supriya Chaudhuri examines the theoretical debates worldwide, surrounding the measuring of quality and excellence in higher education. It also highlights the situation at the institutional level in India using a case study of Jadavpur University.

Chapter 12, titled 'Managing Quality and Excellence at the Institutional Level: A Study of Bharathiar University', by Narayanan Annalakshmi, Rajalakshmi Bhavana and Bhuvana Esther examines the challenges to quality and excellence that confront the state university and the institutional responses taking the case of one state university and an autonomous government college affiliated to the state university. Chapter 13, titled 'The Political Economy of Governance in Higher Education: Temporary Teachers Phenomenon', by Sudhanshu Bhushan drives us to look into the macro and micro picture and understand certain issues and dynamics that guide the temporary teachers phenomenon in higher education.

Pankaj Mittal in Chapter 14, titled 'Leveraging Technology to Solve the Pentagon Puzzle of Higher Education in India', highlights the recent digital initiatives and critically examines the role of technology in confronting the problem of access, equity and excellence.

Nidhi S. Sabharwal in Chapter 15, titled 'Managing Student Diversity in Indian Higher Education Institutions: Achieving Academic Integration and Social Inclusion', brings to the fore the way in which higher education institutions are managing the challenges faced by a diverse student body both inside and outside classrooms.

Thus, the *IHER 2019* will focus on some of the governance and management challenges posed by the emerging higher education context.

REFERENCES

Altbach, P. G. 1989. 'The New Internationalism: Foreign Students and Scholars'. *Studies in Higher Education* 14(2): 125–136.

Austin, I., and G. A. Jones. 2016. *Governance of Higher Education: Global Perspectives, Theories and Practices*. New York: Routledge.

Bush, T. 2003. *Theories of Educational Leadership and Management*. London: SAGE Publications.

Chandra, P. 2017. 'Governance in Higher Education: A Contested Space (Making the University Work)'. In *Navigating the Labyrinth: Perspectives on India's Higher Education*, edited by K. Devesh and B. M. Pratap, 235–264. Delhi: Orient BlackSwan.

Fielden, J. 2007. 'Global Trends in University Governance'. Education Working Paper Series Number 9, the World Bank, Washington, DC.

Ministry of Education (MoE). 1950. Report of the University Education Commission 1948–1949 (Chairman Dr S. Radhakrishnan). New Delhi: Ministry of Education.

Government of India (GOI), June 1966. Education and National Development: Report of the Education Commission (Kothari Commission, 1964 1966). New Delhi: Education Commission.

Government of India (GOI). 2017. *Three-Year Action Agenda: 2017–18 to 2019–20*. New Delhi: NITI Aayog, GOI.

International Federation of Accountants (IFAC). August 2001. *Governance in the Public Sector: A Governing Body Perspective—International Public Sector Study*. New York: IFAC.

Kaufman, D., A. Kraay, and P. ZoidoLobaton. 1999. 'Governance Matters'. Working Paper, the World Bank, Washington, DC.

Kivisto, J. 2005. 'The Government–Higher Education Institution Relationship: Theoretical Considerations from the Perspective of Agency Theory'. *Tertiary Education and Management* 11(1): 1–17.

Malik, G. 2017. *Governance and Management of Higher Education Institutions in India, CPRHE Research Paper 5*. New Delhi: Centre for Policy Research in Higher Education, National University of Educational Planning and Administration.

Mathur, K. 2020. 'State, Market and Governance of Higher Education'. In *Governance and Management of Higher Education in India*, edited by N.V. Varghese and Garima Malik. New Delhi: SAGE (Forthcoming).

Ministry of Human Resource Development (MHRD). 2005. Report of the Central Advisory Board of Education Committee on Autonomy of Higher Education Institution. New Delhi: Government of India.

Mulyadi, M. S., Y. Anwar, and M. Ikbal. 2012. 'The Importance of Corporate Governance in Public Sector'. *Global Business and Economic Research Journal* 1(1): 25–31.

Narayan, A. K., K. Olesen, and S. Ramachandra. 2012. 'Remodelling University Governance in Public Universities to Respond to the Dual Challenges of Academic Research and Commercialization'. *Corporate Ownership and Control* 10(1–6): 597–606.

Neave, G. 1988. 'The evaluative state reconsidered'. *European Journal of Education* 33(3): 265–284.

Neave, G., and F. Vught. 1994. *Government and Higher Education Relationships across Three Continents: The Winds of Change*. Oxford: Pergamon Press.

Olssen, M. 2002. 'The Restructuring of Tertiary Education in New Zealand: Governmentality, Neoliberalism, Democracy'. *McGill Journal of Education* 37(1): 57–87.

Qamar, F., ed. 2016. *Regulation of Higher Education in India and Abroad: A Study of Select Countries*. New Delhi: Association of Indian Universities, MHRD.

Raza, R. November 2009. 'Examining Autonomy and Accountability in Public and Private Tertiary Institutions'. Human Development Network, the World Bank.

Saint, W. October 2009. 'Guiding Universities: Governance and Management Arrangements around the Globe'. Human Development Network, Working Paper, the World Bank, Washington, DC.

Salmi, J. 2007. 'Autonomy from the State vs Responsiveness to Markets'. *Higher Education Policy* 20(4): 223–242.

Tricker, R. I. 1984. *Corporate Governance: Practices, Procedures and Powers in British Companies and Their Board of Directors.* Vermont: Gower Publishing Company.

University Grants Commission (UGC). 1990. Gnanam Committee Report on Alternative Models of Management. New Delhi: Government of India.

Varghese, N.V. 2009. *Higher Education Reforms: Institutional Restructuring in Asia.* Paris: IIEP/UNESCO.

Varghese, N.V. 2014. *Governance Reforms in Higher Education in Africa.* Paris: IIEP/UNESCO.

Varghese, N.V., and M. Martin. 2014. *Governance Reforms in Higher Education: A Study of Institutional Autonomy in Asian Countries.* Paris: International Institute of Educational Planning/UNESCO.

Varghese, N.V., and G. Malik, eds. 2016. *India Higher Education Report 2015.* New Delhi: Routledge.

Varghese, N.V., and G. Malik. 2019. 'Institutional Autonomy and Governance of Higher Education in India'. In *Governance and Management of Universities in Asia: Global Influences and Local Responses,* edited by Chang D. Wang, M. N. N. Lee, and H. Y. Locke, 43–55. London: Routledge.

PART I

Governance and Management: Macro Issues

Chapter 2

State, Market and Governance of Higher Education

Kuldeep Mathur

The relationship between the state and market has undergone a remarkable change in recent years. The role of state in market intervention began to lose its sheen, and public discourse centred around the crucial role of markets in delivering public services. The ensuing neoliberal reforms were an effort to create a favourable environment for the private sector to grow and invest in India's development.

The introduction of neoliberal policies in 1991–1992 and the rise of associated discourse of governance have produced a fundamental shift in the way public institutions are defined and delivery of public services is perceived and designed. These reforms were also closely associated with processes of globalization, allowing for free trade and free movement of capital across national borders. The strategy was to prioritize growth as a state goal, support large corporate houses in achieving this goal and keep labour under control (Kohli 2006). In the last few years, India has been described as an emerging giant and the economic changes that it has brought about are nothing short of revolutionary.

While celebrating the adoption of liberal economic policies for the buoyancy in the Indian economy, not much attention has been paid to the governance reforms that it has entailed. These have implications for democracy and legitimacy of collective decision-making in public interest. For, they are involved in reorienting existing state institutions and introducing new public institutions to pursue the liberal economic agenda. Multiplication of state institutions to perform specific tasks is an important feature of the governance agenda. Is it leading to fragmentation of state management?

What is intended in this chapter is (a) to offer basic premises of neoliberal thinking and then (b) to draw upon the institutional consequences of the neoliberal agenda and (c) point to the direction that transformation is taking place in the education sector. It is argued that neoliberalism has introduced new modes of institutional management in higher education and these can be best understood by understanding its tenets of governance reform. The question is whether the issues that we are facing in these sectors can be resolved by these new institutional arrangements. There does not appear to be an easy answer to this question. As a matter of fact, contradictions and dilemmas are emerging which are leading to further uncertainties.

II

It is a truism to say that liberalization was an effort to create a favourable environment for the private sector to grow and invest in India's growth. In a classic contribution, Lindblom (1978) had suggested that the greatest distinction between one government and another is in the degree to which market replaces government or government replaces market. In a planned economy, the government participates in the control and ownership of industry, services and trade, while in a market-oriented economy these functions are taken over by business and the private sector. In both cases, they have an impact on the way government and its institutions function. Those having faith in democracy fear that while an overly planned economy leads to regimentation and loss of initiative and thus kills entrepreneurship, a market-oriented economy, on the other hand, leads businesses to develop disproportionate power over political outcomes, which in the words of a leading democratic theorist (Dahl 1989 quoted in Bernhagen and Bräuninger 2005: 8) undermines political equality, democratic accountability and the legitimacy of public policy. Scholars and practitioners have directed their attention to these questions, which we also need to look into.

Broadly speaking, neoliberalism is a theory of political economic practices that proposes that human well-being can be advanced best by liberating the individual entrepreneur by providing freedom and skills within an institutional framework characterized by strong property rights, free markets and free trade. The role of the state is to create and preserve an institutional framework appropriate to such practices (Harvey 2007). The core concepts in this theory are of holding individuals responsible and accountable for their own actions and well-being. This principle extends to designing institutions in the realm of welfare, education and health such that the individual expresses his own choices for his own welfare and becomes responsible for them. Together, this is the concept of competition. Individuals bring out the best when they compete with each other, and this is as true for institutions as for individuals. Competition is a way to improve performance and give opportunity to individuals and institutions to excel. Therefore, the culture of competition is to be inculcated by the state and society. The role of the state, in this theorizing, is clearly demarcated. It is to provide an institutional framework for neoliberal practices to thrive.

The major concern that led to the adoption of neoliberal strategy was frustration with the traditional system not being able to fulfil the promises held out. It was a reaction to the growth of inefficiencies in the role of state and its inability to be effective in generating and implementing public policies. In the 1980s and 1990s, the search for efficiency led to the movement for limiting the scope of state activity. Conventionally, education, including higher education, and health were included as public good and hence the responsibility of state. With financial and bureaucratic deficiencies, the state did not seem to undertake its responsibilities fully. With wide acceptance of liberal ideas, the scope of state activities was redefined and both higher education and public health which were earlier supposed to be in the sole domain of state responsibilities were claimed to be private goods, allowing for the participation of the private sector in state endeavours.

Governance, the term given to the provisioning of institutional framework in the neoliberal agenda, in which the role of the state was clearly defined, had two very important implications. One was that the pursuit of good governance became essentially a pursuit of establishing such institutions and processes that would facilitate the functioning of markets. The state began to be seen as a facilitator for non-state actors to operate and not an institution to intervene in society. Consequently, providing support for successful operation of business and civil society became the central theme of the state's role and activity. The second implication, flowing from the first, was that business assumed greater power and influence than other segments of society. Large corporate houses began to see themselves as partners of state in development. Thus, good governance came to mean the development of governing styles in which boundaries between and within public and private sectors became blurred (Stoker 1998). The new formulation underlined that political institutions no longer exercised a monopoly of the orchestration of governance (Pierre 2000). The concept of governance indicated a shift away from well-established notions of the way government sought to resolve social issues through a top–down approach.

In this formulation, the state itself was enjoined to generate public policies in conjunction with non-state actors. It was no more an independent entity intervening or guiding society. Thus, it must be emphasized that it gave up its perceived neutral role and was expected to work in collaboration with business and non-governmental sector.

Thus, the new conceptualization of governance was based on the idea of network relationships of three actors—state, market and civil society. It is this concept of relationship that became the core thrust of the idea of governance. Governance is seen as an interactive process where institutions work together to achieve results. What is significant in this conceptualization is that the role of the government is considerably diluted to give space to the private sector and civil society actors. The idea that public and private sectors are distinct is being subsumed by the idea of cooperation and working together.

In this new world view, the primary role of the government is not merely to direct the actions of the public through regulation and decree, nor is it merely to establish a set of rules and incentives through which people will be guided in the proper direction. Rather government becomes another player in the process of moving society in one direction or the other. Where traditionally government response to needs has been 'yes, we can provide service' or 'no, we cannot', governance mode would be a response like saying 'yes, let us work together to figure out what we are going to do and then make it happen'.

Markets are relied upon for optimal solutions, but markets need certain conditions to succeed. When these conditions do not prevail, markets fail. States could also fail in their obligations. Thus, both failures of market and state can occur. Quest for establishing new institutions which could cope up with challenges from both state and market failures thus began. Public–private partnerships (PPPs) offered new institutional arrangements that would mitigate the perverse effects of the state and market. In this normative formulation, PPPs are associated with desirable attributes of collaboration, trust, responsibility and participation (Utting and Zammit 2006).

The emphasis on PPPs changed the pattern of governance, as well as adaptations in management practices and in perceptions regarding the role and responsibilities of different development actors in the context of globalization and liberalization. This transformation has also been termed as a pragmatic turn in official development practice and as pointed out 'approaches to development interventions, and in particular the role of the private sector, are said to be driven by 'what works' and less by ideology' (Utting and Zammit 2006).

PPPs appeared even more as a pragmatic turn because of the context where the financial circumstances of both the government and private sector were changing. Governments were suffering from a financial crisis and fiscal deficits in the 1980s while the corporate sector was doing well with good returns and technological advancement. The corporate sector was being lauded for its efficient management practices. Government sought to tap these private resources for public good. Across the world, partnership among the three actors—state, market and civil society—began to be promoted as a strategy of good governance. The partnerships promise to avoid duplication of efforts and are seen to draw on their complementary resources and capabilities to design more effective problem-solving mechanisms. They promise to increase responsiveness of policies and create accountability by including other actors—market and civil society—into decision-making processes. They are also presumed to improve compliance with and implementation of political decisions.

The wide appeal of the PPP model was rooted in the political ideals of individual liberty and freedom, long regarded as sacrosanct and which were the banners of rebellion against the oppression of the state. These were, as Harvey (2006: 146) calls, 'central values of civilization' that continue to resonate throughout the world of various shades of democracy. However, the social and economic policies generated by neoliberalism and its lofty ideals yielded mixed results. Increase in income inequalities and poverty became endemic features of development performance in many countries. The whole emphasis on market and downsizing of state institutions failed to give adequate impetus to growth and investment that would provide adequate protection to the poor.

Within higher education, this neoliberal thinking has introduced a new perspective and different way of thinking. Higher education, thought as public good in welfare mode, is now being replaced by seeing it as a response to market and an instrument of improved economic growth alone. The central propositions of neoliberal thinking—self-interested individuals, demand and supply, competition—are believed to bring out the best in allocation of resources and performance. Thus, educational institutions are being judged on the efficiency criterion. To do this, private sector managerial practices need to be adopted in governing institutions and emphasis placed on measuring performance. Consequently, institutions need to concentrate on their core activities, outsourcing other activities. As a general policy, then privatization and PPPs are more appropriate to fulfil intended goals.

III

PPPs began with infrastructure projects as these demanded heavy investments which only the private sector could provide. Now they are being tried in the social sector. While the challenge that policy makers face in the infrastructure sector is that of creating a more favourable enabling state to attract greater private investment, the story of PPP projects in the social sector has an additional challenge. The concern is not only of creating physical infrastructure but also to provide access to it equitably. With these concerns in mind or ignoring them, the government is moving towards different forms of PPPs at various education levels. There are frequent announcements that it is establishing more schools in this mode. Sometime back, an erstwhile HRD minister announced that the government was planning to set up over 2,500 model and 200 central schools on a PPP basis in the country in next two years (*Indian Express*, 29 August 2009). He added that the schools would be set up in PPP as part of our efforts to strengthen the human resource base and then went on to ask the corporate houses to invest in a big way in the education sector emphasizing that developing human resources is key to the success of any nation.

Other institutions and researchers have also joined in stressing the need of introducing PPPs in the education sector for similar reasons and also for fulfilling the commitment of raising literacy levels. A World Bank study (Jagannathan 2001) has explored the working of six non-governmental organizations (NGOs) that extend primary education to rural children in India. It is argued that these NGOs have demonstrated effective grassroots action to enhance the quality of basic education and have also influenced mainstream education through replication of their models and through policy dialogue with the government. While suggesting that NGOs are best suited for small projects and micro-level interventions, the study strongly advocates sustainable and enduring partnership with the voluntary sector that will strengthen the government's efforts to actualize the goal of universal elementary education. In their official documents, both World Bank and the Asian Development Bank have been advocating the policy of 'PPPization'.

The Centre for Civil Society launched a School Choice Campaign in 2007 arguing that what the poor need today 'is not just Right to Education, but the Right to Education of Choice'. It advocates PPP through the use of a voucher system. At a recent conference in 2009, the speakers included representatives of the World Bank and the private sector and stressed the need of quality education by providing choices to the poor. This scheme was called as funding the students and not schools and giving choice to the students through a voucher system.

At the policy level in higher education, the government has reached out to the private sector for advice. Prime Minister's Council of Trade and Industry appointed a committee of two well-known industrialists, Mukesh Ambani and K. Birla, to recommend measures for education reforms. This committee recommended in its report in 2000 (Ambani and Birla 2000) that there needs to be greater association of the private sector in higher education and the government should confine itself to primary and secondary education, leaving higher education to the private sector. What is significant is that it strongly recommended that the 'user pay principle' should be adopted, supplemented by loans and grants to economically and socially deprived students. It appears that the recommendations of this committee have been very influential in guiding later developments.

Thus, the international donor agencies, corporate houses, and some civil society organizations are demanding greater PPP in the education sector. The government, having articulated its commitment to provide education for all through the enactment of the Right to Education into law, is also becoming receptive to these ideas for it is facing resource crunch and lack of capacity to run a responsive and efficient educational system.

The government, having articulated its commitment to PPPs in education, is still at the stage of experimentation. For one thing, the forms that partnerships can take place in education are diverse. Government aid to schools is a form of partnership that has existed since a long time but it does not fit into the current mould. In this partnership, a private entrepreneur or trust provided the school buildings and infrastructure while the government paid for the salary of teachers and regulated the curriculum and quality of teaching. There are also alternatives where the government just provides the land and infrastructural facilities at varying rates of subsidy. There are now many other openings such as financing of services, such as those of Information Technology (IT), underwriting mid-day meals or handing over of a school to the private sector to provide management services.

At the higher education level, the forms it can take is in establishing research collaboration between government and industry, giving space to private entrepreneurs to enter the field and opening up for partnership with foreign universities. For quite some time, large businesses have been a big player in the field of higher education, such as engineering and medical education. These institutions were primarily colleges affiliated to universities which exercised control over their academic norms. These colleges were seen as response to the market need for more professionals as doctors and technologists. By the mid-1990s, promoters of private colleges saw the regulatory control of the affiliating university and state governments as cumbersome, impeding the full utilization of the colleges' market potential. Thus, they wanted university status to wriggle out of control of state governments and the affiliating universities. This resulted in the proliferation of private universities. In addition a new institutional form of deemed university emerged. It was not multidisciplinary like the usual university but enjoyed the benefits of being one. Earlier, the deemed university provision that empowered an institution to award its own degree was sparingly used to allow leading institutions to offer programmes at an advanced level in a particular field or specialization. What is significant here is that each of the private universities/deemed universities was established under separate legislations enacted by state or central government. There was little uniformity in them regarding stipulations on various aspects of education.

The Indian Institute of Science in Bangalore and the Indian Agricultural Research Institute in Delhi were the first two institutions to be declared deemed universities in 1958. This number increased to 29 in 1990–1991 and 38 in 1998 and now stands at 122 as of 2017. Most of the post-1998 deemed universities are private (Agarwal 2007). In the past four decades, the number of universities has grown more than six times. Out of 33,023 colleges, one-third was set up only during past five years. The number of private institutions grew faster than public institutions (Gupta 2016: 360). It must be emphasized that there has been greater growth in technical and medical colleges than in liberal arts institutions. One in seven universities in India is a technical one. The 126 universities out of 882 overall are second only to 500 listed as general in the All India Survey of Higher Education 2017–2018 published by the MHRD, Government of India (MHRD, 2018). Next to engineering, medical universities account for the highest count for specialized universities at 58, followed by agricultural universities at 52. Such a pattern of growth is in response to the market which is now demanding technical workforce in greater numbers.

Some of these institutions are now vigorously seeking alliance with foreign universities to enhance their credibility. This alliance can take many forms, including inviting visiting faculty or sending students to foreign universities for a semester and so on. The current government is actively encouraging this outreach as this provides the ladder to compete with international institutions and have a place in world rankings.

Finding a respectable place for its institutions of higher learning in a world ranking system is not only an aim the government would like to pursue but it is of interest to the private sector too for their individual gain. The interests of both coalesce. This has important policy implications in assuring the private institutions considerable freedom to negotiate with international institutions on the pattern of partnership and collaboration.

Seeking partnerships with higher educational institutions (HEIs) outside the country is also part of the process of globalization. While, earlier, students went abroad to study at institutions of excellence, now the effort is based on institutional mobility. Branch campuses can be established in home countries, and domestic students can avail of foreign degrees that are highly valued in the labour market. What is significant is, as Varghese (2017: 35) points out, 'the internationalization of education in the context of globalization has become a market mediated process, where internationalization is an item of cross-border trade. The new providers of higher education are more often investors rather than educationists, and cross-border trade in education is a lucrative business involving billions of dollars.'

It must also be pointed out here that not only Indian educational institutions have external alliances, they themselves have left Indian shores to establish campuses elsewhere. Such campuses have been established in UAE (Dubai), Nepal, Malaysia, Mauritius and so on.

The entry of entrepreneurs in the field of higher education has introduced another set of problems. Many professional for-profit organizations have entered for personal gain by introducing unscrupulous practices that seem to exploit the students and the community. These practices are not only related to what is taught and how but to financial misdemeanours. There is now capitation fee for colleges which demand high admission fees, and the students are asked to bear the costs of services that may be advertised but not provided. There is now increasing risk that financial costs and fees may be out of reach of a vast number of students and may lead to restricting education to those who have the ability to pay. Economic deprivation may also result in educational deprivation.

Another equally important, if not more, is the fear that for-profit institutions and foreign collaborations may not fulfil India's quest of social equity. Broadening access may leave out the socially deprived segment of the population. Policies of affirmative action have been pursued in government institutions while private institutions are not mandated to do so. Such expansion in education may not fulfil social aspirations unless adequate steps are taken. Recent surveys and data alert us to what the future may hold.

If 'partnerships' have to be equitable and accountable, they need an interventionist state which can or is willing to mediate and use its institutional, financial and regulatory resources to create a level-playing field. However, if the state itself turns out to be the enabler of market only, such an interventionist role is doubtful. Partnerships by their very nature mean equality of partners, but over the years it has emerged that the corporate houses have used their financial and managerial strength to leverage greater advantages for themselves. Clearly, the strength of the corporate sector lies in its ability to refuse to participate in a venture that it does not find profitable.

The government has turned to establishing regulatory bodies that can play a more effective role in seeing that private institutions fulfil social goals and work in an ethical fashion. At the same time, it needs to allow them adequate autonomy to function well. But it is still struggling to develop an appropriate design. (For how regulating institutions and processes have evolved, see Ayyar 2017: 27–36 and also the chapter by Furqan Qamar in this volume.) In 1956, the government had established the UGC to oversee the higher education institutions. It was given the responsibility of funding and setting academic standards for universities. Being a body of academics and experts, it was supposed to act independently of the government. However, this arrangement was found inadequate in view of the changing scenario of higher education. In 2010, the then government introduced several bills in Parliament to regulate HEIs to respond to the emerging situation. Most of them lapsed with the coming of the new government in 2014. A bill to regulate foreign educational institutions was also introduced. As Ayyar (2017: 475) points out, 'even though the Parliament Standing Committee submitted its Report in August 2011, a beleaguered government did not wish to add to its woes by pushing forward a Bill which might evoke controversy.'

Another effort at innovating institutions for regulation is being made. In 2018, the Government of India has sought to replace the UGC, the current regulatory body for universities with the Higher Education Commission of India (HECI). The minister concerned argued in proposing that it reflects the commitment of the government to give greater autonomy to higher education institutes. The new dispensation separates the academic from funding function. The agency will be responsible for ensuring academic quality in education and will have 'powers to enforce compliance to the academic quality standards and will have the power to order closure of substandard and bogus institutions'. Grants will come from the ministry or any other institution established by it. The proposed bill is being debated in public domain and has revived controversies about the nature and role of regulation. A recent editorial in a newspaper captures much of the public concern with the title 'Draft law on revamping higher education governance raises fears of micro-management, more curbs on autonomy' (*Indian Express*, 29 June 2018).

IV

The policy perspective spelt out in the liberal agenda has an impact on the way institutions of higher education are governed and the purpose for which they are established. This has been true for earlier state dispensations too. During colonial times when universities were being established, the British were very clear on what was expected of them. Widely known, the educational policy was framed on the basis of Lord Macaulay's Education Minute, which in its most famous words set the objective of creating a 'class who may be interpreters between us and the millions whom we govern; a class of persons, Indian in blood and colour, but English in taste, in opinions, in morals and in intellect'. Such an objective determined the way universities were governed and the way government relationships with them were established. During this period, universities were under the control of the government. Chancellors had to be informed of decisions taken by the senate or syndicates, and important issues were decided upon only after ascertaining government views (Basu 1989 quoted in Dahiya 2001: 30).

After independence, educationists and public-spirited individuals began to imagine a university fashioned after leading British universities such as Oxford and Cambridge. It was assumed that a university was an institution enjoying considerable autonomy from the government. It was a self-regulating institution, governed by its faculty and students, in accordance with academic norms involved in production of knowledge. For this reason, it was not open to external influence. This ideal view was in conflict with the British where objectives were set by the government, which also exercised control over the institution.

Two early commissions and committees were not able to lay down a clear pattern of governance. Arguing that greater control of universities is not the way to achieve reform, the Radhakrishnan Commission suggested that 'present evils arise from the fact that most of our universities have no real autonomy whatsoever, and have proved incapable of resisting pressure from outside' (Government of India 1950). Having said this, the commission did not offer any legal safeguards but went on merely to say that 'universities should be sensitive to public opinion; they should never let themselves be bullied or bribed into actions that they know to be educationally unsound or worse still motivated by nepotism, factionism or corruption.' The commission's recommendation was 'that the right policy is to give the university the best possible constitution, securing among other things of the wisely chosen external members of the governing board and then leave it free from interference.'

UGC Committee headed by P. B. Gajendragadkar, (UGC, 1971), while accepting the idea that 'there ought to be some level of autonomy to the institutions of higher education' did not lay down any legal framework for it either. It left it to the goodwill and attitude of the government to work out the relationship even when an elaborate Model Act was proposed by the Gajendragadkar Committee with considerable participation of faculty in decision-making.

The result has been that no single pattern of governance has emerged. The structure and organization of institutions of higher learning have varied across the country and so also their relations with government. These differences may be due to their source of funding like central or state government or are what have come to be known as deemed universities. The nature of relations of the government with universities and institutions of higher learning has been fluid, differing across institutions and sponsorship. Central universities and institutions established by the central government have fared differently from those established by the state governments.

The mushrooming of private universities across the country has raised concerns about quality and standards of education. Anecdotal evidence suggests that many of them falter on these counts. What has happened is, as pointed out earlier, since they have been established under different statutes by different state governments and central government, stipulations differ. It has been reported that the government has been concerned about this problem and is now undertaking all such legislations to remove anomalies and produce a 'holistic picture' (Shukla 2018). The UGC and NITI Aayog are jointly responsible for this exercise.

With the introduction of policies for privatization of higher education and establishing institutions in the mode of PPPs, another dimension in the issues of governance is being introduced. From an ideal view, the universities are now seen to have multipurpose functions in which responding to the labour market appears to be gaining precedence. With private investors replacing the government in financing these institutions, universities have begun to be seen as 'stakeholder organizations' where the voice of the faculty is one among many of the stakeholders. While academic considerations may play a role in decision-making, but other functions of raising funds, competing with like institutions, attracting faculty and students through perks and advantages to establish their prestige and so on also become important. (See Bleiklie and Kogan 2007 for a detailed discussion of these issues.)

From an organizational perspective, structure and processes have to be developed to support the pursuit of these other goals too. The entry of the private sector, therefore, brings in its wake managerial practices which are, in any case, celebrated for being superior to bureaucratic processes. The market's call for efficiency promotes competition and cost effectiveness. Evaluating academic performance and creating an aura of excellence become important to compete successfully in education market. This has led to the development of quantitative indicators that can be used to compare national and international universities. It is common practice now to judge the excellence of a university in terms of the rank it has obtained in such listing (Varghese 2017). These rankings are seen as a source of encouragement of competitive spirit among institutions and a spur for it as valued in neoliberalism.

This changed perspective also, then, demands a different kind of leadership. The trend is that the vice chancellor leads an executive team that satisfies the stakeholders in terms not only of academic goals but those of market efficiency. The attributes of the leader required are not only academic but entrepreneurial, and a new term has been coined, that of 'academic entrepreneur'.

Some of these trends are still in the nascent stage but are emerging as more and more private universities and private institutions of higher learning are being established. What is significant is that government is demanding similar practices for its own public institutions. Probably, it is too early to predict how universities will shape up in the milieu of pursuing efficiency and responding to the market but trends point to the development of educational institutions as business enterprises sources for the labour market.

V

It appears that neoliberal solutions of privatization or PPPs may be creating more problems than one can foresee. In a country where backwardness is not defined by economic factors alone, the major goal of any public policy is equity and justice. This was recognized by our founders and incorporated into various dimensions of affirmative action. Goals of neoliberalism and governance hold individual incentives and market values of efficiency in high esteem but it is questionable if they can tread the path of equity and justice. This is not only one but is a foremost challenge. Transformation in purposes of education and ideas what constitutes a university or an institution of higher learning are further challenges that need to be debated and discussed and need policy response.

Regulatory agencies are being proposed as mechanisms to keep educational institutions on track. Past experience has not been particularly a happy one and establishing new ones is already facing problems in their embryonic stage.

What is needed is a reevaluation of the role of the state in education. The government needs to strengthen its own commitment to education. Outlays in this sector have not kept pace with demand and have actually been falling in the last few years. But falling outlays is only one part of the problem and is magnified as the only problem. It is not the only culprit. Educational institutions are being allowed to decay due to mismanagement and neglect of government's responsibilities of taking timely action in appointments of teachers and heads of institutions and release of already budgeted funds. It appears that there is a deliberate effort to allow public institutions to fail and thus create a policy context for privatization and partnership with the private sector. The state needs to rearrange its priorities, by strengthening its own public institutions and demonstrate that non-state actors only supplement state action and not replace it (Mathur et al. 2013).

What is being stressed is that we are responding to the slow decline of public educational institutions as if it just happened because there is a resource crunch without realizing that it is embedded in a coherent philosophy of neoliberalism. Its ideas have become so common place that we seldom recognize it as an ideology, a framework in which policies are determined (Monbiot 2016).

In conclusion, it can be said that the government's commitment to education has shifted to looking at the private sector in fulfilling its ambitions and goals of raising the stature of India in the world of education. The process generated in the neoliberal framework represents education as an input–output model. PPPs or contracting out of services to private players rests on terms on what has to be achieved. A contract is signed in which objectives are clearly defined and quantitatively measured outputs are indicated. Much emphasis is laid, for example, on the number of students passed, number of them recruited after graduation, or expectation from faculty on the number of research papers published or seminars attended.

These measures of quantitative outputs are taken as indicators of excellence in institutions of higher learning. Much attention is paid on devising measuring indices that could rank these institutions and thus permit their evaluation. These rankings are seen as a source of encouragement of competitive spirit among institutions and a spur for a competitive spirit as valued in neoliberalism.

The whole concept of an institution of higher learning is being redefined in this input–output model. The opportunities of intellectual debate or quality of contribution to knowledge find little space in this model. Notions of professional norms are not measurable and therefore not included in its evaluation. The traditional professional culture of open intellectual enquiry and debate has been replaced by institutional stress on performance as measured by measurable indicators (Olssen and Peters 2010). The underlying ethos of higher education is a spirit of curiosity, a spirit of tolerance of differing views. What seems to be evolving in this framework is a narrowly instrumental educational system that closes horizons instead of broadening them.

REFERENCES

The Indian Express. 2009, 29 August. '2,500 model schools to come up in 2 yrs: Sibal'. *The Indian Express.*

The Indian Express. 2018, 29 June. 'An Over-regulator Draft Law on Revamping Higher Education Governance Raises Fears of Micromanagement, More Curbs on Autonomy'.

Agarwal, P. 2007. 'Higher Education in India: Growth Concerns and Change'. *Higher Education Quarterly* 6(2): 197–207.

Ambani, M., and K. Birla. 2000. Report on a Policy Framework for Reforms in Education. New Delhi: Prime Minister's Council on Trade and Industry, Government of India.

Ayyar, R. V. 2017. *History of Education Policy-making in India 1947–2016.* Delhi: Oxford University Press.

Bernhagen, P., and T. Bräuninger. 2005. 'Structural Power and Public Policy: A Signaling Model of Business Lobbying in Democratic Capitalism'. *Political Studies* 53(1): 43–64.

Bleiklie, I., and M. Kogan. 2007. 'Organization and Governance of Universities'. *Higher Education Policy* 20(4): 477–493.

Dahiya, B. S. 2001. *The University Autonomy in India: The Idea and the Reality.* Shimla: Indian Institute of Advanced Study.

Government of India. 1950. *Report of the University Education Commission 1948–1949* (Chairman Dr S. Radhakrishnan). New Delhi: Ministry of Education.

Gupta, A. 2016. 'Emerging Trends in Private Higher Education in India'. In *Indian Higher Education Report 2015*, edited by N.V. Varghese and Garima Malik, 355–374. London: Routledge.

Harvey, D. 2006. *Spaces of Global Capitalism.* 1st ed. London: Verso.

Harvey, D. 2007. *A Brief History of Neo-liberalism.* Oxford: Oxford University Press.

Jagannathan, S. 2001. 'The Role of Non-governmental Organizations in Primary Education in India: A Study of Six NGOs'. Policy Research Working Paper, the World Bank, Washington, DC.

Kohli, A. 2006. 'Politics of Economic Growth in India 1980–2005'. *Economic and Political Weekly* (Parts 1–2): 1361–1370.

Lindblom, C. E. 1978. *Politics and Markets: The World's Political-Economic Systems.* New York: Basic Books.

Mathur, Kuldeep, et al. 2013. *Public–Private Partnership and Public Accountability and Exploration.* Delhi: Centre for Democracy and Social Action.

Ministry of Human Resource Development. 2018. *All India Survey of Higher Education 2017–18.* Department of Higher Education, Government of India, New Delhi.

Monbiot, G. 2016. 'Neo-liberalism—the Ideology at the Root of All Our Problems'. *The Guardian* 15 April, 28(4): 2–5.

Olssen, M., and M. A. Peters. 2010. 'Neo-liberalism, Higher Education and the Knowledge Economy: From the Free Market to knowledge Capitalism'. *Journal of Education Quarterly* 20(3): 313–345.

Pierre J., ed. 2000. *Debating Governance*. Oxford: Oxford University Press.

Qamar, F. 2020. 'Regulation of Higher Education in India'. In *Governance and Management of Higher Education in India*, edited by N.V. Varghese and Garima Malik, 44–70. New Delhi: SAGE.

Shukla, A. 2018, 15 October. 'To Maintain Education Quality, UGC to Tighten Scrutiny of Private Universities'. *Hindustan Times*.

Stoker, G. 1998. 'Governance as Theory: Five Propositions'. *International Social Science Journal* 50: 17–28.

University Grants Commission. 1971. *Report of the Committee on Governance of Universities and Colleges* (Chairman: PB Gajendragadkar). New Delhi: Government of India.

Utting, P., and A. Zammit. 2006. *Beyond Pragmatism: Appraising UN Business Partnerships Markets, Business and Regulation Programme Paper No. 1*. Geneva: United Nations Research Institute for Social Development.

Varghese, N.V. 2017. 'Internationalisation and Cross-border Mobility in Higher Education'. In *Joint Modules and Internationalisation in Higher Education: Reflections on the Joint Module Comparative Studies in Adult Education and Lifelong Learning*, edited by R. Egetenmeyer, P. Guimarães and B. Németh, 21–38. New York: Peter Lang Edition.

Chapter 3

Regulation of Higher Education in India

Furqan Qamar

INSTITUTIONAL DIVERSITY IN HIGHER EDUCATION

Higher education in India is provided by a wide complex web of higher educational institutions (HEIs). At a broader level, these comprise of Institutes of National Importance (INIs), institutes under state legislature (ISLs), universities, colleges and standalone institutions. In order to comprehend the complexities and changes of regulation in higher education, a brief description of various types of higher educational institutions (HEIs) seems imminent:

1. INIs are established under an Act of Parliament and are funded and regulated directly by the ministry of human resource development (MHRD). Most INIs are technical HEIs, but a few multidisciplinary universities have also been declared as INIs. Primarily, INIs comprise of HEIs such as Indian Institutes of Technology (IITs), Indian Institute of Science Education and Research (IISERs), Indian Institutes of Information Technology (IIITs), National Institutes of Technology (NITs), Schools of Planning and Architecture (SPAs), All India Institutes of Medical Sciences (AIIMSs) and National Institutes of Pharmaceutical Education and Research

(NIPERs). The latest addition in the list are the Indian Institutes of Management (IIMs), which were until recently counted amongst the stand-alone institutions.

2. ISLs are specialized HEIs with power to award degrees and established under state legislation. They are small in numbers, and their types are not growing any further.

3. Universities are established either by the Act of Parliament or by the Act of state assemblies and are of many types such as central universities (CUs), public-funded state universities (PFSUs), self-financed private state universities (SFPUs) and institutions deemed to be universities (DUs). CUs are established by an Act of Parliament but are funded and regulated by the University Grants Commission (UGC). PFSUs are established by the respective state governments under an Act of their state legislation and are funded by the respective state governments. Such universities are subject to regulation by the state governments and UGC. SFUs, on the other hand, are, though established by the respective state governments, largely self-funded and rarely receive funding from the government. These types of universities are regulated by the UGC, the respective state governments either directly or through a private higher education regulatory commission.

Institutions deemed to be universities, commonly referred to as DUs, are HEIs but are not established by an Act of Parliament or state assemblies. They are generally established and run by the societies and trusts that are of non-profit nature. These institutions come under the provision of Section 3 of the UGC Act and declared as DUs. Some of them are established and are fully funded by government either directly or through UGC, while others could be only partially funded. A good number of them are self-financed in nature and are not funded by the government.

Within each category, the universities are of different types—unitary, federal or affiliating. Unitary universities are single-campus universities and generally do not have colleges attached to them. On the other hand, federal universities have a limited number of colleges as their constituents or associates and that such colleges are considered integral to the university concerned. The affiliating universities are those that have power to affiliate colleges within their territorial jurisdiction. While most CUs are unitary, there are some which are of federal or affiliating character; most PFSUs are affiliating in character but there are some which are unitary or of federal character. The SFPUs are generally unitary in character and do not have power to affiliate colleges so are the DUs, but some of them may also have their off-campuses either in the same town in which their main campus is located or in other towns. A few DUs have also been permitted to have off-campuses abroad, though such privilege has so far not been accorded to INIs, CUs, PFSUs and SFPUs. In addition, the universities could also be classified in accordance with the types and variety of academic programmes. Those offering a wide variety of academic programmes are referred to as multidisciplinary as opposed to unidisciplinary. In contrast are those that could be called unidisciplinary or monodisciplinary. These are subject- or discipline-specific universities such as technological universities, health science/medical universities, law universities, language universities and so on. There are thus layers and layers within each layer and type.

4. Colleges are such higher educational institution which organize instructions but are not empowered to award degrees, and for that purpose they have to be constituent of or associated with or affiliated to a university—generally the university in whose territorial jurisdiction they fall. The colleges could be government, government-aided and self-financed private. Government colleges are established and fully funded by the government—most of them by the state governments but there are some which are under the domain of the central government. These colleges are owned, managed and financed by the government and are, therefore, public HEIs. Government-aided (often also referred to as private-aided) colleges are established and managed by societies or trusts established by group of private individuals but are financed the government. Self-financed private (or private) colleges are established, managed and financed by the societies or trusts founded by a group of private individuals. Invariably, most of their funds come from fees from students. Colleges are subject to the regulation by the universities to which they are affiliated to, the respective state governments and UGC.

5. Stand-alone institutes (SAIs) are outside the purview of the university system and accordingly cannot award degrees in their own names. They generally offer proficiency-, certificate- and diploma-level courses. However, in some cases the diplomas awarded by them have been considered equivalent to a corresponding degree awarded by universities. Most SAIs are privately established, managed and financed but there are some that have been established, managed and financed by governments.

Table 3.1 presents a glimpse of the number of and enrolment in various types of HEIs so as to fathom their significance and importance and also to hint on the complexities that the regulation of higher education in the country is faced with. It is obvious that while public and private HEIs have coexisted in India for a fairly long time, the numbers and types have multiplied over the past seven decades. Notably, while earlier on, government and government-aided HEIs played a dominant role, the situation today has been reversed with the private HEIs dominating the scene. What add to these complexities are a large number of non-degree-awarding HEIs. Importantly, a wide variety of HEIs fall under the domain of either the central government or state governments, but it is the state sector which are a dominant players as far as the number of HEIs and enrolment are concerned.

Legal and Regulatory Framework for Higher Education

By law, the universities and university-level institutions (ULIs) are considered autonomous with powers to take their own decisions, including to award degrees. Other HEIs have to be affiliated to a university under whose jurisdiction they fall. Universities and ULIs in India, public or private, can be established only by an Act of Parliament or of state assemblies. Importantly, they all are supposed to be established by individual and separate legislations. Besides, the MHRD is also empowered to recognize certain non-university institutions (NUIs) as institutions deemed to be universities on the recommendation of the UGC under Section 3 of the UGC Act. Colleges and institutes, which enrol and employ a bulk of students and teachers in higher education, are not permissible by law to award degrees in their own names, even

Table 3.1 Number of and Enrolment in Various Types of HEIs in India

Types of HEIs	Number		Enrolment	
	Number	%	Enrolment	Percentage Share
Institutions of National Importance (INIs)	**101**	**0.21**	**2,03,197**	**0.56**
Institutions under State Legislature (ISLs)	**5**	**0.01**	**3,709**	**0.01**
Central Universities (CUs)	45	0.09	7,23,679	2.01
Central Open Universities (COUs)	1	0.00	8,61,275	2.39
Public Funded State Universities (PFSUs)	351	0.72	25,96,633	7.21
Public Funded State Open Universities (PFSOUs)	14	0.03	10,90,083	3.03
Self-financed Private Universities (SFPUs)	262	0.53	10,35,729	2.88
Self-financed Private Open Universities (SFPOUs)	1	0.00	26	0.00
Government Deemed Universities (GDUs)	33	0.07	42,921	0.12
Government Aided Deemed Universities (ADUs)	10	0.02	55,994	0.16
Private Deemed Universities (PDUs)	80	0.16	6,52,151	1.81

Total Universities	**797**	**1.63**	**70,58,491**	**19.60**
Government Colleges	8,358	17.07	86,84,532	24.12
Government Aided Colleges	5,083	10.38	54,75,679	15.21
Private Colleges	24,620	50.27	1,23,92,090	34.41
Total Colleges	**38,061**	**77.72**	**2,65,52,301**	**73.73**
Polytechnics	3,239	6.61	15,52,345	4.31
Postgraduate Diploma in Management	269	0.55	52,432	0.15
Nursing	2,676	5.46	2,72,176	0.76
Teacher Training	3,691	7.54	2,79,342	0.78
Institutes under Ministries	136	0.28	38,320	0.11
Total Stand Alone Institutions	**10,011**	**20.44**	**21,94,615**	**6.09**
Total Higher Education	**48,975**	**100.00**	**3,60,12,313**	**100.00**

Source: MHRD (2018).

Note: AISHE 2017–2018 estimates total enrolment in higher education at 36.6 million, whereas the above table computes enrolment in higher education to be 36.01 million; the difference is due to the fact that the table gives enrolment in HEIs that actually responded to AISHE survey.

though they are empowered to organize teaching according to the university-prescribed curricula, and their students are subject to the common examination conducted by the university. Autonomous colleges are, however, given some degree of autonomy with regard to the curriculum, examination, and admission.

Universities in India operate within their territorial jurisdiction as specified in their acts and statutes. Even the central universities and the INIs that are established by the Act of Parliament have limited territorial jurisdiction. Such restrictions constrain universities in their initiatives to establish branch campuses in India or abroad. Even their drive to introduce distance, open, virtual, online mode of higher education is curtailed. All universities, public or private, the DUs and colleges are required by law to seek approval to get listed under Section 2(f) of the UGC Act. INIs are, however, exempted from such requirements. Besides, those intending to access development and research funding from the government are also required to be registered under Section 12(b) of the UGC Act. All ULIs are required to award degrees as specified under Section 22 of the UGC Act. Colleges are subjected to multiple regulations in the form of approval for affiliation, no object certificate from the state governments, registration under Sections 2(f) and 12(b). HEIs offering professional and technical programmes are also required to obtain approvals for each and every programme from the concerned regulatory body or professional council.

Exit, closure or withdrawals of HEIs are in the mandate of the UGC and all other regulatory bodies, but that is usually a tedious and lengthy process. In most cases, these also require permission from the concerned regulatory bodies. Withdrawal for a private university is simpler, but the sponsoring body must give notice to the state government at least six months to a year in advance and waiting until the last batch of students has completed its courses. Upon dissolution, the assets and liabilities rest with the sponsoring body. Again, this provision varies from state to state as some states have not mentioned the provision of managing or transferring the assets and liabilities on dissolution. The exit barrier is reasonable and low. The biggest challenge of following this route by all states is the lack of proper legislation. In states, the exit procedures in case of private universities are not defined.

Even though universities and ULIs are fully empowered by their acts and statutes, the UGC, All India Council for Technical Education (AICTE), National Council of Teacher Education (NCTE) and other regulatory bodies and professional councils play a major role in this regard. While, earlier on, they used to prescribe model curricula and would leave the decisions to the universities, presently their regulations in this regard have become almost binding and mandatory. In many states, state-wide curricula and syllabi committee are constituted by the chancellor, who is the governor of the state and the recommendations of these committees are binding on universities.

Universities and ULIs are free to adopt their own policies and procedures for admission which could be based on the past academic performance or admission test. In professional courses such as engineering, management, medicine, dental, architecture, pharmacy, there have, however, been prescribed national- or state-level admission tests, and often universities are required to admit students using these. Universities and ULIs are autonomous with regard to the system of examination, evaluation and grading. However, the UGC and other regulatory bodies in the country have been issuing guidelines and regulations in this regard as well and the universities are expected and often forced to adopt the same.

In case of general higher education in India, the regulation of faculty recruitment, qualification and compensation is vested with the UGC. Under Section 26 of the UGC Act, it has been given the power and authority to make regulations and determine the minimum qualification for appointment of teachers, pay scales, service conditions for teachers and other academic staff in universities. Every university and other institutions of higher education incorporated established by either under the Acts of Parliament or under state legislation including their constituent colleges recognized by the UGC are covered under this regulation. In case of agricultural and veterinary education, the regulatory power pertaining to determination of qualification and recruitment is done by the Indian Council for Agricultural Research (ICAR). The recruitments in agricultural institutions or programmes are done by the agricultural scientist recruitment board.

Similarly, in case of professional programmes such as medicine, law, engineering or other technical programmes, the pay scales, service conditions and qualifications for teachers and other academic staff in technical institutions are determined by their respective councils such as Medical Council of India (MCI), Bar Council of India (BCI), AICTE, NCTE, and so on. As a common procedure, the recruitment for teachers in all category of institutions and programmes is done through direct selection procedure by advertising the vacant positions in leading national newspapers, other print media or through websites. In case of administrative or non-teaching staff, both direct recruitment and borrowing on the basis of deputation from other organizations are also practised.

Degrees awarded by one university in the country is recognized by all universities in the country as they are all empowered to award degrees as per their acts and statutes. Universities are, however, expected to ensure that they adhere to the minimum norms and standards prescribed in this regard by the UGC, MHRD, other regulatory bodies and the state governments. As regards foreign qualifications, each university is vested with the authority to recognize them according to their regulations. However, as a facilitative mechanism, the Association of Indian Universities (AIU) is now recognized as the nodal agency for the purpose. Presently, foreign qualifications are recognized as equivalent to the corresponding degrees of the Indian universities so long as the qualification has been awarded by a university that is approved/recognised/accredited in its own country; the student has pursued the programme of studies as a full-time regular student either on the campus or on the approved offshore campus of the university; and the minimum eligibility requirement for admission as well as the minimum prescribed programme duration is the same as in India.

Universities in India have been conceptualized as self-governing institutions, and to give effect to this philosophy, their acts and statutes provide for decision-making bodies/university authorities which are given power to make statutes, ordinances and regulations to run their own affairs. Their powers to govern themselves have, however, been circumscribed by the governmental rules and regulations and also by the regulations and guidelines issued by the regulatory bodies. The sum and substance is that higher education in India is subjected to the rules, regulations, guidelines, norms and standards prescribed by more than 16 regulatory bodies and professional councils described later.

REGULATORY BODIES IN HIGHER EDUCATION

Maintaining and coordinating standards, what is now commonly referred to as regulation, for such a complex, diverse, large and rapidly growing sector of higher education are indeed a daunting task. As a natural corollary, a large number of statutory bodies and professional councils have been set up and working in the country for the purpose of coordination and maintenance of standards, improving quality and promoting excellence in higher education, most of them having been established in the post-Independence period. Even though both the union as well as the state governments are empowered to legislate on matters relating to higher education, the responsibility and authority to coordination and determine standards in institutions of higher education or research and scientific and technical institutions vest in the union government (Entry 66 of List I, Constitution of India). Accordingly, the Government of India (GOI) has established a number of institutions for the purpose. Additionally, a number of professional bodies have also been playing a critical role in this regard. Being in the concurrent list of the Constitution, promotion of higher education is a joint and shared responsibility between the union and the state governments in India. Both are empowered to legislate on matters relating to higher education. However, coordination and maintenance of standards in higher education is the exclusive responsibility of the union govern-ment. Invoking entry 66 of the Constitution, the central government has established a number of regulatory bodies. These bodies formulate norms and standards relating to various facets of higher education and also for ensuring their adherence and implementation.

AIU published in 2018 an edited volume on a comprehensive review of the regulation of higher education in India and abroad (Qamar et al. 2018). Chapter 1 of the volume presents a detailed description of the regulatory framework for higher education in India, and a select portion of the chapter is drawn heavily from the chapter contributed by the author in the said volume (Qamar 2018, Qamar et al. 2018).

MHRD: THE NODAL MINISTRY

MHRD, being responsible for education at all levels, formulates policies at the national level, ensures its implementation, undertakes planned development, including expanding access and improving quality of the educational institutions throughout the country. It also provides financial assistance in the form of scholarships and students loan interest subsidy and, most importantly, it allocates funds to state governments, the funding bodies such as the UGC and also directly to the INIs. Individual state governments and union territories with legislature have their own ministries or departments dealing with school education, technical education and higher education. Within these ministries, there are generally directorates dealing with higher and technical education.

Even though higher education may, theoretically, differ from state to state, in reality, the country has a common system of higher education as all HEIs operate within the bounds of a common framework and are subject to common regulatory requirements imposed by various regulatory bodies and professional councils. This critical balancing is also ensured through an advisory and consultative mechanism called the 'Central Advisory Board of Education (CABE)', which is chaired by the union minister for human resource development and is represented by the minister of education from all the states and the union territories; the CABE also has representatives of the regulatory bodies, professional associations, representative bodies and a cross section of specialists and individual experts (MHRD 2005).

While MHRD is the nodal ministry for education and higher education, a few regulatory bodies, though established under the Act of Parliament, work under the aegis of other ministries of the union government. Of late, the ministry of commerce has also started playing a role particularly for promoting export of educational services and the international higher education, though it neither has any control nor any regulatory body under its aegis. Besides these, many other ministries/departments in the GOI have also established and run HEIs but they do not regulate the same. Obviously, such a complex web causes a multiplicity of regulations, which is further compounded by the over-lapping functions that require interministerial consultation and dialogue, which, to some extent, was being done by the Planning Commission and presently probably by the NITI Ayog. Since higher education in India, as mentioned earlier, is in the concurrent list of the Constitution, individual state governments and union territories with legislature have separate ministries/departments of education/higher education, which take decisions with regard to the policy, planning, administration and implementation of the same within their jurisdiction. Normally, their policies and plans are in broad framework provided by the union ministry and the regulatory bodies under the union government.

1. *AICTE:* AICTE is another statutory body responsible for coordination and development of technical education including its qualitative improvement. It also lays down norms and standards for courses, curricula, physical and instructional facilities, staff pattern, staff qualifications, quality instruction, assessment and examinations and grant approval for starting new technical education institutions and for introduction of new courses or programmes.

2. *AIUs:* Essentially a representative body of universities in the country, it is the nodal agency for the recognition/equivalence of qualification for the purposes of admission and jobs and works closely with the MHRD on the issue of mutual recognition of international qualifications and international cooperation. Such qualifications which entitle a person to practice a profession such as architecture, law, medicine are, however, outside the purview of the AIU, and equivalence of these qualifications is done by the respective professional councils charged with the responsibility for registration, licensing and practicing of the profession.

3. *BCI:* A representative body of the lawyers and advocates, BCI regulates legal education. Besides prescribing standards of professional conduct and etiquette by exercising disciplinary jurisdiction over the bar, it also sets standards for legal education and grants recognition to universities and colleges offering programmes of studies in law and legal education at the undergraduate (UG) and postgraduate (PG) levels.

4. **Central Council of Homeopathy (CCH):** It regulates the education, practice and professional standards and maintains a central register of homeopathic practitioners and thus specifies the minimum standards in homeopathy education and practice. Accordingly, it inspects homeopathy colleges and seeks to ensure that they adhere to the prescribed standards.

5. **Central Council of Indian Medicine (CCIM):** It is a statutory body prescribing the minimum standards of education for courses in Indian systems of medicine such as Ayurveda, Siddha and Unani as offered by colleges and universities. It formulates uniform curriculum and syllabus for UG and PG education in these disciplines.

6. **Council of Architecture (CoA):** Besides registration of architects, it prescribes the minimum standards of architecture education including recognition and approval of courses/programmes of studies/institutions engaged in architecture education and training. Interestingly, such programmes and institutions are subjected to the dual regulatory control of the CoA as well as the AICTE.

7. **Dental Council of India (DCI):** It is established to recognize the dental qualifications and regulates dental education, profession and ethical standards in dentistry. Clinical practice in dentistry can be undertaken only by dentists who have obtained their qualifications from dental colleges/universities approved by the DCI and are registered with the state dental councils. Accordingly, it gives approval for introducing a new dental course or for establishing new institutions, its intake capacity in any course of study or training. It is authorized to refuse recognition of the degrees awarded in violation of the provisions.

8. **Distance Education Council (DEC)/Distance Education Bureau (DEB):** The DEC was intended to regulate the higher education provided by the distance and open mode universities and also by the mainstream universities offering programmes through distance learning. The council was established under the Indira Gandhi National Open University (IGNOU) Act and was under IGNOU for a long time. However, recently, the DEC was taken over, and in its place the responsibility was vested in the UGC, which has set up the DEB as a unit within UGC.

9. *Indian Council for Agriculture Research (ICAR):* An autonomous organization under the ministry of agriculture, ICAR is an apex body for co-coordinating, guiding and managing research and education in agriculture including horticulture, fisheries and animal sciences in the country. Effectively, all agricultural universities and other universities with programmes of studies in the above disciplines are subjected to the ICAR guidelines.

10. *Indian Nursing Council (INC):* INC is responsible for the regulation and maintenance of uniform standards of training in nursing at all levels, and to discharge this function, the INC inspects nursing schools and colleges including the examination centres so as to ensure that the uniformity and requisite standards are being maintained.

11. *NCTE:* It regulates teacher education and determines its standards and accordingly grants approval for the introduction of new courses and the establishment of institutions imparting teacher education.

12. *MCI:* MCI is a statutory body charged with the responsibility for establishing uniform and high standards of medical education in India. Given its mandate to grant recognition to medical qualifications, giving accreditation to medical schools, registering medical practitioners, and monitoring medical practice in India, all universities and colleges offering medical education are required to obtain MCI approval, which also includes the intake capacity, programme duration, curricula and pedagogy.

13. *Pharmacy Council of India (PCI):* It prescribes the minimum standard of education in pharmacy, approves courses of study and examination for pharmacists. It recognizes and withdraws recognition of courses and institutions offering pharmacy education. Importantly, the pharmacy courses and institutions are under the dual regulatory control of the PCI and AICTE.

14. *Rehabilitation Council of India (RCI):* Established under the ministry of social justice and empowerment, RCI regulates education and training occupational therapy, speech pathology, audiology, speech therapy, special education and so on. Interestingly, courses in physiotherapy are not regulated by the RCI or for that purpose by any other central regulatory body. They are, however,

subject to regulation by different councils set up by different state governments.

15. **UGC:** Besides providing development and maintenance grants to universities and colleges, UGC has the general duty to promote and coordinate university education. It is empowered by law to determine and maintain standards of teaching, examination and research in universities. UGC is also expected to advise the central government on issues related to the coordination and maintenance of standards in universities and colleges. It is, in a way, an umbrella body as all HEIs come under its ambit.

16. *Veterinary Council of India (VCI):* This statutory body regulates veterinary practice and for the purpose maintains the Indian Veterinary Practitioners Register. It recommends to the central government the recognition and de-recognition of the qualifications granted by the institutions running veterinary-related programmes.

Lately, quality assurance, accreditation and rankings have assumed a far greater significance in the coordination and maintenance of standards in higher education. Earlier, accreditation of higher education institutions was voluntary, which has become mandatory now. For receiving government funding, the institutions are required to undergo the process of accreditation and now there are a number of schemes which can be accessed by the HEIs only if they are accredited. As regards accreditation, there are two main agencies responsible for accreditation and quality assurance in higher education, that is, National Assessment and Accreditation Council (NAAC) and National Board of Accreditation (NBA). Most recently, yet another agency, the National Institutional Ranking Framework (NIRF), has also entered into the fray to promote competitiveness for quality.

1. **NAAC:** It is responsible for institutional assessment and operates under the aegis of the UGC. Established as an autonomous body under the UGC in 1994, the NAAC has been charged with the responsibility of maintaining quality in higher education in India. All kinds of HEIs such as central, state, private, and DUs, INIs, and affiliated and autonomous colleges are accredited by the NAAC.

2. *The National Board of Accreditation (NBA):* Operates under the aegis of AICTE and is responsible for accreditation and quality assurance in professional programmes. NBA is an autonomous body operating under the aegis of AICTE and it accredits the technical and professional institutions. The fields such as engineering, technology, architecture, pharmacy and hospitality are covered under NBA.

3. *NIRF:* This is a kind of arrangement set up by the MHRD to collect and compile data on all HEIs to rank universities and other HEIs, primarily colleges. Beginning from 1996, NIRF is being managed and supervised by a team of select experts with data and logistic support provided by the NBA.

State-Level Regulatory Bodies

In addition to the above national-level bodies, state governments also have set up either on their own or in accordance with the requirements of the central government various bodies and mechanisms for regulating higher education. Prominent among these are the *SCHE* as contemplated in each state. Some states have already established one, and others are in the process. SCHE is expected to facilitate the planning and coordination of higher education at the state level. Recently, many state governments have also started establishing regulatory commission or council for universities and colleges falling under their domain.

Regulation Relating to the Funding and Financing of Higher Education

Traditionally, higher education in India has always been viewed as a public activity. Hence, it has traditionally been a state-funded sector, though things are changing drastically. To be eligible for government funding, the HEIs need to be registered under Section 2(f) of the UGC Act 1956 and be declared fit to receive fund under Section 12B of the UGC Act.

HIGHER EDUCATION FUNDING AGENCY (HEFA)

A very recent development in this regard has been the establishment of the HEFA, which seeks to provide loans on concessional terms to universities, presently the beneficiaries are the centrally funded higher and technical institutions. As per the existing arrangements, the interest on the loan is borne by the government whereas the principal amount is to be repaid by the institutions themselves over a period of time, though certain category of institutions are either totally exempt from the repayment of the principal amount or have to repay only a part of it.

Fee regulatory committees: With the advent of the large number of private self-financing colleges and universities, and also because of the fee reimbursement policy declared by many a state government for the people belonging to the deprived sections of the society studying in the self-financed private institutions, the regulation of fees has also assume importance. Most states have constituted fee regulatory committees consisting of a retired judge, a chartered accountant and a few academicians; the HEIs are required to submit their accounts and other related information to this committee on the basis of which the maximum amount of fees chargeable by these institutions is prescribed.

Clearly, higher education in India is not only highly regulated but is also subjected to multiple regulations. These bodies and councils have issued regulations on almost every aspects of the university and college life—curricula, pedagogy, syllabi, qualifications, experience and salaries and allowances of the faculty and staff, fees, office procedure, administration, governance and so on. While initially these regulations were more of advisory in nature, they have now become mandatory.

A CRITIQUE OF REGULATORY FRAMEWORK FOR HIGHER EDUCATION IN INDIA

UGC since its establishment in 1956 till 1986 was the lone body charged with the responsibility of coordination and maintenance of standards in higher education. Since then, several other bodies have been created with an idea of providing more effective standards for regulating the specific kind of HEIs. Simultaneously, other professional councils, which were essentially constituted to set professional standards and ethics, also became proactive players in the regulation of higher education falling under their professional domains. With all these efforts and with these many different kinds of regulatory bodies working overtime to improve the quality and standards of higher education, the country should have had one of the best systems of higher education in the world. But going by the views expressed by a series of committees and commissions to look into the regulatory overreach or deficiencies in higher education, the regulation of higher education in the country has been far from effective.

In recent times, the regulatory bodies have been found faltering in maintaining standards due to massive expansion in the HEIs including proliferation of private universities under state legislations and DUs under the UGC Act. Most criticisms emanate from their inability to regulate the sector efficiently and thus failing in their mandate of maintaining and coordinating standards and thereby adversely affecting the quality of higher education. They are often accused of perpetuating mediocrity and are thus alleged to be adversely impinging on the drive of the HEIs, particularly the private one, to attain excellence. The public universities have their own grouses and they often lament that the regulatory bodies through their regulations and guidelines effectively make them dysfunctional. The regulatory bodies, on the one hand, have their own case and come up with examples of many a different kind of tendencies in the HEIs that lower the standards and quality of higher education in the country. The reality may lie somewhere in between. Most agree that regulatory framework for higher education need reforms. But most of their suggestions have been in the form of replacing the existing ones with new ones. None have, however, attempted any detailed analysis of what went wrong. None provides any clue as to how do they think that the newer bodies created to replace the existing one would be better than them. The only consensus seems to be that higher education cannot be left to the mercy or vagaries of the market forces and that the higher education system does need some regulators but that regulator has to be effective.

Excessive or ineffective regulation does indeed cause damage to the qualitative growth and development of the higher education sector. Despite the fact that in terms of the number of HEIs ours is the single largest system of higher education found anywhere in the world, it is disquieting that none of our HEIs are ranked amongst the top 100, or even amongst the top 200 universities of the world by any of the global ranking agencies—Academic Ranking of World Universities (ARWU), the Times Higher Education (THE) Ranking or the QS Ranking. There could be many factors responsible for this state of affairs, but the regulatory framework shall have to bear its share of blame.

Ensuring quality, access and affordability in higher education has, theoretically and conventionally, been regarded the responsibilities of the state. Public financing of higher education was justified on the ground of both equity and quality. These were seen as integral to the overall public welfare policy. Regulatory bodies established by the state are considered an important organ to give effect to the public policy, which in addition to the equity and excellence could also provide for expansion and balanced growth of the sector. It could also involve seeking and promoting participation of the private sector, albeit with due regard to the constitutional mandate that such activities in India are to be organized on non-profit basis. A welfare state like ours is expected to provide for and proactively take a variety of enabling actions to provide for the education, including the establishment of universities and other HEIs, and for promoting excellence in all walks of life, including education towards the achievement of the national objectives and goals. These are considered necessary to meet the aspirations of the people.

Universities in India are regarded autonomous as they are established by the Acts of Parliament and legislative assemblies of the respective states, and these legislations do not just give birth to the universities but also lay down the procedures for the functioning of the universities and their institutions. Universities are expected to function with a sense of responsibility and be accountable to the people through Parliament or assembly, for it is an established principle that 'Autonomy to universities does not mean freedom to them whatever they want to but freedom to do whatever they are expected to do.' Various regulatory bodies and professional councils are expected to respect the autonomous status of universities and are supposed to just coordinate, guide, facilitate and regulate the standards of higher education and the functioning of HEIs. The problem arises when the two institutions, created by law transgress their power and authorities and in the process not only undermine each other but compromise on the core of their basic functions and responsibilities.

Anecdotal evidence abounds to comment that the regulatory bodies in higher education have failed to discharge their responsibilities effectively or to propel higher education in right direction and with the speed that was expected of them. The author undertook a research to find out empirical evidence to support or contradict the prevalent views about the regulatory framework in higher education. Based on the research, the author published an article (Qamar 2017) and a monograph (Qamar 2018). The empirical evidence only reinforced the popular perception that the regulation in higher education is found seriously faulty. In fact, the data clearly pointed out that the quality of higher education in the country has been inversely proportional to the intensity of the regulation.

It has been over a decade since the National Knowledge Commission (NKC) reached the conclusion that higher education in India was over-regulated but undergoverned and called for the establishment of an Independent Regulatory Authority in Higher Education (IRAHE) to replace all the existing regulatory bodies in higher education including the UGC and the AICTE (GOI 2006). The committee for the Revival and Rejuvenation of Higher Education, which was set up to follow up the NKC, too reached a similar conclusion though using an altogether different argument and logic and suggested for creating a National Commission for Higher Education and Research (NCHER) in place of UGC and AICTE. Following the announcement in Budget 2017, media reported the possibility of a Higher Education and Empowerment Regulatory Agency (HEERA) being established soon. Despite such high-pitched demands, an overhaul of the regulatory system and processes in higher education as yet seems only a distant dream. Now, the latest development is that a newly conceptualized body called HECI is being contemplated to replace the UGC.

Regulation of higher education in India suffers on several counts: multiplicity of regulatory bodies with overlapping functions and responsibilities leading to chaos and conflict; their ineffectiveness to check mushrooming of a large number of poor-quality HEIs; their inability to ensure quality and promote excellence and to discriminate between performing and non-performing HEIs; and prevent malpractices in higher education. One may also add to the list their inability to evolve and effect an enabling framework for the entry and operation of the quality foreign educational providers in India. At the same time, barriers for the Indian higher educational institution to become global players have also been high. Importantly, while they seek to regulate entry, operation, processes and outcome of HEIs, they have ended up becoming stumbling blocks in the path to the progress and promotion of excellence.

Worrisome as the prevailing situation is, there is hardly an objective evidence that the existing sets of institutions and mechanisms are beyond redemption and must necessarily be done away with and replaced by a new set of institutions. Alas, the Yashpal Committee (MHRD 2009) that was constituted to objectively examine the deficiencies in the working and performance of the UGC and AICTE took an altogether different turn and chose to focus on larger issues relating to the governance and regulation of higher education. There indeed were some concrete comments on the working of the UGC and AICTE by the Hari Gautam Committee and M.K. Kaw Committee indicating on reforming these institutions could not see the light of the day, presumably because the dominant view since 2007 has been on replacing these two and few other regulatory bodies such as the NCTE and the DEC.

The idea that a new institution shall be more effective than the old one, however, has its own limitations. The assumption that the existing regulators have outlived their utility and suffer from design defect to cope with the challenges of contemporary times does not necessarily reflect the reality. Design defects are only a part of the story because organizations may also fail due to the people they comprised of and the processes through which they operate. A closer analysis of the facts suggests that such assumptions are often unfounded, and change is suggested just for the sake of change. Further, there is also no guarantee that the new regulator would be free from the perceived defects in the existing regulator or that the new regulator would deliver better than the old ones. From 1956 till 1986, the UGC was the sole regulator in higher educator. Starting from 1987, many of the responsibilities of the UGC were taken away from it and vested in a plethora of other agencies that were established. The experience tells us that the newer ones proved no better, if not worse.

India is too diverse and too large in its geography and demography and is unique in its socio-cultural and political context and what has worked in one country will not work at all in our context for the simple reason that what works in an individualistic society is not likely to work in a pluralistic society because such societies have their own compulsions. This effectively means that the scope of learning from other economies is only limited and the country shall have to experiment and evolve its own ideas and framework. The idea that organizations suffer on the count of people of which they are made of and that the new institution shall bring in better people too are fraught with the limitations that even in the new set-up people shall have to be drawn from the same national common pool and that there is every possibility that the newer institution shall soon be saddled with more or less the same kind of people.

While most of the commissions and committees set up recently have espoused replacing the existing regulatory bodies by a new one, it could also be possible to reform the existing bodies such as to improve their working and performance. Bashing and battering and thereby weakening the existing institutions, which the talk of reform has actually done so far, are not going to work. We actually need to empower them further to require them to become responsive to the rapidly changing needs and circumstances. This could easily be achieved by ensuring that the right kind of people, people with high integrity, credibility and accomplishments are identified and given the responsibility. At the same time, the regulatory bodies be required to reexamine and reengineer their processes to shun and shed all such activities and functions that are trivial to their core functions. Anyone familiar with the working of the existing regulatory bodies knows well that there are a lot of them that could easily be done away with or delegated to other subordinate or partner institutions and thereby freeing them to focus on the core and critical. Most such people- and process-oriented reforms could be easily accomplished without the need for a new amendment in the existing legislation and would be easier and faster to implement.

A regulatory body, by whatever name it is called, is essentially an organ of the state to give effect to the public policy and higher education could be no exception. Questions about the efficacy of the regulation of higher education, particularly about the way the regulation has been effected so far, notwithstanding, the need for regulation in higher education shall continue to remain a reality and higher education being too important to be left to market forces, the state shall have to play a critical role.

The regulatory body is expected to frame rules of the games for the entry and operations of the institutions under its purview; set standards of operations and performance; monitor progress and performance against the stated standards; take corrective action against institutions found faltering on adhering to norms, standards and benchmarks set for their operation and accomplishments; and deter misuse and malpractices so as to safeguard the interests of the stakeholders, including the larger public interest. Additionally, a few regulatory bodies in higher education have also been charged with the responsibility of funding and grants-in-aid. Given the gamut of roles and functions described above, the following may have to be addressed in the new regulatory body being in higher education:

Presently, these functions are being performed by as many as 16 different regulatory bodies and professional councils—just a few under the ambit of MHRD and the rest under various other ministries/departments. The new-generation regulator can, at the best, remove multiplicity of regulatory bodies under MHRD. This would effectively mean that the multiplicity of regulatory bodies, which have been a major bane of higher education regulation, shall continue to exist and interfere with higher educational systems and processes.

The challenge could be overcome by empowering the new regulator as the sole regulator of higher education and thereby rendering the remaining bodies as only professional councils responsible for setting and enforcing the practice of their respective professions. At the most, the professional councils may provide input to the new regulator for setting standards and benchmarks for such qualifications and degree that are the minimum prescribed entry qualification for registration and licensing for practice of a profession. Further, the representatives of the professional councils could be involved as a member of the peer team for institutional and programme accreditation of HEIs. This will effectively mean an end to multiple peer team assessment, evaluation and inspection of higher education institutions by different agencies.

Existing regulatory bodies in higher education hardly engage with the states, which account for an overwhelming proportion of enrolment in higher education, leading to a gap between the national-level policies and programmes and the practices and requirements at the provincial level. The disconnect could be addressed by providing for a coordination and consultation council as the top policy, planning and regulatory standards. The council could comprise of the office bearers (chairperson, vice chairperson, members) of the new regulator, experts drawn from different disciplines, representatives of the professional councils and representatives of state, preferably the chairperson/vice chairperson of the State Council of Higher Education (SCHE). All policy decisions should be taken in consultation and coordination with this council and effected by its office bearer supported by its bureaucracy.

With the institutional accreditation having been made mandatory and the national rankings catching up fast, the regulation of higher education needs to be linked with these two such that the regulatory body prescribes the minimum norms and standards for the entry and operation of the HEIs in the country in as much detail as possible and should monitor their implementation and progress in terms of the performance of HEIs in accreditation and ranking. Institutions would register themselves with the regulator and should be free to function without the requirement of inspection and approval by the regulatory body so long as they undertake to comply with the prescribed norms and standards. The new regulatory body would act, and act decisively and drastically against an institution which is found to be defying or deviating from the prescribed norms and standards. With such a division of roles and responsibilities whereby the monitoring could be done through accreditation and action to be taken by the regulatory body, the rules of game shall be well laid out.

This leaves us with the funding functions and grants-in-aid. As per the present scheme of things, the state universities and their colleges are getting funds from the respective state governments and the central funding is being routed through Rashtriya Uchchatar Shiksha Abhiyan

(RUSA). The centrally funded technical institutions are funded directly by the MHRD. The central universities which are being presently funded by the UGC, a regulator in higher education, could also be disbursed funds directly by the MHRD and the process could be facilitated greatly if a norm-based funding model could be evolved. This shall free the regulator to focus on setting norms, standards and benchmarks and shall enable the HEIs to enter and operate autonomously, of course within the bounds of the norms and standards so set.

CONCLUSIONS AND POLICY IMPLICATIONS

The essential objectives for the regulation of higher education are to achieve an envisioned goal of enlarging and expanding the frontiers of knowledge, in a systematic manner, for the service of humanity. The regulation must, therefore, provide a framework of opportunities, possibilities and limitations, prescribed in the larger interest of public in a transparent manner, bringing in certainties in defining obligations of every player in the system, that is, the regulator, the HEIs and the receiver of the higher education so that the time and money invested for providing, sharing and acquiring knowledge could become meaningful not only for the direct stakeholders but to the society at large. In contemporary times, the regulatory framework has to also additionally provide for the mobility of students and staff, the entry and operation of international education providers and establishment and operations of the offshore campuses of the domestic HEIs. This aspect has to essentially cover the global recognition of qualifications leading to seamless mobility of students and staff across borders.

A good regulatory system may also ensure sustainability and smooth functioning of the HEIs and processes. This could be done through a variety of ways including promoting competitiveness. Importantly, the regulatory system must prevent malpractices operating within the education system. Critically, the regulatory framework must move with the changes in the economy. The conventional methods of the regulation may no more be effective. Ideally, under the present circumstances, it must provide for comprehensive and critical information to all stakeholders to enable them to take informed decisions. At the same time, it is also a truism that the standards of higher education across different disciplines and throughout the country cannot be uniform, but a minimum standard of education and quality has to be maintained. Further, the quality and standards have to be dynamic and must keep pace with the changes in time and space.

A few recent initiatives to curtail the ambits of the regulatory bodies are welcome developments but shall serve only a very limited purpose. The idea of the graded autonomy as announced by the government aims to free the best-performing HEIs from adherence to the UGC regulations. It is an excellent idea but would benefit a smaller number of high educational institutions as fewer would be able to meet the minimum eligibility conditions as the privilege is limited only to the best-ranked HEIs. Similarly, the identification and announcement of the institutions of eminence also aims at freeing such universities from regulatory restrictions but this privilege too shall be available only to a maximum of 20 universities.

Taken as a whole, the challenge before the nation and the higher education system is to simplify regulation and do away with unnecessary conditions and impediments in the entry and operation of HEIs; provide for and ensure adequate academic freedom and autonomy to the HEIs; ensure that the prescribed regulations become effectively implementable; maintain transparency and accountability in the working and performance of the higher educational system at all levels—the regulator as well as the HEIs—and promote coordination amongst different organs and bodies responsible for the regulation and facilitation of the higher educational process. In fact, the ultimate objectives of the regulation should be to build institutional capacity and effectiveness to attain and maintain highest academic standards and quality.

REFERENCES

Government of India (GOI). 2006. *National Knowledge Commission Report of the Working Group on Undergraduate Education*. New Delhi: GOI.

Ministry of Human Resource Development (MHRD). 2005. *Report of the Central Advisory Board of Education Committee on Autonomy of Higher Education Institution*. New Delhi: Government of India.

Ministry of Human Resource Development (MHRD). 2009. *Report of the Committee to Advise on Renovation and Rejuvenation of Higher Education* (Yashpal Committee). New Delhi: Government of India.

———. 2018. *All India Survey of Higher Education 2017–18*. New Delhi: Department of Higher Education, Government of India.

Qamar, F. 2017, 2 May. 'Higher Education, Low Regulation'. *Indian Express*.

———. 2018. *Reforming the Regulatory Framework for Promoting Excellence in Higher Education*. New Delhi: Association of Indian Universities.

Qamar, F., V. Bhalla, A. Pani, and Y. Singh, eds. 2018. *Regulation of Higher Education in India and Abroad: A Study of Select Countries*. New Delhi: Association of Indian Universities (AIU).

Chapter 4

The State Councils of Higher Education
A Case for Strengthening Intermediary Agencies

I. Ramabrahmam and G. Umamaheswararao

GENESIS

The 42nd Amendment to the Constitution[1] placed 'education' in the concurrent list from the state list four decades ago. While it acknowledged the role played by states in 'higher education', it also emphasized the need for a central-level regulation for uniformity and effectiveness. The policy supremacy of union government is established through setting up of a number of regulatory bodies such as University Grants Commission (UGC), All-India Council for Technical Education (AICTE), Medical Council of India (MCI) and so on. Keeping in view the fact that the majority of enrolment is in state-level institutions, the need for an intermediary agency at the state level to coordinate with central bodies was deemed necessary. The National Policy on Education (NPE) 1986, amended in Programme of Action (POA)

---

[1] The Constitution of India (42nd Amendment) Act, 1976, says 'Education including technical education, medical education and universities, subject to the provisions of entries 63, 64, 65 and 66 of List I; vocational and technical training of labour.'

1992, suggested state governments to establish state councils of higher education (SCHE) for planning and coordination of the development of higher education.[2] However, many of the states have not constituted a council until recently as 17 of 36 state and union territories only have initiated to set up a council through legislation.

However, one important shift in the policy regime is starting of a new funding agency. In 2013, Rashtriya Uchchatar Shiksha Abhiyan (RUSA), a centrally sponsored scheme (CSS), was launched with the objective of reinforcing the tertiary education sector with power to allocate funds with an objective of ensuring access, equity and excellence as envisaged in the 12th plan. It is proposed to channel funds from the central ministry to SCHEs. This necessitated the establishment of SCHE to avail funds under RUSA in states. Thus, the scheme attempted to revive the institution of SCHE, which was underutilized due to lack of scope for participation at the national level and lack of representation in executive bodies at university and college level. Tracing the genesis of SCHEs will enable us to understand the role of the councils in the overall framework of governance in higher education.

LEGAL FRAMEWORK

In pursuance of the recommendations of NPE 1986 (modified in 1992), the UGC set up a committee to identify the gaps in the facilities in existing institutions by using the computerized management information system (MIS). It also recommended to develop an effective mechanism for coordination and planning at state level as there existed no policy for the growth and development of higher education in India. The committee consisting of educationalists and key officials from the ministry of human resources development (MHRD) was entrusted to frame the guidelines for SCHE as well as define its objectives, structure and functions, that is, academic, advisory and administrative. The committee stressed on the need for an effective mechanism to promote

---

[2] It also recommended the small states, perticularly the North-Eastern states, to have a joint Council of Higher Education as it may not be possible to have separate councils at the state level and the responsibilities are entrusted to the council.

and coordinate the state-level activities to fill the gaps between the state and central policies through the SCHE. The committee evolved guidelines which were approved by the UGC in 1987 (modified in 1988). The SCHEs were to design the programmes to strengthen the higher education system at the state level. The policy articulation on this issue is clearly described in NPE 1986 and POA 1992 (Government of India 1992). It was therefore proposed to establish SCHE as statutory bodies with powers to carry out functions which include (UGC 1988): (a) prepare programmes in each state; (b) scrutinize development programmes of universities and colleges; (c) assist and advise the UGC in respect of maintenance of quality; (d) support to state governments in determining the block (maintenance) grants; (e) encourage autonomous colleges for initiating new programmes; (f) monitor progress and assess the performance; and (g) advise the state governments in setting up new institutions.

Prior to creation of SCHEs, there have been several agencies to regulate college and higher education in states. The Directorate of Collegiate Education (DCE), one such agency, has been responsible for formulating rules regarding admissions and regulation of the activities of government and private colleges in different states.

ROLE OF DCE IN THE STATES

Higher education at the state level was managed by different departments under different names. In states such as Andhra Pradesh and Tamil Nadu, Directorate of Public Instruction (DPI) used to manage education at all levels—primary, secondary and higher education. In the case of Maharashtra, Directorate of Education was responsible for the same. However, with the number of colleges growing in states, the concerned state governments felt the need to separate the departments for intermediate and degree education. DCEs came into existence in Kerala (1957), Rajasthan (1958) and Karnataka (1960). Soon, other state governments also followed the suit by creating separate departments for school and higher education. For example, erstwhile Andhra Pradesh created Commissionerate of Collegiate Education (CCI) in 1975. The core objectives behind creating these agencies were to expand college education to backward and rural areas, reinforce women education, introducing vocational courses on need base, and so on. Matters relating to government, government-aided and self-financing arts and science colleges, training colleges, oriental colleges, opening of government colleges, sanction of new course and so on are managed by DCEs. The functions of the DCEs can be broadly listed as follows:

- Ensuring quality education through degree and PG colleges;
- Administrative control and inspecting government degree colleges;
- Grants (grant-in-aid) to private-aided colleges;
- Encouraging private participation in higher education;
- Development of infrastructure;
- Auditing the financial functioning of colleges;
- Assessing the developmental requirements of government colleges and releasing grants;
- Distribution of scholarships;
- Restructuring of courses based on need and market demand;
- Encouraging colleges to opt for autonomous status and assessment and accreditation;
- Organizing training programmes for lecturers and principals;
- Formulation of targeted schemes for academic and administrative development of colleges;
- Encouraging use of IT and modern technology in colleges.

In addition, DCEs perform certain additional functions, for example, DCE in Rajasthan also issues permanent and temporary no-objection certificate (NOC) to private colleges. Kerala Collegiate Education Department deals with the provident fund for the aided colleges in addition to its regular functions. The DCEs function through several sections, that is, establishment section deals with the postings, transfers, promotions of government college employees; planning and coordinating section is responsible for making proposals for new colleges, faculties, subjects and budget, and also looks after the infrastructure facilities; academic section deals with the admission policy, policies related to orientation programmes, foreign scholarships and awards, and conduct of fair examination. There are other sections dealing with issues related to legal, accounts, personnel and private institutions.

Private Regulatory Agencies in States

Private university/educational institutions regulatory commissions/acts are being created to regulate the state-level private universities/private HEIs in several states, such as Madhya Pradesh, Himachal Pradesh, Arunachal Pradesh and Rajasthan. Few other states have also proposed similar legislations to regulate the functioning of private universities. The purpose of establishing these regulatory commissions is to facilitate a 'regulatory mechanism' and act as an 'intermediary agency' between the state and central governments for 'ensuring standards of admission, teaching examination, research extension programme, qualified teachers and infrastructure and protection of interest of students in the Private Educational Institutions (PEIs)' in accordance with the guidelines issued by regulatory bodies at the centre or states.

Composition of the Regulation Committee

The private HEIs' regulatory commission/committee in Himachal Pradesh, Madhya Pradesh and Arunachal Pradesh consists of three members: one chairman and two members selected from amongst persons of eminence in public life, in the field of higher education or government officials above the secretary level. These members are appointed by the respective state governments. However, the Uttar Pradesh Private Higher Educational Institutions Regulatory Commission bill, 2016, proposed to set up an eight-member committee including chairman. The commission shall collect funds from the PEIs and mobilize funds from other sources and through the loans from the government.

POWERS AND FUNCTIONS OF THE PRIVATE HIGHER EDUCATIONAL REGULATORY COMMISSION/ACT

The powers and functions of the regulatory commission in all the state are broadly the same as described earlier. The commission shall ensure that the admissions in PEIs are based on the marks achieved in the Common Entrance Tests (CETs) organized by the centre or at the state level. In case of no such CETs in any state, the marks obtained in the qualifying exam determine admission of a student. The commission directs the PEIs to set up a committee for redressal of grievances of students/parents. The commission may create a separate committee to inspect PEIs in the concerned states. The commission has the power to monitor and regulate the fee in PEIs.

Though the DCEs operate in almost all the states in India, a need for a uniform coordinating agency in the states to implement guidelines of UGC and other regulatory agencies was felt. While the DCEs worked as independent agencies at the state level, an agency to coordinate between the state and central policies would help in developing higher education institutions on par with the central government. Therefore, SCHEs were proposed at the state-level working independently from DCEs.

STATE INITIATIVES TO CREATE SCHEs

Several states established SCHEs through an act with the goal of planning and coordination of higher education according to the guidelines of the UGC. Several other states have also created SCHEs through an executive order pending clearance in the state assemblies. Though the national policy recommended setting up of a coordinating mechanism at the state level three decades ago, only 10 out of 29 states and 1 out of 7 union territories have followed until now. The states which have established the council include Andhra Pradesh (1988), Tamil Nadu (1992), West Bengal (1994), Uttar Pradesh (1995), Kerala (2007), Karnataka (2010), Telangana (2014), Maharashtra (2016), Chandigarh (2015) and Haryana (2018). On the other hand, Arunachal Pradesh, Bihar, Gujarat, Jammu and Kashmir, Madhya Pradesh, Punjab, Rajasthan and Puducherry (UT) proposed to pass the act in respective legislative assemblies.[3] The Department of Higher Education, Gujarat, has established Knowledge Consortium of Gujarat (KCG) through an executive order to enhance the standards of higher education. Maharashtra also constituted an SCHE through a government resolution, but the state is yet to specify its composition, functions and

---

[3] After it was mandatory as part of RUSA, the above states (9) and UTs (2) initiated steps to establish a council.

responsibilities. Chandigarh (UT) has constituted SCHE by the order of Higher Education Administrator on April 13, 2015, by following the guidelines of RUSA. It can be said, therefore, that there appears to be a gap between centre's stipulation and state governments' role. Though NPE stressed the need for state-level coordinating bodies, it is yet to be totally adhered to by the states.

Structure and Composition of SCHEs

In a country of wide diversity, the structure of the SCHEs varies from state to state. While states such as Andhra Pradesh, Telangana, Uttar Pradesh and West Bengal and so on have appointed an *academician* as a chairman/vice-chairman of the SCHEs, states such as Tamil Nadu, Karnataka, Gujarat, Kerala, Maharashtra and so on have appointed or nominated *administrators* and some states have appointed *minister* of *education* for the same. Again, the office of secretary in the council is held by either an educationist or an administrative officer. Eminent academicians/educationalists are nominated by the government as the council members from reputed institutions in the states. Vice chancellors (VCs) of state universities are nominated as members. Secretaries to government from various departments are appointed as ex-officio members. States such as Kerala and Karnataka have created executive body, general body, and advisory body of the council. For example, Kerala SCHE consists of three agencies. The *advisory body* consisting of chief minister, minister of education, minister of law, minister of health, minister of agriculture, leader of the opposition of the state assembly, one member of parliament (MP) from the state, representatives from SC, ST, and women group from within the state legislature and so on in order to guide functions of the council. The *governing body* includes minister of education, VCs of state universities, SC/ST/ women representatives from the academic councils of state universities, secretaries and directors from the various departments among others. This enlarged the scope of participation in matters relating to the state universities. Third, the *executive body* consisting of vice-chairman along with one permanent secretary, five part-time secretaries, one VC and the secretary to government, ministry of higher education. This body is supposed to look into day-to-day functioning and activities of the council. The Karnataka State Higher Education Council created two councils: *one* is *general council* having VCs, key ministers and secretaries from the government, a nominee from the UGC, SC/ST and women representatives from reputed institutions among others. The *second* is *executive council* consisting of two VCs from state universities, four of the ten academicians nominated by rotation by the council for a period of 20 months, principal secretary to government and so on plays a vital role in decision-making and policy matters. Apart from the above councils, there are ten academicians and ex-officio members in the SCHE. The other existing state councils maintain uniformity in the structure of councils. The composition of the SCHEs is provided as below (Table 4.1).

Powers and Functions of SCHE

The guidelines of the Report of the Committee on Setting up State Council of Higher Education (UGC 1988) state that the state-level planning and coordination be carried out by the SCHE. It is expected to be a bridge between the institutions and the state government and work closely with the UGC.[4] The state councils are expected to play a significant role in planning and coordination with other national bodies, education department, UGC, and so on. These councils also review the development of higher education institutions in the state.

The power and functions of the councils as specified in the report of UGC include planning and coordination, academic, and advisory functions. In addition, Uttar Pradesh and Rajasthan have included *financial and other functions* in their acts, while Kerala has included only general functions in the act along with the advisory, governing and executive councils.[5] Therefore, one can identify the similarities and dissimilarities in the functions of SCHEs. What follows is a broad classification of functions of SCHEs under four broad categories.

---

[4] UGC (1988). Report of the Committee on Setting up State Council of Higher Education.

[5] The functions and powers are compiled from the SCHE Act of the state governments.

Table 4.1 Composition of the State Councils of Higher Education

SCHE	Full Time Members	Ex-Officio Members	Other Members
APSCHE/ TSCHE	Chairman 2- Vice-Chairmen (Educationists)	Secretary- Education Dept., Secretary- Finance Dept., Secretary- LE&T Dept., Secretary-UGC Vice-Chancellors of the Universities	4 Members – Educationists 1 Member – Industry 1 Member – Technical Expert 2 Members – Others **Special Invitees** Commissioner, Technical Education, Commissioner-Collegiate Education, Director- Intermediate Education.
Karnataka SHEC	Chairmen (Edn. Minister) Vice-Chairmen (Educationists)	9 Principle Secretaries to Government-Finance, Primary & Secondary, Medical Education, Higher education, Agriculture, Horticulture, Animal Husbandry & Veterinary Sciences, Law &Justice, Social Welfare Commissioner- Collegiate Education Director - Technical Education Director -Medical Education Commissioner-Pre-University Board. One UGC Nominee	Secretary-The Executive Director VCs of the Universities Ten eminent academicians from various disciplines **Special Bodies** General Council Executive Council

(Continued)

Table 4.1 Continued

SCHE	Full Time Members	Ex-Officio Members	Other Members
Kerala SHEC	Chairmen Edu. Minister Vice-Chairmen Academician	Member Secretary Academician The Registrar- below the rank of a Joint Secretary to Government	32- Advisory Council; 35- Governing Council; 9- Executive Council.
Rajasthan SHEC	Chairmen Edu. Minister Vice-Chairmen Academician	Secretary- HE & Technical Education Department Secretary- Public Works Department- Finance Department Secretary- Planning Department Director of Collegiate Education Director of Technical Education Director, Sanskrit Education State Project Director 3- VCs from the Universities	12 Eminent personalities in various fields of study Two Principals of autonomous or affiliated colleges A nominee of the Union Government Two academicians of the rank of Professor having five years teaching experience
TNSCHE	Chairman Edu., Minister Vice- Chairman Academician	Secretary-FAC Addl. Chief Secretary to Governor Secretary, Higher Education Addl. Chief Secretary, Finance Dept., Secretary, UGC Director of Collegiate Education Director of Technical Education	1 Member – Academician 1 Member – Scientists/Engineers 1 Member – Industry 2 Members – Vice-Chancellors 3 Members – Co-opted by Council 1 Full time Member – Secretary

UPSCHE	Chairman	3 Secretaries, Education Dept., Finance Dept., Planning Dept.,
	2-Vice-Chairmen	Secretary, UGC
	Educationists	Director of Higher Education
		Director of Technical Education
		3 Members – VCs
		3 Members Academicians from Education, Law & Engineering
		1 Member Principal of College cooped by Council
		1 Member Industrialist – Co-opted by Council
WBSCHE	Chairman Edu., Minister	Addl. Chief Secretary, Dept. of HE, Sci. & Tech., and Bio-technology-Vice-Chairman,
	Vice-Chairman	Secretary, Higher Education Dept.,
	Academician	Secretary, Finance Dept.,
		Secretary, UGC, Nominee
		Secretary-AICTE, Nominee
		Secretary, DEB, Nominee
		VCs of the Universities
		Director of Public Instruction,
		Director of Technical Education
		Director of State Archives,
		Chairperson, WB College Service Commission
		Secretary, WBSCHE
		Joint Secretary, WBSCHE

Source: Compiled from acts of different state councils in India and from different websites.

Planning and Coordination

The SCHEs prepare consolidated programmes; liaison with UGC; make perspective, annual and budget plans for the development of higher education; and forward the proposals to the UGC. The Uttar Pradesh SCHE is also expected to explore industry and other related avenues. The SCHEs frame the guidelines to start new colleges or introduce additional subjects or departments in the existing colleges according to the rules of the state government and the UGC and explore additional resources. Besides, UP and Rajasthan SCHEs coordinate research funding at national and international levels for the promotion of scientific research in universities and colleges under its jurisdiction. SCHEs in Andhra Pradesh, Telangana and West Bengal additionally monitor the development programmes in higher education in their respective states. The Andhra Pradesh SCHE (APSCHE) is working as a regulating agency for all the private (including engineering and polytechnic colleges) and affiliating colleges in the state. Thus, in principle, the public and non-public institutions are under control of State Higher Education Council.

Academic Functions

The SCHEs are expected to initiate measures to promote innovations in curriculum development, restructuring courses and updating syllabus in universities and colleges; promote and monitor the programmes organized by the autonomous colleges; suggest necessary steps to strengthen the standards of examinations conducted by the universities and autonomous colleges; enable teachers' training in universities and colleges, monitor the academic staff colleges, encourage quality publications; improve programmes to enhance the cooperation between the faculty and facilitate mobility of teachers and students in and outside the state; advise on regulating the admissions; encourage physical and cultural activities; motivate to interact with the other agencies with regional planning and development; prepare report on the working of the universities and colleges in state and send a copy to the UGC. SCHE in Uttar Pradesh, however, sends its reports to the state government. Andhra Pradesh, Telangana and West Bengal conduct separate entrance examinations for admission to institutions. Thus, one can see the expanded and diverse role of SCHEs. Apart from this, states such as Uttar Pradesh (UP), Rajasthan and Tamil Nadu extended the scope of SCHEs in establishing centres of excellence in the universities and provide national and international linkages for further development in frontier areas of knowledge as the function of SCHE. They advise to set up State Centre for Scientific Research to coordinate the research activities among the universities, the UGC, AICTE and other agencies in relation to higher education.

Advisory Functions

The important advisory functions of SCHE are to formulate policy in determining disbursement of block grants; set up a state research board; and link research agencies and industry with state agencies. Attempts are made to evolve uniformity in statutes, ordinance, and regulations in state universities. Advisory functions vary from state to state. Andhra Pradesh and Telangana work with regional offices of the AICTE. Uttar Pradesh and Rajasthan expect their SCHEs to raise funds for innovative programmes for the sustainable growth of higher education through consultancy and liaising with institutions at national and international levels. APSCHE formulates proposals to augment quality in teaching and research by recommending setting up a Research Board, Accreditation Council, Institutional Performance Review Board, and Inter University Board at state level. Thus, the councils made earnest efforts to promote quality in governance of higher education.

Financial Functions

State councils in North Indian states took lead in financial management by monitoring grants-in-aid to universities and colleges. Besides administering student welfare fund, national scholarships, other scholarships, travel grant, publication grant, the SCHEs also advise states in release of research grants received by the council from national and international funding agencies. They also advise the state governments on steps to make institutions self-sufficient and viable and monitor funds for higher education to ensure matching grants received from centre.

The Chandigarh SCHE administers funds received from RUSA and distributes them as per state higher education plan.

Activities of SCHEs

As stated earlier, the SCHEs in India are perceived as intermediary agencies between centre and state governments to implement national policies of higher education (NUEPA 2018). The major activities as expected from the selected SCHEs have been discussed earlier. In addition to the common activities such as conducting workshops, seminars, teacher training programmes, and quality improvement programmes and so on, the SCHEs have their unique identity as mentioned below.

Andhra Pradesh: The council (a) initiated an online database of the universities and colleges, (b) conducts common admission tests (to graduate and postgraduate students), (c) prepared a report on Common Accounting and Finance rules to maintain the transparency in financing, (d) initiated a project on Andhra Pradesh Higher Education English Communication Skills to enhance the English language proficiency and employability skills[6] of 100,000 college students and 2,500[7] teachers in the state.

Kerala: The Kerala State Higher Education Council has been working actively since its establishment to address the issues of higher education in the state. It has submitted several reports to the government of Kerala for a state policy, Assessment and Accreditation Council, strategy to bridge between industry and education and so on. Further, the state government approved proposals to implement a choice-based credit and semester system, state faculty training academy and so on on the recommendation of SHEC.

Telangana: The TSCHE introduced online admission through a programme called Degree Online Services Telangana (DOST) aimed at checking misuse of scholarships and other benefits.

West Bengal: The WBSCHE monitors distribution of funds to universities and colleges through the West Bengal Council Higher Education Fund, which receives grants from centre, state and other sources.

---

[6] Available at: http://www.apsche.org/apsche_new/eng_csp.php.

[7] Available at: http://www.apsche.org/apsche_new/Pdf/ECSPPR.pdf.

Thus, the diverse role of SCHEs in different states is evident from the above discussion. Though the nature and functions of councils vary from state to state, there are some common challenges faced by SCHEs all over India. Some of the major challenges are discussed below.

CHALLENGES

Although the state councils are a creation of NPE-1986/POA/UGC, there exists no mechanism in place to achieve the goals. The UGC rarely convenes meetings of SCHEs for effective monitoring of its agenda. The MHRD calls council meetings of IITs. Many issues of coordination are discussed there. In respect of SCHEs too, the same initiative may facilitate coordination. It can help in identifying best practices of SCHEs. The UGC does not associate SCHE even as special invitees in its meetings. Interestingly, according to a senior functionary, it is doubtful whether state councils are on the mailing list of UGC. Thus, vertical linkage with national regulatory bodies remains a challenge.

Furthermore, the effectiveness of existing councils is questioned in view of the lack of functional control over state-level institutions. Coming to horizontal linkages, the state councils do not have statutory link with executive and academic councils of universities under its ambit. To what extent the SCHEs enjoy autonomy is a question and calls for review. There is a significant gap between the power and functions allotted to SHECs and the role these play in practice. World Bank Report (2014) titled 'State Higher Education Councils in India: Opportunities and Challenges' explained how far the members of the councils succeeded to exercise the given powers. An analysis of the gaps with respect to selected Indian states is presented in the World Bank Report. Organically, the councils consist of secretaries to government—education, finance and college administrative regulator on councils. The councils appear to be excluded from the process of selection of VCs, of faculty and determining grants. In both horizontal and vertical linkages with policy machinery, SCHEs seem to be out of the purview. The initiative of NIEPA to bring SCHEs and funding bodies such as UGC on a platform is not only laudable but may lead to redefining the role of SCHEs vis-à-vis other educational bodies for effective impact.

REFERENCES

Government of Andhra Pradesh. 1988. The Andhra Pradesh State Council of Higher Education (APSCHE) Act, Act 16 of 1988, G.O. Ms. No. 199, Education Department dated 17 May.

Government of Haryana. 2018. Haryana State Higher Education Council Act, Haryana Act No. 4 of 2018, G.O., 28 March.

Government of India. 1992. *National Policy on Education—Programme of Action 1992.* New Delhi: Ministry of Human Resource Development.

Government of Karnataka. 2010. Karnataka State Council of Higher Education Act, Act 16 of 2010, G.O., 26 July.

Government of Kerala. 2006. The Kerala State Higher Education Council Ordinance 2006 replaced by The Kerala State Higher Education Council Act, 2007, Act 22 of 2007 G.O. (P) No./2007/H.Edn, dated 15 October.

Government of Tamil Nadu. 1992. The Tamil Nadu State Council for Higher Education (TANSCHE), Act 40 of 1992 (as modified up to 30 June 1994), G.O. 10 July.

Government of Telangana. 2014. The Andhra Pradesh Reorganisation Act, 2014—the Andhra Pradesh State Council of Higher Education Act, 1988 (Act No. 16 of 1988), Act No. 6 of 2014, G.O.Ms. No. 5, Higher Education Department, dated: 2 August.

Government of Uttar Pradesh. 1995. Uttar Pradesh State Council of Higher Education Act 1995, Act 22 of 1995, G.O., 25 August.

Government of West Bengal. 1994. The West Bengal State Council of Higher Education Act 1994, West Bengal Act 37 of 1994, The Calcutta Gazette Extraordinary dated 27 July.

National University of Educational Planning and Administration (NUEPA). 2018, July. *Report of the Consultative Meeting on State Higher Education Council, Centre for Policy Research in Higher Education.* New Delhi: NUEPA.

University Grants Commission (UGC). January 1988. *Report of the Committee on Setting up State Councils of Higher Education.* New Delhi: Government of India.

World Bank Report. 2014. *State Higher Education Councils in India: Opportunities and Challenges.* Washington, DC: South Asia Human Development Department-Education.

Chapter 5

Accountability Measures to Improve Governance

M. Anandakrishnan

UNIVERSITIES AS ORGANS OF CIVILIZATION

The University Education Commission headed by Dr S. Radhakrishnan characterized the universities as organs of civilization as follows (Government of India 1950):

> He indeed must be blind who does not see that, mighty as are the political changes, far deeper are the fundamental questions which will be decided by what happens in the universities. Everything is being brought to the test of reason, venerable theologies, ancient political institutions, time-honoured social arrangements, a thousand things which a generation ago looked as fixed as the hills. If India is to confront the confusion of our time, she must turn for guidance, not to those who are lost in the mere exigencies of the passing hour, but to her men of letters, and men of science, to her poets and artists, to her discoverers and inventors. These intellectual pioneers of civilization are to be found and trained in the universities, which are the sanctuaries of the inner life of the nation.

Universities are institutions that are meant to sustain human practices and activities of a very special kind. They are, of course, concerned centrally with higher education and research, but their concern in these fields is very different from that of other institutions of higher learning and research which are devoted to imparting knowledge and skills that are essential to competent and creative pursuit of what might be called 'technical professions'.

Universities perform multiple roles for a diverse range of stakeholders, all of whom have high expectations. If universities have to stand up to such expectations, their governance system should be imaginative enough to play an effective role in governing the university as a living entity not just to deal with today's problem but to assist towards a smooth growth process. In order to have a proper balance of freedom and accountability, the government may ensure fiscal accountability, accountability for quality teaching–learning process and research and protecting the interests of vulnerable and disadvantaged section of the society. The remaining issues should be left to the discretion of higher educational institutions (Sandhu 2015).

CONTROL ON ACCOUNTABILITY

In developed countries, governments generally required universities to accept some form of external quality assessment as an accountability measure. Universities and colleges are accountable for their outputs or outcomes. The justifications for such control or accountability include: (a) higher education produces wider social and economic benefits and therefore such benefits must percolate to the whole society; (b) equity considerations require that low-income students are not disadvantaged; and (c) students, employees and the wider society need to have confidence in the quality of higher education qualifications.

Educational institutions will continue to feel the pressure and demands for accountability. Control of costs, elimination of duplication and evidence of other efficiencies are the focus for legislatures and higher education regulating and coordinating agencies. Similarly, demands for greater productivity in higher education will continue to be heard with greater frequency than at any time in the past (Leveille 2006).

EXPANSION TRENDS

Higher education is critical to India's aspirations of strengthening its reputation as a major competitive player in the global knowledge economy. The system is huge and complex, and there is a consensus that reforms are imperative. Issues of fair access and affordable participation in higher education are critical if India is to empower its people with educational opportunities that will allow individual potential to be fulfilled and provide more Indian graduates with opportunities for employment and abilities to compete in an international arena. India's robust economic growth has been driven mainly by higher productivity of educated and trained human capital in the face of greater competitiveness of the global economy. Future growth is increasingly contingent on ushering in a knowledge-based economy that would require increased enrolment and improved quality of the higher education system. At least 10 to 20 per cent of institutions should be rated among the premier institutions in teaching, research, publications, patents, innovations, social recognition, international reputation and so on. Another 20 to 30 per cent of the institutions should have standards benchmarked against the better quality institutions around the world.

ROLE OF GOVERNING BODIES

India's higher education sector has undergone a phenomenal expansion—with even more envisaged. Further expansion of the higher education sector without essential prerequisites in place, especially in relation to good governance, would not serve the nation's best interests and could undermine the sector's long-term development. A good governance system ensures that educational institutions are run by an independent and fully empowered board with representation from key constituents such as government, faculty, alumni, donors/industry and students. A good governance system helps create a stimulating ecosystem to attract talented faculty and motivate them through a performance-based reward structure. An enlightened governance system encourages faculty to engage in external research and consulting to stay abreast of new developments and to bring external knowledge into the classroom. It motivates alumni to contribute generously and willingly both funds and facilities for the development of the institution. It stimulates a culture of innovation, encourages large-scale faculty development programmes and improves productivity. The role of the governing body is vital in developing global collaborations and partnerships with academic, research and productive organizations.

It is not easy to create an ideal governance system since its constitution as also its powers and functions have to be adjusted to cater to several special circumstances. Even so it is possible to establish a governance system that is functionally autonomous and accountable so as to fulfil the mission of the institution effectively. The expansion of the higher education system has brought to the fore several critical issues relating to governance of the higher educational institutions. Historically, the educational institutions in India enjoyed considerable degree of autonomy vested in the heads of the institutions and the academic community guided by enlightened peers. This advantage has now been eroded substantially in the government-funded as well as the private institutions.

TYPOLOGY OF INSTITUTIONS

In general, the central and state governments in India have established multi-faculty universities; some of which are unitary and others are of affiliating type. Affiliating state universities are more common than affiliating central universities. Many of them often affiliate several hundred colleges. The enrolment of students in affiliated colleges alone accounts for roughly 90 per cent of the total in the higher education system. In addition, there are professional universities serving technical, medical, law and agricultural fields established by state governments. The professional universities are either unitary or affiliating. A third category consists of open universities established by central and state governments. These offer open and flexible education, through distance mode, using correspondence courses and modern education technologies. A fourth category is a set of institutions, not established by central or state acts but charted by the University Grants Commission (UGC) as 'deemed to be universities' in a variety of disciplines, governed either by the government-funded managements or by non-governmental organizations or by private families. These are established through registered trusts or societies and run in accordance with the UGC Guidelines or Regulations (UGC 2010). More recently, many private universities established by the acts of the legislatures of some states have come into existence.

Apart from universities and deemed-to-be universities, there are also several institutions such as Indian Institutes of Technology (IITs), National Institutes of Technology (NITs), Indian Institutes of Management (IIMs), and Indian Institutes of Science, Education and Research (IISERs) and so on offering professional undergraduate, post-graduate and research programmes, established as Institutes of National Importance, through Acts of Parliament.

Technical education is offered in all of the above categories of institutions. However, nearly 85 per cent of enrolment in technical education is in the engineering colleges affiliated to general or technical universities. Nearly 90 per cent of such colleges are privately owned. The need for adequate stress on improving governance arises out of the national and international experiences on the failures of higher educational institutions. Such failures relate to improper accountability and abuse of the board of governors, at one extreme; and nonparticipation of board of governors at the other, creating a lack of confidence, or worse, a lack of integrity, in governance, and with a danger of undermining the sector as a whole. Good governance ensures that stakeholders, including students, faculty, institutional management, as well as those from the wider society, have full confidence and trust in our institutions—and that those who have governance responsibilities and accountabilities carry these out effectively.

DEGREE OF AUTONOMY

The Kothari Commission emphasized that the proper sphere of autonomy of institutions broadly emphasizes (a) freedom to function to achieve academic excellence and (b) freedom to administer the institution through its own rules and regulations. Such autonomy has now become a veritable myth on account of (a) too much linkage with political powers of the state and (b) financial constraints faced by the institutions. Many states have come to apply more control on autonomous functioning of universities and colleges by various means and methods. Financial support has become most powerful instruments in the hands of state governments to curtail the autonomy of the universities and colleges. The autonomy relates to appointment and promotion of teachers, determination of courses of study, methods of teaching and selection of areas and problems of research. The National Policy on Education visualized that higher education should become dynamic as never before. One of the main features of the programmes and strategies to impart the necessary dynamism to the higher education system consist of the development of autonomous colleges and departments. The system of affiliated colleges does not provide autonomy to deserving colleges to frame curricula, courses of studies or their own system of evaluation (Gandhi 2013).

In case of centrally funded government institutions such as IITs, IIMs, central universities, IISERs, NITs and so on, it is reasonably certain that the interference and control of the government is minimal. Usually, the boards and the heads of these institutions have the freedom to evolve their academic policies and strategies except in areas where it concerns the fundamental national policies (e.g. reservations and pay commission norms). The governing boards of these institutions include just one or two officials of the central government.

At the same time, there are also several centrally funded institutions, especially those in the category of DUs and some of which are under different ministries, which have a large proportion of government officials in their governing bodies where the interference effect is high and troublesome. This is particularly worrisome in the case of state-funded institutions, where there is an unduly large proportion of government official in the governing boards interfering in all aspects of the university functions. In case of college-level institutions run by the states, the official control from the directorates is nearly total in all respects (Anandakrishnan 2010).

DIMENSIONS OF ACCOUNTABILITY

Accountability is a moral obligation of a university whether it is supported by public funds or privately financed. The ability of colleges and universities to provide for effective accountability engenders public trust. An institution with good accountability measures will not attract intrusion of government in its affairs. Accountability within the university should be based on very strong performance management systems for faculty and staff alike. Good universities are characterized by strong systems of performance management and review. In India, in recent years, many centrally funded institutions have adopted a system of external peer reviews to assess their performance once in five years. This system is quite comprehensive to include all aspects of the various functions of the institution, including teaching, research, administration, development, projects, funding and so on. The review reports are placed before the governing boards for appropriate actions mainly to adopt measures to eliminate accountability weaknesses.

The governing body in consultation with the head of the institution, faculty and outside experts should explicitly spell out the strategy and agenda for the future development of the institution. The governing body should indicate the implementation strategy including sources of finance.

The state-funded and private universities are yet to adopt such peer review systems. Hence, their accountability remains questionable.

Yet, another important aspect of accountability relates to systems to monitor the performance by students not only during their years in the institution but also thereafter. This should be assessed by the employment rates of graduating students, how quickly graduates secure full-time employment and how well they are paid.

Finally, good accountability requires strong internal audit requirements. Any public institution should have a strong, independent and professional internal audit process so that they can confidently face the external audit system, which is unavoidable in public-funded institutions.

DIFFICULTIES WITH CURRENT ACCOUNTABILITY SYSTEM

The faculty attributes are measured by empirical approaches. Often there is too much documentation and hence faculty may spend time in documenting than on real academic work. There is more distrust of the faculty claims than trust. Excessive monitoring upsets academic ambience. Hence, it is necessary to design an accountability system that emphasizes the approach to academic functions rather than on outcome. Feedback from colleagues should have sufficient weightage (Selvan and Warnick 2018).

PRIMARY ACCOUNTABILITIES

The primary accountabilities of institutional governing bodies are:

- To approve the mission and strategic vision of the institution, long-term business plans and annual budgets, ensuring that these meet the interests of stakeholders.
- To put in place suitable arrangements for monitoring the performance of the head of the institution.
- To ensure the establishment and monitoring of proper, effective and efficient systems of control and accountability (including financial and operational controls and risk assessment, clear procedures for handling internal grievances and for managing conflicts of interest.)
- To monitor institutional performance arrangements, which should be, where possible and appropriate, benchmarked against other institutions nationally and internationally (including any concerns for accreditation and alignment with international quality assurance systems).
- An annual report on institutional performance should be published widely. It should include identification of key individuals and a broad summary of the responsibilities and accountabilities that the governing body delegates to management, or those which are derived directly from the instruments of governance.
- There should be a balance of skills, experience and competence among governors, sufficient to enable a governing body to meet its primary accountabilities and to ensure stakeholder confidence.
- Normally, governing bodies have a majority of independent members, defined as both external and independent of the institution. Autonomous institutions would be free from direct political interference in order to ensure academic freedom.

SELF-ACCOUNTABILITY

Benjamin (2003) postulates that it is our capacity for self-accountability that keeps us functioning ethically and responsibly. While people may be accountable to others, they may not be as accountable to themselves when there is no one else to observe, monitor or hold them responsible. Self-accountability is the cornerstone of ethics: It is who you are and what you do when no one is watching. When you have a well-developed sense of self-accountability, you are honest with yourself and are answerable and responsible for what you say and do. You have the ability to look beyond the immediate moment to consider the consequences and know if you are willing to pay them. You have personal ethics. Personal ethics is the precursor to professional ethics, since we are not likely to be more ethical in our professional life than in our personal life. If we are dishonest in our personal life, we are likely to be dishonest in our professional life as well.

If the notion of self-accountability consists of ethical and responsible behaviour, then there will be no room for conflict between self-regulation and external regulation. In India, the Right to Information (RTI) Act requires institutions to respond to queries from interested persons about matters concerning the institution. If the practices and functions of a university are ethical and responsible in all its endeavours, there would be no cause for concern about accountability in disclosure of information on any of the processes of the university.

EFFECTIVE ACCOUNTABILITY

Assessment aims at improving the quality of education but is necessarily constrained by budgets. A focus on student learning outcomes can be a bridge that links the two. Effective and useful accountability measures should have two qualities. First, they must be unambiguous. Second, they must be linked in some way to indicators of quality. It turns out that student learning outcomes constitute useful measures of quality in and of themselves. They are consistent with the stated missions of higher education, and improving them is a valid indicator of improved institutional performance. Such indicators, when combined with cost data, could also be used effectively as measures of changes in institutional fiscal efficiency or overall performance over time (Frye 1999).

ACADEMIC FREEDOM AND AUTONOMY

It is widely recognized that academic freedom and autonomy, though linked, are not the same. Academic freedom is a universal concept, needed by universities, public or private. Autonomy, in contrast, is a relative value and may legitimately differ in its contents from place to place and from time to time. The issue of autonomy can usefully be broken down into two major parts, procedural and substantive. In the United States, the accountability movement in higher education has operated at both the national and the state level. But in each case, there are three possible layers at which to function: those relating to legality, those to efficiency and those to effectiveness (Berdahl 2010).

Providing academic accountability is difficult, especially in a democracy with high aspirations for higher education, strong populist tendencies, and constrained public resources. Colleges and universities are creatures of the state that established them. Governing boards at best provided benevolent, nonintrusive oversight, offered political and fundraising support, looked after the administration of the institutions. Sometimes, boards delegated authority to the head of the institution (Zumeta 2000).

AUTONOMY AND ACCOUNTABILITY

Autonomy should be viewed concurrently with accountability. Accountability is not meant only for auditing and regulatory functions. It is intended to promote and encourage better performance of managerial and administrative responsibilities in conformity with the objectives of a University. The governing board has the responsibility to determine the nature of functions of persons in different positions towards accountability without interference from outside. Accountability also demonstrates the social responsibility justifying the investments in the institution.

ACCOUNTABILITY TOWARDS GOALS

Every institution has the primary obligation to fulfil its declared mission faithfully and demonstrate the connection between the resources and achievements as a part of the accountability process. The governance system facilitates this process. The use of modern management tools will enhance the accountability functions.

The accountability functions should not be viewed as a bureaucratic exercise, unconnected with the academic and intellectual dimensions. The ethical dimensions of the accountability should be preserved.

EFFECT OF POLITICAL INTERFERENCE

In India, there is substantial evidence of political interference, especially in the state-funded institutions. Similarly, the private institutions suffer from undue control from the management. The accountability is interpreted as fulfilling the wishes of the political system or the private investors. Agencies charged with accrediting and ranking such institutions should assess the degree of interference in their functions and ensure true accountability is shown towards the goals of the institutions and not influenced by the political concerns.

As state universities rely on state governments for funds, the state officials tend to expect a degree of loyalty from the institutions in return for their support. When the academics took independent positions on issues, politicians resent it. They sought to curb the autonomy by bringing the institutions under close scrutiny of government. Often, the politicians and officials look upon state-funded universities as extensions of government departments resulting in increased government intervention in the affairs of the academic community. The only way to tackle such a situation is to amend the act of the university to reconfigure its board of management to limit official representation to the minimum, not exceeding two, and eliminate membership of politicians. This requires an enlightened government. The composition of the syndicate of Anna University, Chennai is an example of such a composition.

UNIVERSITY GOVERNANCE

Governance addresses how universities and higher education systems define and implement their goals, manage their institutions—physical, financial, human resources, academic programmes, student life and monitor their achievements. Universities now had to deal with complex issues relating to admissions, appointments, curriculum and financing as also their public image.

The key objectives of a university as generally understood are to disseminate, create and preserve knowledge and understanding by teaching, research, extension and service and effective demonstration and influence on society. It includes promotion of the spirit of intellectual inquiry and sustained pursuit of excellence. A major goal is to encourage individuality and diversity within a climate of tolerance and mutual understanding. The university is meant to extend the benefits of knowledge and skills for development of individuals and society by associating the university closely with local and regional problems of development.

CHANGING NATURE OF UNIVERSITY GOVERNANCE

Some of the rapid changes in recent decades have major implications for university governance. The changes are reflected in vastly increasing numbers, changing curricula, growing student strength, higher expectations on faculty competence, newer fields of study for graduation, compulsions of research performance by students and faculty and so on. These shifts require new forms of relationship between the university and the state, in case of publicly funded institutions and the university and the trust or the society supporting the university in case of private institutions.

ROLE OF GOVERNING BOARDS

For universities to perform these functions effectively, the government and external agencies should refrain from intervening in their internal governance. Governments should recognize that conserving the autonomy of these institutions is essential to protect academic freedom, the advance of knowledge and the pursuit of truth.

The ultimate responsibility for governance of the institution rests in its governing board (or executive council or syndicate). The board should establish effective ways to govern while respecting the culture of decision-making in the academy. The board should approve a budget and establish guidelines for resource allocation using a process that reflects strategic priorities. Boards should ensure open communication with campus constituencies. The governing board should manifest a commitment to accountability and transparency and should exemplify the behaviour it expects of other participants in the governance process. Governing boards have the ultimate responsibility to appoint and assess the performance of the head of the institution. Boards of universities should play an important role in relating their institutions to the communities they serve.

Notwithstanding the differences among the funding responsibility or accounting pattern of the university, it is necessary to ensure the full autonomy of the university by arm's length relationship between the governing body and the funding agency. The involvement of all the stakeholders in the governing body such as the faculty, students, public, donors, the state, alumni and so on is necessary for ensuring the credibility of the policies proposed by the governing body. The university should accept full responsibility for accountability to the society.

The governing body should avoid overregulation and micromanagement of the institution. It should lay down broad policy guidelines and performance targets and leave to the head of the institution and the members of the faculty and staff to fulfil the mandate. The board should ensure periodic external peer review of the institution by eminent educationists, researchers and administrators. The present trend in the composition of governing bodies of prestigious universities is to involve a majority of eminent external members and keep to a minimum the *ex-officio* government officials or the representatives of the sponsoring body.

CURRENT PATTERN OF GOVERNANCE

The two major governing bodies of older universities are the senate and the syndicate. The senate, meant to be a representative body, is quite unwieldy with representation from all and sundry with strength of two hundred or more presided over by the chancellor. Though it has the ultimate power on all matters concerning the university, its decisions often lead to a chaotic situation. All newer universities have avoided the senates in this sense.

Nowadays, syndicates (or executive council or board of management) manage most universities. In the case of state and central universities and most deemed universities, the vice chancellors chair the syndicate or board of management. The unwieldy size of some governing bodies, up to 35 members, is a matter of concern for effective management. Good practice models suggested that 10 to 15 members is the best size for effective decision-making, while still benefitting from a diversity of viewpoints.

TYPICAL COMPOSITION OF GOVERNING BOARDS OF DIFFERENT UNIVERSITIES IN INDIA
Centrally Funded Institutions

The typical size of the executive council of a central university, chaired by the VC, is 15 with one official from the MHRD and one from the state where it is located. In the case of the Institutes of National Importance such as IITs, NITs, IIITs, an eminent educationist or industrialist chairs the board of governors. The size of their board of management is around 12 to 15 with deans besides four distinguished persons nominated by the council. This includes the representatives of the state government where the institution is located and from the neighbouring states where there is no IIT. They may be educationists or officials. The number of central government officials is generally one and sometimes none. Similarly in the case of the NITs, the size of the board is about 13 members with one official from the MHRD and one official from the state where it is located.

Deemed Universities

The deemed universities may be centrally funded or privately sponsored. The UGC regulations (UGC 2016) for deemed universities prescribed that the board of management of deemed universities should have a minimum of 10 and maximum of 15 members chaired by the vice chancellor. In the case of private deemed universities, the number of representatives of the sponsoring body should not be more than four.

State-Funded Institutions

The composition of syndicates of some of the older universities is as follows: Calcutta University Syndicate: The total strength is 40, but the secretary, higher education, is the only government representative. The management councils of state universities in Maharashtra have 20 members with three government representatives, the secretary, higher education, the director of higher education and the director of technical education. (Table 5.1)

NATURE OF INTERFERENCE

Uttar Pradesh universities have no government officials. Most other states have utmost 2 or 3 officials. Tamil Nadu universities have as much as seven officials. The presence of government officials in the governing boards/syndicates can be helpful if they function as regular members of the bodies in assisting the university in securing the full support of the government and negotiate the paths of power. This is what happens in most of the centrally funded institutions. However, in the case of state universities, the government officials tend to dominate and insist on having their way. They serve to convey the demands of their political bosses at the cost of the autonomy of the university.

The adverse effect of government officials is immense when there is a prolonged absence of the vice chancellors as in the case of many universities in Tamil Nadu. At such times, the acts provide for governance by what is called a 'convener committee' consisting of three members of the syndicate. In the case of syndicates with several official

Table 5.1 *Total Strength of Management Council/Syndicate*

State	University	Total Strength of Management Council/ syndicate	Government Officials
West Bengal	Calcutta University	40	1
Maharashtra	State Universities	20	3
Tamil Nadu	Madras University	23	7
	Madurai Kamaraj University	22	7
	Anna University	13	Originally 2 Presently 5 Besides one MLA
Kerala	Kerala University	25	4
	MG University	25	4
	Cochin University of Science and Technology	20	3
Karnataka	Bangalore University	22	5
	Mangalore University	19	5
	Mysore University	21	5
Punjab	Punjab University	18	2
Gujarat	Gujarat University	27	3
	Sardar Patel University	25	2
	MS University	25	3
Odisha	Biju Patnaik University of Technology	18	5
	Utkal University	13	1
	Sambalpur University	10	1
	Indira Gandhi Institute of Technology	18	7 (Minister, MP, two MLAs, 3 Officials)

State	University	Total Strength of Management Council/ syndicate	Government Officials
Andhra Pradesh	Andhra University	14	3
	Acharya Nagarjuna University	13	3
	Sri S.V. University	15	4
	JNTU Kakinada	15	3
Telengana	Osmania University	5	4
Uttar Pradesh	Lucknow University	25	0
	VB Singh Purvanchal university	21	0
Madhya Pradesh	Barkathullah University	24	2
	Jiwaji University	17	2
Bihar	Patna University	23	2
	Magadh University	14	2
Assam	Gauhati University	21	3
	Dibrugarh University	21	3

Source: Compiled from official sources.

members, officials invariably dominate the convener committee as chairpersons and members. The chairperson is invariably the secretary, higher education and the director of collegiate education or the director of technical education as a member with an academic as a third member. Only the day-to-day functions of the university get attention. The academic and developmental aspects of the university are ignored. Convocations are postponed causing difficulties to students seeking to go abroad for higher studies.

Time has come for the university community and the concerned public personalities to try to eliminate the provisions for the representation of government officials and members of Parliament and MLAs in the governing bodies of the universities. The public should agitate against prolonged vacancies of vice chancellors and other statutory senior officials such as registrar, finance officer and controller of examinations.

GLOBAL TRENDS IN AUTONOMY AND ACCOUNTABILITY

Describing the global trends in autonomy and accountability, Saint (2009) states that

> As university systems around the world have become larger and more complex, governments have found it more effective to disengage from direct management control of individual institutions and instead, to steer them at arm's length by increasing their autonomy while putting in place mechanisms of accountability to ensure that enhanced freedoms are not misused. Apart from governments' inability to administer dozens of institutions, thousands of academic staff, and tens of thousands of students, the move towards increased institutional autonomy seeks to respond to the accelerating pace of change by enabling greater management flexibility, responsiveness, efficiency, and space for innovation. At the same time, new accountability mechanisms create positive and negative incentives, as well as various types of system oversight bodies, to monitor and reward institutional performance in the pursuit of public policy goals. Many of these incentives are financial. They are provided through formula-based funding, institutional performance contracts, and competitive awards. Others are based on reputation, as imputed through accreditation or institutional rankings. However, the topic of the present discussion is university leadership. Thus, trends in university autonomy and accountability will be reviewed here only as they pertain to university leadership as it is expressed in the roles and responsibilities assigned to institutional governing boards and senior officers.

UNIVERSITY GOVERNING BOARDS

The findings of Saint (2009) are summarized as follows:

- University governing boards come in all shapes and sizes. They may be called university councils, boards of trustees, administrative councils, university assemblies, senates, syndicates or something else. Yet all institutions of higher education have some type of highest decision-making body to which university leaders are accountable.

- The mandates, composition and procedures of governing boards also vary, as does the process for appointing their members. The choices made in defining each of these attributes often make the difference between autonomous, responsive and imaginative leadership and restrictive, rigid and conformist administration—or something in the middle.

- The mandates given to university boards vary widely from one country to the next. In virtually all cases, boards are tasked with defining a strategic vision for the institution, setting institutional policies, monitoring institutional performance and ensuring good stewardship of the institution's assets. Many (but not all) are charged with approving the university's budget. Some are asked to take on responsibilities for quality assurance and the equivalence of academic awards. Others are allowed to define salary structures, terms of employment for academic staff and/or recruitment of the institution's chief executive. A few are empowered to set student fees and determine student intake numbers. In general, higher levels of institutional autonomy can be found where boards are given more of these responsibilities.

- The means of appointing board members are essentially four: (a) the head of state or prime minister may control the selection directly (e.g. Lao PDR and Thailand); (b) the minister of (higher) education may be given appointing authority (e.g. Malaysia and Zimbabwe); (c) a formula may be defined whereby various stakeholders or constituencies elect their representatives to service on the board (e.g. Argentina and Brazil) or (d) board members may choose their own replacements through a self-perpetuating process.

- Fully self-perpetuating boards are most common within private universities, especially in the United States.

- How the chairperson of the governing board is appointed is another key indicator of university autonomy. The chair holds the powers to call meetings, set the agendas, appoint subcommittee membership, cast tie-breaking votes and generally influence the direction of discussion.

- State-funded universities in many Asian countries including India contain a combined governance and executive body called a syndicate, composed of 12 to 25 members, which functions under the purview of the senate and is therefore only roughly analogous to a governing board. However, the syndicate performs many of the functions normally allocated to a governing board, such as managing university assets, developing the institutional budget, making staff appointments and so on. In both countries, the head of state appoints some or all of the syndicate's members—even those from the academic community.

CONCLUDING REMARKS

The accountability measures to improve governance would include:

- The affirmation of universities as self-governing institutions with ultimate decision-making authority vested in a governing board.
- More diverse composition of governing board members, especially with regard to the incorporation of persons from outside government and the university community.
- Increasing use of formulas for determining board membership, often on the basis of elected representation, in place of government appointment of board members.
- Reduction in the overall numbers of governing board members.
- Occasional supplementation of governing board expertise through the establishment of formal or informal advisory bodies.
- Some inclusion of international members on governing boards in order to keep abreast of global happenings, a practice that seems likely to increase in the future.
- A clear shift to empowering governing boards to select university chief executives rather than government.
- Increased transparency, the use of merit-based criteria and competitive evaluation in the recruitment of university chief executives.
- Willingness to adopt worldwide recruitment of senior official of university.
- Greater concentration of decision-making authority in the chief executive and management team.

- Accountability on the academic side requires good universities to embed in policy and in practice very strong systems of peer review for teaching and research.
- It also is necessary to create strong internal performance indicators.

REFERENCES

Anandakrishnan, M. 2010, November. 'Accountability and Transparency in University Governance'. *University News* 48(45):18-23.

Benjamin, B. 2003. 'Ethics and Self-Accountability'. *Massage Today* 3(12).

Berdahl, R. 2010. 'Thoughts about Academic Freedom, Autonomy and Accountability'. *The Magna Charta Observatory Seminar*, Turkey, Istanbul, November.

Frye, R. 1999. 'Assessment, Accountability, and Student Learning Outcomes'. *Dialogue* (2): 1–12.

Gandhi, M. M. 2013. 'Autonomy and Accountability in Higher Education—An Indian Perspective'. *IOSR Journal of Research and Method in Education* 3(5): 33–37.

Government of India. 1950. *Report of the University Education Commission 1948–1949* (Radhakrishnan Commission). New Delhi: Ministry of Education.

Leveille, D. E. 2006. 'Accountability in Higher Education: A Public Agenda for Trust and Cultural Change'. *Research and Occasional Paper*. Berkeley, CA: Center for Studies in Higher Education, University of California.

Saint, W. 2009. 'Guiding Universities: Governance and Management Arrangements around the Globe'. Human Development Network, Working Paper, the World Bank, Washington, DC.

Sandhu, R. 2015. 'Autonomy and Accountability in Higher Education'. *International Journal of Research in IT, Management and Engineering* 5(1): 15–22.

Selvan, K. T., and K. F. Warnick. 2018. 'A Global Vision for Academic Scholarship and Professional Development'. FERMAT, Education 3. Available at: https://www.e-fermat.org/education/selvan-edu-2018-03/.

University Grants Commission. 2010. *UGC (Institutions Deemed to be Universities) Regulations 2010*. New Delhi: Ministry of Human Resource Development.

University Grants Commission. 2016. *UGC (Institutions Deemed to be Universities) Regulations 2016*. New Delhi: Ministry of Human Resource Development.

Zumeta, W. 2000. 'Accountability: Challenges for Higher Education'. In *The NEA 2000 Almanac of Higher Education*, Washington, DC: National Education Association: 57–71.

PART II

Governance and Management: Institutional Issues

Chapter 6

Governance and Management of Affiliated Colleges

Mohd Muzammil

India is one of the few countries where affiliating universities do exist and have colleges affiliated to them in very large numbers. The British government introduced the affiliating system in the 18th century, which continues to exist and has also grown much in size and intensity. In neighbouring Bangladesh, a similar picture also emerges with regard to university affiliation system (Muzammil 2017). Affiliated colleges are characterized by two main features: (a) prescription of courses and conduct of examination are done by the affiliating university and (b) the rest of the functions colleges perform almost independently. Affiliating universities hardly exercise any other control over their colleges.

EVOLUTION OF AFFILIATING SYSTEM

The evolution of affiliated colleges is older than the establishment of universities in India. It was the East India Company, then the British Parliament and later under the direct British rule in India that shaped collegiate higher education in different parts of the country. The East India Company is said to have set up the Calcutta Madrasa as an institution of higher learning in 1781, Banaras Sanskrit College in 1791 and

Fort William College in 1800. In the beginning, universities in India were also awarding First Arts (FA) degree, which was the Intermediate level of education (GoI 1950). Thus, FA (Intermediate) also came under university affiliation. Higher education was declared as one of the duties of the British government by the Charter Act of 1813. The Serampore College was set up in 1818 near Calcutta. With the setting up of the universities at Calcutta, Bombay and Madras in 1857, colleges were affiliated to these universities which were modelled on the pattern of the University of London—an affiliating university which focused on entrance tests for admission and conduct of examination (University of London Act 1898).

The system of higher education in India started with affiliating universities and constituent colleges. Many universities were set up by combining two or more colleges to make an operational unit of a university. Like in Uttar Pradesh, King George's Medical College (KGMC), which is now King George's Medical University, Isabella Thoburn (IT) College and the Canning College provided the base for enacting University of Lucknow in 1921. The IT College was set up in 1870 and Canning College in 1867 and KGMC in 1911. Earlier when universities were set up in Calcutta, Bombay and Madras in 1857, colleges were affiliated to these universities. Many old colleges in United Provinces namely Agra College, Agra (set up in 1823) and Bareilly College, Bareilly (1837) were later affiliated to Calcutta University.

The constitution of the three universities in Calcutta, Bombay and Madras was such that they were purely examining bodies, on the model of London University and each university admitted to its tests only those students who were enrolled in affiliated colleges. Thus viewed, the formal beginning of affiliated colleges to Indian universities dates back to 1857. Admission to graduate programmes was monitored by these universities in affiliated colleges. The role of the university was limited to the conduct of examinations. The universities did not focus on promotion of serious academic achievements and research in affiliated colleges. The defects of the affiliating system were soon realized in England in 1898 but not in India even now! It created provisions for admission and examination of what it called internal and external students who were reading in schools (colleges) affiliated to the University of London (1898).

The Calcutta University Commission (Sadler Commission) 1920 had opined that unless secondary education was reorganized well, meaningful improvement would not be possible in collegiate education at the university level. This necessitated organizing boards of secondary education in India. Consequently, that was done and looked upon as a major reorganization of pre-university education in this country.

TYPES OF AFFILIATION

Under the present system, an important function of affiliating universities is to affiliate colleges and confer degrees on their students. Each university, under the directions of the state government, lays down the conditions of affiliation, sends out teams of inspection and grants affiliation on the basis of their recommendation. In granting affiliation to a college, both the state government and the university are involved. When affiliated colleges were also given grants-in-aid by the government, the state government was concerned with financial matters and university was taking care of academics. Gradually, self-financed colleges (SFCs) were allowed to function and seek affiliation from a university without commitment of the state/central government in its financing.

With regard to the procedure of affiliation, the mechanism is not clearly defined across the country. In some states, affiliation is granted by universities without reference to the state government, while in some others, affiliation is a joint affair. The system of grants-in-aid is relatively on a decline as new colleges are coming up as SFCs affiliated to universities. This is one of the reasons why affiliation has become easy and the number of colleges is rising fast.

Affiliated colleges can be analysed in detail group-wise: (a) constituent colleges, associated colleges and affiliated colleges, (b) colleges of essentially residential universities and those of affiliating universities, (c) affiliated colleges in general and autonomous colleges, (d) aided colleges and SFCs, (e) general colleges and women's (or specialized) colleges. The constituent colleges enjoy special status as these are those colleges that made the university come into being as an independent unit of higher education. The category of affiliated colleges came later. On the other hand, associated colleges are situated often in close proximity of the university and function as a compact unit of the affiliation system.

There is another classification of colleges, viz. government colleges, aided colleges and SFCs. Government colleges again are of two types: colleges under the state government and colleges under the local bodies. However, the latter is a very insignificant category. The role of central government in owning affiliated colleges in the country is also minimal. SFCs, on the other hand, are generally looked upon as a category of new generation colleges/institutes as compared to aided and government colleges affiliated to the same university. Although some of the SFCs are doing very well, most of them leave much to be desired and are often dubbed as inferior.

Several questions arise while debating upon the issue of affiliation. One option is that as of now the affiliated colleges should remain with state universities. Another option is (and which looks convincing) that some of these if not all be affiliated to private universities whose number is gradually rising in all states and has already reached almost double the number of affiliating state universities in a state like Uttar Pradesh.

GROWTH OF THE AFFILIATING SYSTEM

The system of higher education in all states of the country has now grown into a very large system and the workload on affiliating universities has gone up many folds over the years in view of increase in the number of affiliated colleges. It is also true that there has gradually been tremendous increase in enrolments in existing affiliating colleges, and newly opened colleges. Offering larger number of courses and other types of quantitative expansion have together raised the responsibilities of universities manifold. Along with the issues of affiliated colleges, the task of managing universities is also becoming unwieldy. Many large universities in many states are now having more than 1,000 colleges affiliated to them!

Usually, even the number of colleges running into 700 to 800 with each affiliating university poses the problem of huge quantity mostly in admission and examination-related works. Now most of the universities are having centralized admission for affiliated colleges and they allot seats to different colleges and in the online process of admission, mostly students in rural areas find it very difficult to enrol themselves in the concerned college. Consequently, a unique situation is often obtained which is characterized by vacant seats in certain colleges and aspirants remaining un-admitted due to procedural complexities. In subjects such as engineering, biotechnology, management, many colleges also adopt parallel entry of students and thus are able to fill seats to a great extent. The network problem in computers in rural areas seems to be the biggest threat that limits ultimate admissions in many colleges whereas the students in catchment area are willing to be enrolled in the particular course that the affiliating college is offering.

SIZE OF THE COLLEGIATE SYSTEM

At the national level, counting only affiliated and constituent institutions of central and state universities, there are over 40,000 affiliated colleges of the 278 affiliating universities in the country. The largest 16 affiliating universities of the country do have 500 to 1,000 colleges affiliated to them. Some 156 universities of the country do have less than 100 affiliated colleges each. The college density (defined as the number of affiliated colleges per lakh of eligible population in the age group of 18–23 years) varies from 7 in Bihar to 59 in Telangana with a national average of 28 only. About 77.8 per cent of the colleges are in the private sector—both aided and SFCs taken together (MHRD 2017).

Further, from the view point of affiliation, there are two types of state universities: first category comprises those which are largely residential universities such as Jawaharlal Nehru University (JNU), and secondly, many others that are known as very big affiliating universities such as CSJM Kanpur University (in Uttar Pradesh) which has the distinction of having the largest number of affiliated colleges, followed by Dr B. R. Ambedkar University (in Agra) and University of Pune (in Maharashtra). However, it is also true that gradually all universities have become affiliating universities and all universities have also started developing their own campuses.

Now, in order that universities remain viable institutions to manage their affairs reasonably well, there is the need to have more universities and more autonomous colleges. The existing autonomous colleges may be considered gradually to be converted into universities. Time has now come when the biggest and most viable college of a district (with 70–80 degree colleges in the district) may be converted into a lead college and then a university. Conversion of cluster of colleges into separate universities is also a suggestion of similar nature.

The size of universities in terms of the number of affiliated colleges is increasing. There must be a limit to this expansion. Universities which started with small number of colleges are now affiliating several hundred colleges and the number is swelling annually. With regard to the optimal size of a university, commissions and committees appointed earlier at the national and sub-national level opined that quantitative expansion be examined along with equity and quality (Varghese and Malik 2016). For quantitative expansion, around 150 to 200 colleges should be the maximum limit for an affiliating university. The spatial spread and the density of colleges also need to be taken care of while suggesting opening of new universities. The system of administrative and academic management of universities will have to be relooked once the restructuring in numbers is attempted (MHRD 2016; Qamar 2018).

THE MECHANISM OF GOVERNANCE

Often governance in HEIs is looked upon as the process which covers management, administration and leadership (Middlehurst and Elton 1992). Accordingly, educational management in colleges includes planning, organizing, controlling and evaluating with a view to make the institution efficient and effective. Educational administration of colleges involves implementation of the policy within the given framework of the established system often created by the university concerned and the state. It relates to orders, commandments, statutes and ordinances and rules and procedures. The leadership at the institution level takes decisions, provides directions and coordinates activities with a view to create positive working environment. For improving quality at the institution level, visionary management is important along with efficient and effective administration and dynamic leadership (Powar 2005). Technological improvement is helpful in ensuring quality but perhaps more important is the human factor—the teacher whose adequate knowledge and training hold the key for quality improvement in colleges of higher education. Good education must be seen as development and not as a means of development (NCERT 1970).

Governance applies to creating facilities in which the affiliated colleges can function properly and efficiently. This mainly includes academic and infrastructural facilities. On the other hand, management is mainly concerned with utilization of facilities of the college itself to the maximum possible extent and to maximize the output with given input. If output level is given then minimizing the input costs becomes the main aim of management. A well-governed system at the college level is characterized by rule of regulations and ordinances that have been put in place by higher authorities and transparent implementation of the same by the college management. It is also recognized by the responsiveness of the college authorities to the stakeholders—viz. students, teachers, guardians and the society in general. The decisions in the college also need to be taken in a democratic manner with consensus of the main stakeholders. This will ensure that the management holds the feature of participation of all concerned in its working and also ensures equity (of all forms and types), efficiency and effectiveness in governance and management.

GOOD GOVERNANCE

Best practices of efficient educational management and good governance of colleges may need to be exchanged between colleges and universities and across countries. The British experience of the governance of the university system is a point in hand which is worth emulating in India (Muzammil 2012). Opportunities will have to be explored for memoranda of understandings (MoUs) to be signed among universities and institutions for pooling resources and improving academic management of the participating organizations. The academic criteria as suggested by NAAC may be adopted till State Assessment and Accreditation Council (SAAC) is put in place at the states level and it develops its own criteria for the state concerned keeping in mind the regional requirements and specific challenges.

Improvement in surveillance is an essential ingredient of good governance. With a view to make governance effective, the present number of regional higher education officers (RHEOs) needs to be addressed. One option is that at the district level, there may be a district higher education officer (DHEO) in all districts, and the present RHEO may be designated as regional higher education director (RHED) and a few more such posts be created keeping in mind the workload of academic governance and administrative surveillance.

Owing to weak academic surveillance, the facilities for quality teaching and research are lacking at the college level. Monitoring of doctoral research in colleges needs to be done strictly to improve the quality of research and put a check on mushrooming of spurious dissertations. Performance of students needs to be examined at the institutional level by using multifarious criteria for judging the overall personality development of students. Academic monitoring portals may be placed on the net to maintain continuous surveillance. The existing academic bodies such as IQAC and the (proposed) SAAC may be involved in this task of academic monitoring.

If the number of colleges becomes very large, academic monitoring becomes a gigantic task. What do we actually mean here when we say academic monitoring and what should be the criteria to measure the academic performance of the students and the institutions? In general, the teaching, learning and examination performance is termed as 'academic' that also includes the overall educational ambience of the institution concerned.

THE COLLEGE MANAGEMENT SYSTEM

While the physical, financial, and academic management of affiliated colleges is related with efficient use of available physical and financial resources and optimization of outcomes (with given resource base), governance, on the other hand, primarily relates to the voluntary and statutory ability of the affiliating university and the college itself to provide enabling 'facilities' that are necessary for efficient functioning of an independent college. With government grants having been frozen or converted into block grants, colleges are left to supplement resources through self-generated funds and are compelled to run on 'commercial basis' which raises many educational and ethical issues.

In this discussion, many conceptual issues are involved, the knowledge of which will help make the higher education system more efficiently managed and better governed. It will also look at availability of resources at the college level from managerial consideration, its augmentation by its own self and the affiliating university and the way resources are being made available through grants of various types and voluntary support. Finally, management of optimal utilization to ensure better learning outcome becomes all important. Financial grants and donations of money and other resources will need to be examined in relation to the actual requirements of these and the extent of their fruitful utilization. The task of examining the status of governance will focus on the 'ability' of the affiliating university and the college concerned to make available infrastructural and other facilities in the presence of which working of the college could be improved.

For strengthening teaching and learning, teachers (as resources) may need to be adjusted as per exact requirement across colleges of similar type. They may also need to be moved from parent departments to newly created departments in the frontiers of knowledge in the same subject within the institution to help strengthen teaching and research outcomes. This is an important dimension of academic management which is seldom attempted. Consequently, in its absence, quality in affiliated colleges is at stake. The internal quality assurance cell (IQAC) at the college level is an essential component of good governance and management of academic resources at the disposal of the institution. It may need to be strengthened and made more transparent and effective. Efficient management of teaching may think of introducing project work in graduate courses to make the academic study more contextualized to suit the personal aptitudes of students and socio-economic requirements of the region and the country. All in all students services need to be improved at the college level.

Efficient and effective management along with good governance is related with the optimum size of the higher education system in any state. Externalities and spread-out effects start weakening after a limit. For instance, as many as 22 universities were born out of Agra University over time (since its inception in 1927) spread over in several states! In view of the overloaded affiliated universities that are virtually breaking down (due to overload of colleges), we have already recommended to the government of Uttar Pradesh that about 200 colleges to affiliating universities and about 150 colleges to residential universities should be the upper limit of the number of colleges affiliated in order that the governance and management remains efficient and effective (GoUP 2015).

For well-organized management of specific types of colleges (as mentioned earlier), there seems to be a case of having separate universities for these specific types of colleges and institutes. An affiliating medical university may be established for the existing medical colleges that are as of now affiliated to different state universities. Similarly, it also seems wise to have a homeopathic university, a university of dental science, and university for management education and the like for affiliating the specific colleges imparting the related education. The proliferation of BEd colleges all over the state and law colleges also demand that there should be an affiliating education training university and an affiliating law university at the state level.

Courses of study on yoga and naturopathy are coming up on a priority basis in affiliated colleges, and physical education is already in a special status with universities and colleges. Demands have started coming up to have a separate AYUSH university and a separate state-level university for physical education. If that is done, the overload of multifarious colleges with state universities will surely be reduced. Then, specific colleges will be affiliated to specific universities.

THE PROCESS OF ADMISSION

As enrolment ratios are rising, admissions in colleges will rise further in years to come. The increasing demand for higher education in colleges can be met in two ways: by expanding the existing colleges and by opening new colleges. The size of the colleges has an important effect on their costs and efficiency and it is therefore important to have a suitable admissions policy for affiliated colleges.

In graduate classes, admissions are based on subject combinations, and the problem is related with choice of subjects. Usually, the problem lies with the elective subjects. The preference of the students does not match the permissible combination of subjects. Consequently, such subjects are allotted that the student is not aware of due to lack of transparency in the admission process. It is only at the examination time that the student comes to know the subject combination that has been allotted by the university to him/her. In such situations, college students suffer and have to run from pillar to post to have necessary corrections made in the university.

Students from far off districts find it most difficult to have the corrections made as often the online system does not work properly, and they have to visit the university's admission centre physically. It results in the loss of time, energy and money. Further, examination forms are filled in colleges, and the forms are then forwarded to the university concerned. In this process, often there are gaps of data and errors, both technical and manual which results in delays in declaration of results. Policy recommendations based on several commissions earlier had desired that bulk of the postgraduate admissions and admissions for research be made in the university itself and in constituent colleges rather than in affiliated colleges.

CONDUCT OF EXAMINATION

The process of conducting examination was very easy when the system was small and there were few affiliated colleges with the university. Gradually, with mushrooming of colleges and an enormous increase in the number of students (counting into lakhs and answer sheets running into millions), the conduct of examination has become a stupendous task. With secrecy associated with all university examinations at all stages, leakage of question papers, delay in publication of results and several malpractices tarnishing the reputation of the examination are often reported. Mass copying has become a common phenomenon. In many colleges and universities, students have been demanding 'the right to copy at the examinations' as a fundamental right! Credibility of the examination in the affiliated colleges is at stake. The entire examination system has gone into disrepute.

Given the increasing number of enrolments in affiliated colleges, conduct of examination and evaluation both are becoming unwieldy and nearly unmanageable affairs for many affiliating universities across states. The first problem in affiliated colleges is that all colleges cannot be made centres of examination. So, they are asked to send their students to a nearby centre for examination. This creates problems particularly for girls. Sometimes, girls are allowed to appear from the same college and boys are sent out to another college. For smooth conduct of examination in affiliated colleges and to distribute question papers and answer sheets orderly, the affiliating university often sets up nodal centres. Blank answer sheets and question papers are sent out a couple of days in advance to the nodal centre under the supervision of the nodal centre in-charge and an official deputed for the purpose by the university concerned. Similarly, for collection of written answer sheets of the examination, the nodal centres are responsible for collecting answer sheets from all colleges under their purview and sending them to the university examination/evaluation centre.

Thus, the conduct of examination even once in a year of about 5–6 lakh students and evaluation of 6–7 million answer sheets is a herculean task indeed. This is a big constraint in switching over to the semester system in affiliated colleges. Continuous assessment and academic monitoring of students in affiliated colleges is therefore a remote dream. This is one of the reasons why the traditional annual system of examination is continuing in affiliated colleges in states such as UP, Bihar, MP, Rajasthan and many others.

MANAGING QUALITY TEACHING AND RESEARCH

Quality of teaching and learning decreases as enrolment increases beyond proportions. There is a trade-off between quantity and quality. With a view to improve quality of higher education, there is an increasing trend of switching over to semester system in many colleges. One important argument to improve quality through semester system is that it creates curricular space and continuous learning. This aim will be defeated when as much time will be gone twice a year only in conduct of examinations, evaluation of answer sheets and post-examination work of computation of results.

Teaching in these colleges is the most neglected part, and there is virtually no supervision by the university concerned of the teaching quality in affiliated colleges. The current situation is characterized by the fact that the teachers are focused on their own privileges and are neglecting their basic duties and the result is that teaching—which is the most important function of a college—suffers miserably. The involvement of teachers in the corporate life of the college is so absorbing that little time is left for their attention to teaching work. The same is the case with research which is being conducted even in small affiliated colleges where research facilities are very scanty, virtually non-existent (Muzammil 2015).

Despite these odds, the colleges are taking leads in preparing a very large number of doctoral theses in subjects in which they are recognized for conducting research by the university concerned! We have seen their dissertations being prepared under facilities and conditions which are not even fit for UG teaching in that subject. The result is that the quality of investigation and research leaves much to be desired. We must remember that colleges like universities are there in place for pursuit of knowledge and scholarship, examinations and award of degrees are only incidental to it. Unfortunately, this is not being realized and more so in colleges.

COLLEGES WITH POTENTIAL FOR EXCELLENCE

Many affiliated colleges present a better picture than others. A few years back, the UGC launched a scheme for the colleges aiming at those colleges which were promising institutions. Under this scheme, the focus was on fostering excellence in teaching and research in affiliated colleges. The scheme provides financial support to help improve colleges, their academic and physical infrastructure, introduce innovative teaching methodologies and implement modern learning and evaluation methods. The UGC identified 282 colleges with 'potential for excellence' and supported them with financial assistance (UGC 2013).

The largest number of such colleges was found to be located in Maharashtra (49) followed by Andhra Pradesh (24), Uttar Pradesh (23), Karnataka (19), West Bengal (18) and Tamil Nadu (17). Following closely, Kerala (13) and Odisha, Punjab and Rajasthan (12 each) were identified with substantial number of colleges having 'potential for excellence'. It is also noteworthy that only select universities did have colleges with potential for excellence. The 49 identified colleges in Maharashtra belong to 9 state universities and 24 in Andhra Pradesh belong to 6 state universities.

In most of the smaller states/union territories of the country, only one college is identified as a college with potential for excellence. The states are Arunachal Pradesh, Chandigarh, Goa, Jammu and Kashmir, Meghalaya, Nagaland and Puducherry.

AUTONOMOUS COLLEGES

The scheme was launched by the UGC with a vision to advance the quality of undergraduate education by partially delinking some colleges from the affiliating structure of the universities and promoting the concept of autonomy in deciding curricula, prescribing syllabi, evolving pedagogy and appropriate assessment techniques.

The UGC has identified 441 autonomous colleges spanning over 21 states and 85 universities. The commission made special financial provision for these colleges which were given academic autonomy of various types (UGC 2013). The largest number of autonomous colleges is found in Tamil Nadu (155), followed by Andhra Pradesh (78), Karnataka (49), Odisha (37), Madhya Pradesh (35), Maharashtra (28) and Uttar Pradesh (11).

The autonomy to affiliated colleges in various universities is given with a view to: (a) partially delinking some colleges from the traditional affiliating structure, (b) experimenting with innovative approaches to pedagogy, (c) granting autonomy in designing courses and (d) giving autonomy also in designing curricula and syllabi.

The idea of autonomy has assumed special significance under the newly developed accreditation framework of NAAC. While many colleges are vying for getting autonomy, many colleges having received 'autonomous status' wish to surrender the autonomy. Similarly, many good colleges are not willing to apply for autonomy, and (surprisingly) some big autonomous colleges wish to surrender autonomy expressing their inability to carry it through. Dau Dayal Girls PG College under Dr B. R. Ambedkar University, Agra surrendered its autonomy and returned to original position of an affiliated college. A row of opposition came up when the UGC team visited St Stephens College Delhi for granting autonomous status. The students and teachers feared that they would lose academic autonomy and the college will be autonomous only to raise fee (Pandey 2018). The politics of teachers' associations and students unions often comes in the way of academic reforms. The resistance of the teaching faculty to convert the college into an 'autonomous' college came in as a debatable issue.

AFFILIATED COLLEGES AND RUSA

RUSA is the national higher education mission which aims at quality improvement in higher education by providing strategic funding for quality improvement to eligible institutions (university departments and government and aided colleges) (MHRD, 2013). The role of central government in general category states is 60 per cent and the remaining 40 per cent is the state contribution. It also aims at improving equity and inclusion in higher education by promoting access to higher education among under privileged sections of society. But affiliated colleges often complain and rightly so that they are marginalized in the allotment of funds under RUSA. The main beneficiaries are the universities followed by the government colleges. Affiliated aided colleges occupy the last place. Affiliated SFCs do not come under the purview of RUSA so they have to depend upon their own resources for quality improvement.

RUSA is aspiring now at the national and state level what the National Knowledge Commission (NKC) opined earlier in 2007. The enrolment ratios are to be improved in higher education along with that in elementary education (the impact of SSA) and that in secondary education (after the implementation of RMSA). To help facilitate achieving this goal along with quality education, the requirements are having (a) better colleges under universities, (b) clusters of colleges under a lead college *state-level affiliating university* for colleges, (c) more autonomous colleges or more deemed to be university institutions and (d) in view of fast increase in higher education age cohort we may need all these simultaneously in states where higher education is yet to be developed properly. Policy decisions need to be taken in favour of all or few of the above and related modalities would also be needed to be prepared and put into place accordingly.

A BLUEPRINT OF MONITORING

Academic monitoring is an important issue in affiliating colleges. Various concepts of 'academic' need to be examined and the most relevant ones be taken into account. Academic for our purposes has relations with students, teachers and the principals and higher education authorities. It is also to be decided in what ways it needs to be related to knowledge testing. The system of higher education stands for students and promotion of research activities. Achieving excellence in the two should be the aim of our academic monitoring exercise. The concept of student's progression as explained by the NAAC is the guideline that may be followed in this regard. It can also be contextualized as per the local requirements and challenges of higher education.

The learning abilities and improvement in learning levels of students is the first step in that direction. Improvements in learning do reflect academic achievements of the students and the institutions. It is also important to note that academic monitoring is often related with self-evaluation and also self-improvement. For teachers 'academic monitoring', it may also be expressed in terms of the following three types of monitoring: (a) monitoring by peers/colleagues, (b) monitoring by superiors/seniors and (c) monitoring by students. Academic monitoring once put into place will surely help in improving both teaching and learning qualities. It will result in benefiting both—the teachers and the students alike. Surely, the largest beneficiary will be the society and the nation.

A comprehensive academic monitoring can help in many ways in converting ineffective instruction into effective education and bring about an improvement in the teaching–learning process in the higher education sector. This seems to be the biggest issue today that needs to be tackled on priority. The mechanism put forth herewith will enable us to achieve the same.

A system of constantly progressive evaluation may be required to make improvements continuously in all directions. For this purpose, a three-tier monitoring mechanism is suggested to be in place in the present circumstances and with minimum dislocations:

1. Internal academic monitoring involving IQAC of the affiliated college concerned.
2. District/sub-district level monitoring by nodal monitoring committees (to be created) for which a lead college of the area may be identified for the purpose. This middle level committee will work as a facilitator to help the colleges in performing their task well.
3. University level monitoring by a central monitoring committee led by the college development councils and by suitably strengthening these councils in the future. A full professor may be appointed as dean/director to make the college development council effective.

Academic monitoring is also very closely related to monitoring of the attendance of the students and the teachers in institutions and the mechanism of how to ensure these. There is strong resistance on the part of the affiliated colleges to be ready to accept educational reform measures. An instructional schedule prepared and given out to students by teachers will be important and helpful. The punctuality of teachers and 'planning the class lecture' will go a long way in ensuring regular and effective classroom teaching and creating an overall improved academic ambience.

CONCLUDING REMARKS

Academic performance of affiliated colleges, which has been grossly neglected, needs to be monitored. Supervision is needed in matters of serious academics and research in affiliated colleges. For strengthening teaching, teachers may be made to move among colleges to impart education. They may be transferred from parent departments to newly created departments in the frontiers of knowledge in that subject to help strengthen teaching and research guidance.

The internal quality assurance cell (IQAC) needs to be strengthened and made more effective. The IQAC may think of introducing project work in PG courses to make the academic study more contextualized and professional to suit personal requirements of students, institutional profile and social demands of the time. The academic criteria as suggested by NAAC for affiliated colleges may be adopted till state assessment and accreditation council (SAAC) is put in place. The number of RHEOs needs to be increased. Their number has been stagnant for decades together across states. They look after administrative supervision of the affiliated colleges.

Many affiliated colleges having PG departments and research guides approved by the university are now conducting researches leading to PhD and DLit degrees. This facility created in the name of giving colleges the same academic status as that of a university department is being resorted to with impunity. Production of substandard theses is a common sight. Monitoring of doctoral research in affiliated colleges needs to be done strictly to improve the quality of research and put a check on mushrooming of spurious dissertations. Pooling of research facilities among colleges is a helpful solution to this problem.

Academic monitoring portals may be placed on the website to maintain a continuous surveillance and the existing academic bodies from IQAC to (proposed) SAAC be involved in this task. This will go a long way in improving e-governance of affiliated colleges. Good performing viable colleges may be identified to be converted into lead college in the district effective governance. At present, the affiliation system of higher education is burdened with several administrative interventions—many of these are regressive in effect. Therefore, enabling facilities need to be created and improved for better governance and efficient management.

A recommendation of the Kothari Commission still lies unimplemented truthfully. It said:

We recommend that there should be a *Council of Affiliated Colleges* in every affiliating university consisting of the representatives of the university and colleges. It may also be advisable to associate with it, as members a few representatives of other universities in the State and from outside. The functions of the Council, to be laid down by the statutes of the University, would be to advise the university on all matters relating to affiliation of colleges, to help in implementation of policy of the university in this matter, to keep a close contact with colleges with a view to helping them in proper development, and to evaluate periodically whether the standards of colleges are being steadily raised. This is by no means an easy assignment and it can be discharged satisfactorily only if members with a high sense of duty and keen understanding of educational problems are selected. (NCERT 1970)

College development councils in many affiliating universities are in place but engaged only in routine work, unaware of the above recommendation.

When the Twelfth Five-Year Plan was being framed, a subcommittee of the plan panel had observed that the affiliation system was detrimental to the growth of higher education (Chopra 2012). The panel observed, 'It is seen that at times the universities engage continuously in the management of affiliated colleges at the cost of other pressing academic pursuits.' The panel felt that even big affiliating universities should not have more than 100 colleges and the condition to grant affiliation to a college should be determined at the national level and all universities should follow them. This recommendation too remains unimplemented, virtually ignored altogether.

REFERENCES

Calcutta University Commission. 1920. *The Report of the Calcutta University Commission (Sadler Commission) 1917–1919*. Calcutta: Calcutta University Commission.

Chopra R. 2012. 'Planning Commission to Junk University Affiliation System?' *India Today* 11 January. Available at: https://www.indiatoday.in/india/north/story/planning-commission-university-affiliation-system–89276-2012-01-11 (Accessed on 20 November 2018).

Government of India. 1850. *Report of the University Education Commission 1948–49* (Radhakrishnan Commission). New Delhi: Ministry of Education. Available at: http://www.academicsindia.com/Radhakrishnan%20Commission%20 Report%20of%201948-49.pdf (Accessed on 20 November 2018).

Government of Uttar Pradesh. 2015. *Report of the Committee on Optimum Number of Colleges and Academic Monitoring in Higher Education in Uttar Pradesh* (Under the Chairmanship of Dr Mohd Muzammil constituted by Government of UP). Lucknow: Department of Higher Education.

Middlehurst, R., and L. Elton. 1992. 'Leadership and Management in Higher Education'. *Studies in Higher Education* 17(3): 251–264.

Ministry of Human Resource Development (MHRD). 2013. *Rashtriya Uchchatar Shiksha Abhiyan (RUSA).* New Delhi: Government of India.

Ministry of Human Resource Development (MHRD). 2016. *National Policy on Education 2016—Report of the Committee for Evolution of the New Education Policy* (TSR Subramaniam Committee Report). New Delhi: NIEPA, Government of India. Available at: http://nuepa.org/new/download/NEP2016/ReportNEP. pdf (Accessed on 16 September 2018).

Ministry of Human Resource Development (MHRD). 2017. *All India Survey on Higher Education 2016–17.* New Delhi: Department of Higher Education, Government of India.

Muzammil, M. 2012, 6–12 February. 'Governance and Funding of Higher Education in England: Lessons for India'. *University News,* 50(6): 7-13.

Muzammil, M. 2015, May. 'Ensuring Quality and Excellence in Quantitatively Growing Affiliating Universities of Uttar Pradesh'. *University News,* 53(20): 83-88.

Muzammil, M. 2017. Convocation Address to the Second Convocation of Atish Dipankar University of Science and Technology (ADUST). Dhaka, Bangladesh, 17 May (mimeo).

National Council of Educational Research and Training. 1970. *Education and National Development School Education: Report of the Education Commission 1964–66.* Volume 3, para 13.54, 1970, 619–620. New Delhi: NCERT.

Pandey, M. 2018. 'St Stephens College in Delhi Like to Get Autonomy, Can Set Its Own Syllabus'. *Hindustan Times* 19 May. Available at: https://www. hindustantimes.com/education/st-stephen-s-college-in-delhi-likely-to-get-autonomy-set-its-own-syllabus/story-GpViaX2Hxzig6XzLt2B17H.html (Accessed on 17 September).

Powar, K. B. 2005. *Quality in Higher Education.* New Delhi: Anamaya Publications.

Qamar, F. 2018. Problems with Creating World-Class Universities in India. *DNA,* 10 September. Available at: https://www.dnaindia.com/analysis/column-problems-with-creating-world-class-universities-in-india-2661226 (Accessed on 15 September 2018).

University Grants Commission. June 2013. *Indian Higher Education—Quest for Excellence: A Compendium of Flagship Programmes of UGC.* New Delhi: Government of India.

University of London Act 1898. Available at: http://archives.libraries.london. ac.uk/resources/1912historicalrecord.pdf (Accessed on 6 September 2018).

Varghese, N.V., and G. Malik. 2016. *India Higher Education Report 2015.* New Delhi: Routledge.

Chapter 7

Management of Autonomous Colleges
A Movement from Academic Colonialism to Freedom and Democratization of Higher Education

G. D. Sharma

THE SYSTEM OF UNIVERSITIES AND COLLEGES IN INDIA

Indian university system came to be established in 1857 when first three universities were set in three port towns of India, namely Calcutta (now Kolkata), Bombay (now Mumbai) and Madras (now Chennai). Prior to this, a couple of colleges were set up during the British rule to meet the engineering, administrative and medical needs of British rulers. These colleges were affiliated to British universities. When these three universities were set up, colleges in respective regions were affiliated to these universities. The concept of affiliation arose from the practice that universities initially were examination conducting bodies and subsequently they assumed the role of teaching, research and evaluation. During the subsequent period, when universities were set up in different provinces, these universities also affiliated the colleges, conducted examination of students and awarded degrees to success-ful candidates. Teachers in colleges mainly played the role of giving instruction/teaching to students as per the given syllabus approved by the academic council of the universities. Colleges also engaged in sports and cultural activities and in the overall development of students. The academic development of students was as outlined in the syllabus provided by universities and the focus was to pass and obtain the grade in the examination. Since universities were set up under the provision of act of state legislation as was being done in Britain, management of universities was as provided in the act and statutes of universities. Act and statutes gave autonomy to universities to take academic and administrative decisions as per the administrative and academic ordinance of universities. Although universities were set up by the state, these were autonomous in their management and governance. Affiliated colleges to universities were managed by the sponsoring body—trust/society or the government department of higher education, as per provisions of affiliation by the university. Curriculum, a method of instructions and system of evaluation, was as per the direction of universities, the general administration was as per the government rules for government colleges and as per provision of Societies Act/Trust Act and guidelines of affiliating universities. Hence, universities were autonomous to frame their curriculum, carry out instructions and evaluate students and award degrees as approved by the academic and Executive council of universities. But colleges on academic side governed by the provisions of affiliation of colleges and administrative side by government rules or the provisions of Trust/Societies Act and guidelines given by the university. Colleges did not make any decision with regard to syllabus, instructions and evaluation of students. Teachers and principals of colleges did become part of university decision-making bodies, as experts or as nominated members by the university authorities. But colleges did not enjoy any academic and administrative autonomy, but to carry out instructions in the classroom and managing day-to-day and annual academic, social, cultural and sports activities. The advantage of this system was a sort of uniformity in the system of syllabus, instructions and evaluation of students within the jurisdiction of the university to which colleges were affiliated. The disadvantage was that teachers could not apply their learning and introduced the programmes of studies they considered appropriate to domain knowledge and appropriate to the region these were located. Another disadvantage was that the system was producing prototypes of students with uniform knowledge inputs and their evaluation was based on these inputs. Irrespective of the fact, such knowledge and skills are needed in the production and distribution system of the region. Colleges could hardly relate their domain knowledge with the knowledge needed for the development of the region and could meaningfully engage college graduates or encourage them to engage in solving the problems of the region.

The process of affiliation of colleges continued as the colleges and universities grew over the period before India became independent and also after India became independent. The numbers of colleges were nearly 500 and there were nearly 25 universities when India became independent.

THE BEGINNING OF THE CONCEPT OF AUTONOMY

The concept of affiliated colleges was done away within the UK and in many countries, colleges came as an autonomous body to decide the curriculum, carry out instructions, evaluate students and award the degrees to successful students. The lead in this model of higher education was taken by the United States of America and many other European countries. Hence, there existed a system of higher education different from that in colonial ruled India and postcolonial independent India. The problem of the affiliated system of higher education became very visible around late 1970 when graduate unemployment became a matter of concern. A study done by this author on graduate employment in India pointed out that unless structural changes take place in higher education or the economy, the problem of graduate unemployment would continue as the system is producing prototypes of graduates with a large proportion graduating as arts, science and commerce graduate and having nearly 30 per cent of unemployment (Sharma and Apte 1976).

An attempt to assess the situation of school and higher education before formulating a national policy on education, some of the limitations of the affiliating system was pointed out in the document 'challenge of education'. The situational analysis also indicated the experiment and innovations done with regard to academic management of colleges in Tamil Nadu.

AN INITIATIVE BY DR MALCOLM ADISHESHIAH

A visionary vice chancellor of Madras University, Dr Malcolm M. Adisheshiah, who has also served as deputy director general of UNESCO Paris gave autonomy to nearly 14 colleges affiliated to Madras University. The autonomy was to college to frame their syllabus, carry out instructions and evaluate students. University agreed to award degrees to students as per recommendations of college. As per the law of the land, degrees can be awarded only by the universities constituted by an act of legislation. Hence, universities awarded a degree on the recommendations of the evaluation done by the colleges. The autonomy of colleges was also given to attempt innovation in the system of teaching and evaluation. Autonomous colleges adopted a semester system and introduced programmes of studies relevant to the needs of the region.

STUDY OF AUTONOMOUS COLLEGES

Followed by Madras University, many other universities also gave autonomy to some of their affiliated colleges. This experiment was studied by the National Institute of Education Planning at the request of the University Grants Commission (UGC). NIEPA organized a study visit by 21 college principals drawn from different parts of the country and carried out the study of the experiment being done by autonomous colleges in Tamil Nadu (NIEPA 1985a). The report of this study visit formed the basis for formulating the policy on higher education and scheme of autonomous colleges for promoting the concept of autonomy by the UGC. The second National Policy on Education was announced in 1986 (NIEPA 1985b).

NATIONAL POLICY OF EDUCATION 1986: REFORMS IN HIGHER EDUCATION

The National Policy on Education 1986 and Programme of Action 1992 (GOI 1992) envisaged three major reforms in higher education. First being the promotion of the concept of autonomous colleges so as to free colleges from the academic colonial system and enable them to take academic decisions including framing of curriculum, the system of teaching and evaluation. The second one was the introduction of the concept of professional development of college and university teachers through setting up of the academic staff colleges in selected universities preferably having centres of advanced studies and with regional distribution. The purpose was to provide opportunities for teachers to attend general orientation and subject refresher programmes. A study conducted by National Commission on Teachers in higher education has pointed out that only 13 per cent of teachers in colleges had an opportunity to attend the seminar and workshop in their 30 years of career, and 40 per cent of university teachers had this opportunity. Hence, there is a need for providing an opportunity for college and university teachers for orientation and subject refreshers programme. Academic staff colleges (now named as UGC HRD centres) were created to meet this need. The third and most important reform was introducing the concept of state-level council of higher education, on lines of UGC, so as to coordinate within the state and with the central government for the development of colleges and a logical step of National Council of Higher Education—an interministerial body headed by prime minister to coordinate overall development of higher education. Of these three reforms, the last one did not take place; a state council was set up only in a few selected states. Academic staff colleges were set up in several universities.

The concept of autonomous college was encouraged through a scheme of grant of autonomy to colleges and special funding provision by UGC for this reform. Colleges were granted autonomy through a well done procedure and quality check through accreditation by NAAC. The latest scheme provides a grant of autonomy to government, government-aided and private self-financing colleges that have existed for 10 years, initially for the period of 10 years with a provision of extension after the review. The UGC provides funds for carrying out following reforms to the tune of ₹9 lakh per year for undergraduate colleges of arts, science and commerce—one faculty only and ₹15 lakh for more than one faculty colleges in these streams and ₹10 lakhs and 15 lakhs both for undergraduate (UG) and postgraduate (PG) level, respectively for single and multi-faculty colleges:

- Upgradation of the syllabus on regular basis making it skill oriented with quantifiable outcomes
- Orientation and re-training of teachers
- Redesigning courses and development of teaching/learning material
- Workshop, seminars, conferences and meetings
- Examination reforms
- Furniture for office, classrooms, library and laboratories, library equipment, books/journals
- Renovation and repairs not leading to the construction of a new building
- Extension activities
- Office equipment, teaching aids and laboratory equipment
- Guest/visiting faculty
- Capacity building for teachers
- Development of area study programmer.

However, self-financing colleges will not be provided autonomy grant (Autonomous College Scheme, University Grants Commission, 2018).

THE PROGRESS AND PROBLEMS OF IMPLEMENTATION

The concept of autonomy for colleges was basically challenging a well-entrenched system of affiliation of colleges for more than a century, that is, 1857 to 1986—precisely 130 years. It envisaged that leadership of University would introduce the provision of autonomy to colleges in their respective universities acts. It also envisaged state governments to support this move. Above all, it envisaged that teachers, students and principals of colleges would welcome it. But in practice, the concept faced challenges from some state governments—particularly West Bengal which did not agree with the concept. Teachers' association also opposed it, fearing that it is a move to withdraw financial support and privatize the colleges. They also feared that it will dent the organization of teachers' union and so on. The opposition from teachers is still seen even after 30 years. A case of Delhi University's St. Stephen College is an indication of apprehension and opposition of teachers to the concept of autonomy to colleges.

Some universities and state governments, particularly in the southern part of the country, came forward to implement this reform and benefit from this change. The lead was also taken by some of the Christian mission colleges and other trust and society sponsored colleges. Some state governments also came forward to give autonomy to government colleges. Mention may be made of Rajasthan state government, which gave autonomy to five government colleges in five districts of the state. But after experimenting it for about five years, it withdrew the autonomy to colleges. Government functionary felt that it is changing from uniformity and also posing a challenge to government hierarchical system. Madhya Pradesh government also gave autonomy to government colleges. However, Tamil Nadu, Andhra Pradesh, Karnataka and Maharashtra implemented it very progressively.

ISSUES IN THE MANAGEMENT OF AUTONOMOUS COLLEGES

The following are issues that have emerged during the process of management of autonomous colleges:

The Academic Management: University versus Autonomous Colleges

The concept of autonomy envisages that colleges would frame curriculum suited to their region keeping in view the growing domain knowledge in different fields of studies. Autonomous colleges under the provision of Board of Studies and Academic Council attempted to reform their curriculum as per the need of society and growing knowledge. However, within this broad structure of university curriculum, nomenclature of courses, college was required to frame the curriculum as the degree-granting power was with the university. University also functions as per Board of Studies and Academic Council's decisions and as per their acts, ordinance and statutes. Hence, scope for a change in curriculum by the college was not possible. Hence, academic autonomy was restricted to the broad structure of the university curriculum pertaining to a subject discipline. If a subject discipline is not available in the university statutes, the university cannot award the degree. Hence, freedom to frame curriculum was restricted to broad structures and subject disciplines being offered by the university to which colleges were associated as autonomous colleges.

The Method of Transaction of Curriculum/Programmes of Studies

The autonomy of colleges also envisaged that the method of transaction of knowledge should follow the semester system. That is 90 days of teaching and followed by semester examination. This system offered college students to prepare well and get better grades in their subject/programmes of studies. But universities continue to follow the annual system of examination, it was assumed that students in this system in practice do not get high grades. But when the students from the system of annual examination and students from the system of semester system compete for admission in the PG degree programme, the high score of students in the semester system puts students from annual system of examination to disadvantage. Hence, universities decided to discount certain per cent marks of students seeking admission for PG programme in the departments of the university concerned. This practice discouraged the students, faculty and leadership of autonomous colleges. Hence, reform in teaching–learning process attempted by the autonomous colleges in the form of semester system, project work and so on was put to a disadvantage. Thus, universities approach indirectly discourages and checked the academic freedom of autonomous colleges.

The linked aspect was students of autonomous colleges could not have university positions of first, second and third as the students of affiliated colleges had in the whole university. Students of autonomous colleges got their positions within the colleges owing to the system of college-level evaluation.

Recruitment of Teachers for New Programmes

Government and private-aided colleges' faculty members are paid by the government department and funded by the government.

The recruitment of a faculty member for new programmes of studies has to be therefore done with the approval of government both in the case of government colleges and private colleges aided by the government. To recruit a new faculty member, therefore, was a difficult task, as colleges have to negotiate with the directorate of higher education of the state government for additional faculty in the case of government colleges and in the case of private-aided colleges additional funds for new faculty members. Given the scenario if state attempted to withdraw the financial support to secure new faculty post it was almost impossible. This position of a shortage of funds also affected the innovations needing for infrastructure or laboratory and library upgradation.

Negotiating with New Management Structure

Thus, the management of autonomous colleges has to negotiate with following governing structure and external factors:

The UGC: For guidelines and financial assistance for the operation of autonomous colleges. UGC provided funds to autonomous colleges for carrying reforms in curriculum, training of teachers and establishing a system of evaluation in the colleges.

The State Government: For recruitment of teachers and staff, infrastructure, laboratory and library development.

The Governing Body of Trust and Society: For approval of activities and additional financial support as also day-to-day governance as any additional resource requirement has to be further negotiated with the local management committee/body.

The System of Participative Management: As per the guidelines of UGC, the system of participative management, both academic and general management, has been introduced. These include the academic council, board of studies, controller of examination, teachers and students' participation in the management of colleges. All aspects have to be negotiated through this process. The provision of industry and university participation in curriculum reforms has also been introduced in academic council.

The Teachers Union and Associations

Autonomous College Teachers Association remains a distinct body from rest of university teachers' association. Teachers have an apprehension that their bargaining power with regards to service conditions and other benefits may be affected.

All India Federation of Teachers Association has opposed the concept on the grounds of weakening the teachers union. The position has been somewhat changed on the ground that service conditions of teachers of autonomous colleges should not be adversely affected.

The Process of Teaching: Learning and Evaluation

In autonomous colleges, the process of teaching–learning and evaluation is expected to change, as stated above, through introduction of semester system, introducing the concept of assignment, project and field work and continuous evaluation of students. This invariably requires more involvement of teachers and students and an increase in their workload. Whereas remuneration and service conditions of teachers in affiliated colleges, with relatively less workload, is the same. This makes affiliated college teachers to oppose the concept of autonomous colleges. UGC guidelines and pay committee of UGC has introduced higher positions in autonomous colleges, yet implementation being slow, it does not inspire teachers of affiliated colleges to opt for autonomy.

Freedom to Innovate and Change: Experiment by Autonomous Colleges

The colleges which opted for autonomous status have bargained for their freedom to innovate and change. These colleges, in spite of limitation and issues narrated above introduced semester system, changed the curriculum keeping in view new social and market demands introduced a new method of teaching and evaluation such as project work, fieldwork, assignment and continuous evaluation. Teachers and students have worked for more than the required hours to make the experiment a success. Introduction of students' feedback has added to change and introduction of transparency in the system of evaluation. This is in spite of fear expressed by a critique of the autonomous colleges that owing to internal evaluation teachers may exploit or harass the students.

A review of working of autonomous colleges and workshop of autonomous colleges in the 21st century conducted by the UGC in 1998–1999 and report published in 2001 under the title of Autonomous Colleges in 21st Century, edited by RP Singh, published by Originals, Delhi 2001, have clearly brought the progress on several aspects of reforms as also apprehension and limitation of working of the concept.

Some innovations in curriculum, method of transaction of knowledge and system of evaluation as highlighted in the report may be narrated here:

Introduction of New Courses

Some of the new courses introduced by autonomous colleges are following: The subjects include

- Computer orientation in almost all the courses
- Wild-life biology, biochemistry, environmental botany, medical botany, plant products
- Mineral bonification and materials handling drilling technology, synthetic drugs, adulterants in foods
- B.E. Mechatronics (four-year course)
- Aqua-culture in zoology
- In economics or commerce: advertising, sales and sales promotion, publicity, taxation practice, consumer education, office management and secretarial practice, entrepreneurship
  - Industrial psychology
  - Healthcare and hospital
  - Tourism in history courses.

Some Unusual Courses Include

- The science of creativity and personality development
- Mathematics for non-mathematics students
- Regional/local events/personalities contributing to the freedom struggle
- Life oriented education for the empowerment of women
- Women's writing

(*Source:* Whither Autonomy: Its Place Today and Tomorrow—AS Desai, Ibid.)

Introduction of New System of Evolution

The system of evaluation included the following aspects:

i.	Monthly one-hour tests (two best out of three)	10 per cent
ii.	Seminars/workshops	5 per cent
iii.	Project wok/assignment	5 per cent
iv.	Model examination	30 per cent
v.	Terminal examination	50 per cent
	Total	100 per cent

Besides the format of the question paper which may include questions like long answers, short/very short answers or one out of multiple choices. Students should be assessed for their reasoning power and the ability to convert information into its application.

The difference between the university system and autonomous colleges at the time of introduction of the concept and around 1998 were as shown in Table 7.1.

Some of the reforms namely semester system and choice-based credit system implemented by the universities under the UGC guidelines to universities were in fact voluntarily implemented by the autonomous colleges even at the very beginning of the concept of autonomy.

Table 7.1 *The Difference between University and Autonomous College*

University	Autonomous College
(a) Semester is optional	(a) Obligatory
(b) There is no credit system	(b) Credit system is followed
(c) Sufficient credits are not a condition for promotion	(c) Minimum credits of 12 is required for promotion next year
(d) Attendance 75 to write the university examination. Less than that, condonation fee Collected	(d) The same procedure is followed
(e) For UG there is one valuation only	(e) Double valuation both for UG and PG
(f) Continuous assessment is not obligatory	(f) Continuous assessment is compulsory; however, there is no minimum for CA. But for terminal, 18/50 for UG and 23/50 for PG is compulsory

Source: Xavier (2001).

This was the situation when in spite of a good scheme of autonomous colleges with financial support was launched in 1986–1987 and the matter was discussed in the CABE meeting to promote the concept, yet India had only about 200 autonomous colleges till 2000 when the above review workshop was conducted. It was only when under the concept liberalization several self-financing colleges were setup and colleges grew at a high rate. An analysis of growth and development of autonomous, as is seen from the analysis below, also reveal a similar trend.

GROWTH AND DEVELOPMENT OF AUTONOMOUS COLLEGES

The Distribution of Autonomous Colleges by States

As of 2018, 24 states have made provision for granting autonomy to colleges and 104 universities in these states have granted autonomy to colleges. A total number of colleges which have been granted autonomy and many have passed through several cycles of autonomy are 621 colleges. Of this, 170 are government colleges and 451 are non-government colleges. Of this, nearly one-third colleges (28 per cent) are in Tamil Nadu. This is followed by Andhra Pradesh (84 colleges), Karnataka (70 colleges), Telangana (57 colleges) and Maharashtra (47 colleges). These five states out of 24 states account for more than half of the autonomous colleges in India (UGC, 2018a, 2018b). For details, see Table 7.2.

Table 7.2 *Distribution of Autonomous Colleges by States, 2018*

Name of the State	Total	Percentage
Andhra Pradesh	84	13.53
Assam	2	0.32
Chhattisgarh	11	1.77
Goa	1	0.16
Gujarat	4	0.64
Haryana	1	0.16
Himachal Pradesh	5	0.81
Jammu & Kashmir	3	0.48
Jharkhand	5	0.81
Karnataka	70	11.27
Kerala	19	3.06
Madhya Pradesh	39	6.28
Maharashtra	47	7.57
Manipur	1	0.16
Nagaland	2	0.32
Odisha	44	7.09
Pondicherry	3	0.48
Punjab	9	1.45
Rajasthan	5	0.81
Tamil Nadu	181	29.15
Telangana	57	9.18

Name of the State	Total	Percentage
Uttar Pradesh	11	1.77
Uttarakhand	4	0.64
West Bengal	13	2.09
Total	621	100

Source: Compiled from UGC list of autonomous colleges, UGC (www. ugc.ac.in).

THE GROWTH OF AUTONOMOUS COLLEGES

The growth of autonomous colleges over the year 1986 when the policy was formulated to 2018 indicates that colleges have grown very slowly until 2005 and it was during 2006–2011 the period when many self-financing colleges were set up and autonomous colleges also had high growth. This continued up to 2012–2018 (Table 7.3 and Figure 7.1). The high growth in autonomous colleges could be due to the fact that Tamil Nadu state gave autonomy to a large number of self-financing colleges. The concept of self-financing private colleges has grown significantly after the year 2000 until 2012. During this period, a large number of colleges got established as self-financing private colleges. There appears to be a close relationship between the growth of self-financing colleges and the growth of autonomous colleges.

Table 7.3 Growth of Autonomous Colleges over the Period 1979–1985 to 2012–2018—All India

Years	1979–1985	1986–1990	1991–1995	1996–2000	2001–2005	2006–2011	2012–2018
Growth of auton-omous colleges	8	61	6	25	34	204	283

Source: UGC (2018).

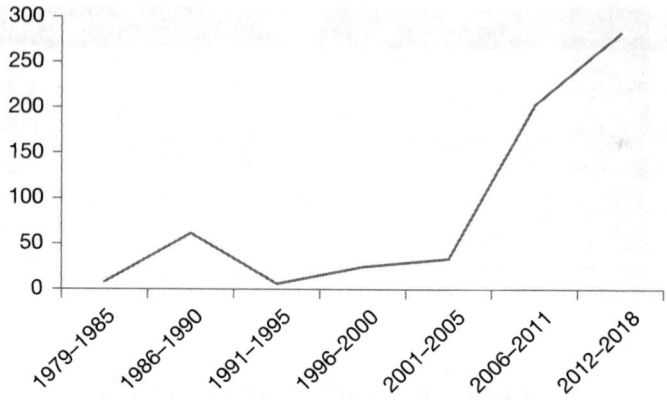

Figure 7.1 *Growth of Autonomous Colleges over the Period 1979–1985 to 2012–2018*

Source: UGC (2018).

The state-wise growth of autonomous colleges (Table 7.4) shows that growth of autonomous colleges during 2006–2011 and 2012–2018 is mainly owing to growth of colleges in Tamil Nadu, Karnataka, Andhra Pradesh and Telangana. Odisha also had a good share of growth during this period.

The high proportion of autonomous colleges in the states, as mentioned above, also has a large proportion of self-financing–private-unaided colleges. The latest Annual Survey of Higher Education report mentions that (MHRD 2018):

> 78% Colleges are privately managed; 64.7% Private-unaided and 13.3% Private aided. Andhra Pradesh and Telangana have about 82% Private-unaided colleges and Tamil Nadu has 76.2% Private-unaided colleges.

The growth of autonomous colleges is during the above period and largely among self-financing private colleges. This is in spite of the fact that these colleges do not receive any grant/funds from the UGC for carrying out required reforms in syllabus, teaching and learning process and evaluation of students. The autonomy offers them freedom and opportunity to orient their programmes of studies and system of evaluation to suit the need of the employment market.

Table 7.4 Growth of Autonomous Colleges during 1979–1985 to 2012–2018, by States

	1979–85 1st Auto	1986–90 2nd Auto	1991–95 3rd Auto	1996–2000 4th Auto	2001–2005 5th Auto	2006–11 6th Auto	2012–18 7th Auto	Total
Andhra Pradesh		6			2	**20**	**56**	84
Assam							2	2
Chhattisgarh		9					2	11
Goa							1	1
Gujarat			1				3	4
Haryana							1	1
Himachal Pradesh				5				5
Jammu & Kashmir							3	3
Jharkhand						4	1	5
Karnataka					4	**42**	24	**70**
Kerala							19	19
Madhya Pradesh			2	9		10	7	**39**
Maharashtra		11		3	1	14	29	**47**

(Continued)

Table 7.4 (Continued)

	1979–85 1st Auto	1986–90 2nd Auto	1991–95 3rd Auto	1996–2000 4th Auto	2001–2005 5th Auto	2006–11 6th Auto	2012–18 7th Auto	Total
Manipur							1	1
Nagaland						1	1	2
Odisha		2		1	7	23	11	**44**
Pondicherry					1	1	1	3
Punjab							9	9
Rajasthan						1	4	5
Tamil Nadu	8	27	1	7	17	68	53	**181**
Telangana		5	1		2	12	**37**	**57**
Uttar Pradesh		1	1			3	6	11
Uttarakhand						1	3	4
West Bengal						4	9	13
Total	**8**	**61**	**6**	**25**	**34**	**204**	**283**	**621**

Source: Compiled from UGC list of autonomous colleges.

THE FUTURE OF THE CONCEPT OF AUTONOMY TO COLLEGES

Some of the aspects pertaining to the future of the concept of autonomy to colleges may be discussed here.

The Concept of Autonomy and Private Self-financing College

The above analysis reveals that the number of autonomous colleges grew rapidly during the period 2006–2011 and 2012–2018. The growth is mainly in five states of India, namely Tamil Nadu, Andhra Pradesh, Telangana, Maharashtra and Odisha. These states also have a large number of self-financing colleges. The concept very much suits the self-financing colleges as they have responded to social and market needs in curriculum and developed certain abilities and skills so that students could have better placement. The concept of autonomy gives them the freedom to revise the curriculum, carry out innovations in teaching and learning as also in the evaluation of students. These colleges also do not require negotiating with state government as they do not receive funding from the state government. They negotiate with university on academic aspects and are able to take advantage of the concept of autonomy. Several issues and limitations highlighted above are somewhat absent or present in a very manageable form. Hence, there is likely acceptance and growth of autonomous colleges in the future. It is also very important to consider whether self-financing colleges can be financially supported for carrying out reforms.

The Concept of Autonomy and Government and Government-Aided Colleges

However, the concept of autonomy to government and government-aided colleges has suffered in the past as some of the government colleges in Rajasthan state were reversed to affiliated colleges. The growth of government and government-aided colleges has been slow. These also account for 27 per cent of a total number of autonomous colleges. These colleges have negotiated with several governing structures and for financial help. Therefore, their growth has been slow. It would continue to be so in future because of several limitations/issues as highlighted above.

But the question is whether this trend should continue or some policy intervention is needed. In our view, in order to benefit students enrolled in government and government-aided colleges, which normally charge relatively less fee and admit students with merit and needy students, they should also have the opportunity to implement the reforms.

POLICY INTERVENTION

The policy intervention is needed to relieve such colleges from limitations of recruitment of staff, limitations of developing infrastructure and labs and the introduction of new methods of teaching and learning and evaluation. State government should evolve a new mechanism of funding the autonomous colleges and a new system of governance so as to give colleges autonomy in real sense and comparable with that of self-financing autonomous colleges. This we consider as essential to encourage government and government-aided colleges interesting experimenting with the concept and introduce needed reforms in the colleges. This is also necessary to avoid a situation that students paying full cost are enjoying the benefit of reforms and those who are paying less fee are deprived of this benefit, in spite of the fact their colleges are ready to take autonomy but for limiting governing, funding structures and process.

DEGREE-AWARDING AUTONOMOUS COLLEGES

Universities imparting higher education are autonomous by definition as they are constituted by an Act of Parliament, Act of Legislation or under Section 3 of UGC Act and so should be colleges imparting higher education. In our view, the concept of affiliated colleges is a vestige of academic colonialism which should be completely done away with. All colleges which have worked to prove their ability should be given autonomy irrespective of government, government-aided and self-financing colleges. Some of the autonomous colleges which have proved their ability and worth may be given degree-awarding status by introducing a new clause along with deemed to be university clause as degree-awarding autonomous colleges.

This would be one of the required and long-awaited reforms to democratize the higher education and free them from the colonial legacy of affiliated colleges.

REFERENCES

Desai, A. S. 2001. 'Whither Autonomy: Its Place—Today and Tomorrow'. In *Autonomous College in 21 Century*. XVIII, edited by R. P. Singh, 1–8. New Delhi: Originals.

Government of India (GOI). 1986. National Policy on Education 1986. New Delhi: Ministry of Human Resource Development.

Government of India (GOI). 1992. *National Policy on Education—Programme of Action 1992*. New Delhi: Ministry of Human Resource Development.

Ministry of Human Resource Development (MHRD). 2018. All India Survey of Higher Education 2017–18. New Delhi: Department of Higher Education, Government of India.

NIEPA. 1985a. *Report on a Study Visit to Autonomous Colleges in Tamil Nadu, NIEPA*. New Delhi:

NIEPA. 1985b. *Challenge of Education: Background Document as Input for Discussion for the Formulation of National Policy on Education, NIEPA*. New Delhi: NIEPA.

Sharma, G. D., and M. D. Apte. 1976. Graduate Unemployment in India. *Economic and Political Weekly* 11(25): 915–925.

Singh, R. P. 2001. *Autonomous College in 21 Century*. XVIII. New Delhi: Originals.

University Grants Commission (UGC). 2018a. List of Autonomous College. Available at: https://www.ugc.ac.in/oldpdf/colleges/autonomous_colleges-list.pdf.

University Grants Commission (UGC). 2018b. Scheme for Autonomous Colleges. Available at: https://www.ugc.ac.in/pdfnews/5353052_Scheme-of-autonomous-colleges.pdf.

Xavier, V. J. 2001. 'Examinations—Loyola College Experiment'. In *Autonomous College in 21 Century*. XVIII, edited by R. P. Singh, 63–68. New Delhi: Originals.

Chapter 8

Governance and Autonomy
A Study of Central and State Universities

Garima Malik

INTRODUCTION

Higher education in India is going through rapid expansion and diversification. With a gross enrolment ratio (GER) of 25.8, India still has a long way to go for universalization. The rise in the number of institutions and explosion in student enrolments have raised concerns about quality of higher education imparted in the public and private institutions.

India also needs sweeping institutional reforms to overcome the problems of governance (Chandra 2018). The poor governance of the public institutions and the profit motives of the private institutions are reasons for low quality (Chattopadhyay 2012). In a massified higher education system, public funding to universities has not kept pace with the rapid expansion. This has many implications for how universities are run and the emergence of private universities has changed the higher education landscape considerably (Varghese and Malik 2016).

The university traditionally has been in close relations with the state and distant relations with the market. Over time, the state has taken a backseat and market has become dominant in higher education decision-making. The globalization process has further reinforced and accentuated this trend. Consequently, the state has moved away from its direct controlling role to steering from a distance. The market processes have introduced neoliberal policies in financing of higher education. Many public universities have privatized their operations and many countries have permitted private higher education institutions.

The chapter looks at the governance structures in universities and how autonomous universities are in their functioning. The chapter argues that central universities in general enjoy more autonomy and liberal funding while state universities are subject to more control and relatively limited public funding. The empirical basis for this chapter is the Centre for Policy Research in Higher Education (CPRHE) study coordinated by the author on governance and management of central and state universities and their affiliated colleges in different states.

The chapter is divided into different sections. The next section examines the changing role of the state in higher education governance. The third section defines institutional governance and autonomy. The fourth section examines various committees and commissions on autonomy. The fifth section delves deeper into the state–university relationship, while the sixth section highlights within-university relationships. The final section concludes the chapter.

CHANGING ROLE OF THE STATE IN HIGHER EDUCATION GOVERNANCE

There have been major reforms to governance in many systems with the state stepping back to allow universities to govern themselves. Thus, the state has a new steering function, and there is greater emphasis on university management capacity. The modern university is very different in character from its counterpart in the mid-20th century. There are several implications of the transformations of society for higher education. The number of students has increased rapidly as has the composition changed. The students are no longer from elite families and many of them will not occupy elite positions in society. There is also a growth of institutions which though are relabelled as universities do not have the same characteristics of traditional universities. In addition, there are new courses, new curricula and new teaching and learning technologies and new conceptions of science and technology. Even the way universities are organized has changed, and they are now being run like 'big corporate bureaucracies' (Scott 2000).

Tapper and Salter (1995) argue in the context of British universities that autonomy has not disappeared, rather it has been reformulated. They also make a distinction between autonomy of academic staff and institutional autonomy, further asserting that while universities have become more autonomous, the power of dons has declined.

Lo (2010) starts with an examination of the concept of autonomy and then of how decentralization has influenced the state–institution–individual relationship in Taiwan's higher education by using a three-level hierarchical model. The first level is concerned with the state–educational institution relationship. Thus, the autonomy of the institution to govern itself in terms of personnel, budget and curriculum decisions is seen. The second level deals with the state–individual relationship, which mainly examines the issue of individual autonomy against the state, more specifically the emergence of professional control in education. Finally, the last level examines the autonomy granted to self-governing bodies and individuals within the organizations and in relation to each other. It shows the relationship between authorities, administrative, professional and community in a decentralized governance framework. In the state–individual relationship, the individual autonomy is seen against the state's control and supervision. At this level, the control the state exercises over the professional codes and practices of teaching is the major source of contention, that is, the government's control over pedagogical or academic freedom. A distinction is made thereby between the autonomy of an organization and that of the individual, and at this level it is about the representation and participation of individuals in the management of educational institutions.

With the advent of globalization, the market forces are entering, and the role of the state is changing from a controlling one to a regulating one. Globally in the context of New Public Management (NPM), the state has moved to 'steering from a distance', as distinct from direct control. An important reason for initiating governance reforms in many Asian countries was the changing role of higher education in the knowledge-based economy in the context of globalization. Neoliberal policies have led to public funding not keeping pace with the massive expansion taking place. This has led to self-financing courses in public universities and other innovative forms of financing of higher education as public institutions are being encouraged to raise finances on their own (Malik 2017).

The state support for education declined after the 1980s when the fiscal capacity of the states was affected by the structural adjustment policies which led to public expenditure being reduced and subsidies being cut and a decline in investment in many sectors including education. This is the same time that there was increased deregulation and entry of market forces and an encouragement of the private sector in previously public sector–dominated areas. Such market-friendly reforms led to a reduction of subsidies in education and movement of resources to other productive sectors. Governance and management structures have thus moved from a state-controlled model to a state-supervised model (Neave 2003).

The forces of globalization led to the growth of market orientation in the higher education sector, consequently leading to the privatization of public institutions and a rapid rise of private universities which were seen as an alternative to public universities (Mathur 2017). This was further reinforced by the cost recovery measures in public universities. The costs were increasingly borne by households, that is, students instead of the state and private higher education providers and cross-border higher education providers became increasingly important in this new and changed scenario of higher education (Varghese 2008).

INSTITUTIONAL GOVERNANCE AND AUTONOMY

Universities were originally conceived to be autonomous entities. Moreover, the scale and diversity of higher education in contemporary times implies that it is very problematic for governments and ministries of education to exercise close centralized control. Governments have from time to time advocated and legislated for more autonomy for higher education institutions. This makes it important to define 'autonomy' and what type of autonomy will suit governments, higher education institutions and other stakeholders. Higher education institutions also advocate for more autonomy, but the perspectives of governments and higher education institutions are not always in congruence. This creates a problem in understanding and implementation of autonomy for higher education institutions. In the case of government, it is the extent to which they interpret freedom and accountability, and in the case of the higher education institutions it is determined by the governance, management and leadership of the institutions (Bhushan 2016: 412–427, Prakash 2011). Thus, even when autonomy is granted, there are variations in institutional responses or the implementation of that autonomy (Turcan et al. 2016).

In moral and philosophical terms, autonomy is never absolute. So too the words freedom and independence associated with autonomy are relative terms. The analysis of university autonomy focuses on four key areas: organization, finance, staffing and academic. The European Universities Association Scorecard refers to these dimensions of autonomy and examines 29 countries bringing out differences between them. However, the study does not explore how institutions exercise autonomy powers and the complex relationships between the four areas that can enhance or limit autonomy. Thus, Turcan et al. discuss 'the law of unforeseen consequences' which provides a more holistic approach.

Governance is the mechanism by which various stakeholders influence decisions, how they are held accountable and to whom. Governance refers to 'the formal and informal exercise of authority under laws, policies and rules that articulate the rights and responsibilities of various actors, including the rules by which they interact'. Thus, it encompasses 'the framework in which an institution pursues its goals, objectives and policies in a coherent and coordinated manner' to address the following larger questions: 'Who is in charge, and what are the sources of legitimacy for executive decision-making by different actors?' (Eurydice 2008: 12).

Huisman (2009) tries to better understand governance in higher education by using the traditional approach and conceptual framework of governance, and also through departures from the traditional approach by highlighting various country experiences.

Management implies the implementation of decisions, involves specification criteria for the allocation of resources to various activities, the allotment of responsibilities and tasks to various groups, and the evaluation of performance. Management refers to the implementation of a set of objectives pursued by a higher education institution on the basis of established rules. It answers the question 'How are the rules applied?', and is concerned with the efficiency, effectiveness and quality of services provided to internal and external stakeholders. Although there is a distinction between governance (with its emphasis on the process of setting policies and long-term goals as well as the strategies for reaching these goals) and management (which is action-oriented), the links between these two concepts should also be appreciated (Eurydice 2008).

Autonomy is the freedom enjoyed by an institution to determine its own goals and priorities, to develop its own study programmes, to select its own leaders, to employ and dismiss staff and to determine enrolment size (Saint 2009). Substantive autonomy refers to academic and research areas while procedural autonomy refers to non-academic areas. Substantive autonomy involves freedom to design curriculum, evolve research policy, determine student admission policies, staff recruitment criteria and criteria for the awarding of degrees. Procedural autonomy, on the other hand, refers to freedom to prepare and administer budget and financial administration, appoint non-academic staff and procure and enter into contract with others outside the institution (Varghese and Malik 2015, 2019).

Autonomy is the freedom of an institution to run its own affairs without control from any level of government (Anderson and Johnson 1998). The study by Anderson and Johnson was one of the earliest comparative studies on university autonomy, and it provided an overview of 20 countries which were categorized into three groups: (a) Anglo-American group, which included Australia, Canada, Ireland, New Zealand, South Africa, the United Kingdom and the United States and (b) European group which included France, Germany, Italy, the Netherlands, Russia and Sweden and (c) Asian group which included China, Indonesia, Japan, Malaysia, Singapore, Sri Lanka and Thailand.

Furthermore, OECD (2008) report is a comprehensive report outlining the main trends and policy approaches as well as practical examples in areas related to institutional autonomy, governance, accountability and the role of the state.

Over the past few decades, the predominant direction in higher education polices in Europe has been towards giving more autonomy to universities. The implementation and pace of reforms have, however, varied from country to country. Estermann et al. (2011) is a comprehensive study comparing the levels of and trends in university autonomy in Europe. It prepares a scorecard on which the autonomy of 27 countries is assessed across four dimensions: academic, organizational, financial and staffing. Also, Varghese and Martin (2013) analyses recent experiences in introduction of institutional autonomy based on interviews in selected countries in Asia, namely, Japan, Indonesia, Vietnam, China, Cambodia and Laos.

COMMITTEES AND COMMISSIONS ON AUTONOMY

The debate on university autonomy and governance is critical to reforms in the higher education sector in India. If we look at the constitutional mandate, the Indian constitution has provisions to ensure that the state provides education to all its citizens. The Indian Constitution in its original enactment defined education as a state subject. Under Article 42 of the Constitution, an amendment was added in 1976 and education became a concurrent list subject, which enables the central government to legislate it in the way that it deems fit.

There is a need to examine what different committees and commissions have to say on autonomy (Varghese and Malik 2015). Some of the recommendations of the University Education Commission (1948) were that the government should not dominate the educational process (GOI 1950). While higher education is an obligation of the state, state aid should not be confused with state control over academic policies and practices. Teachers should be free to speak on controversial issues like all other citizens. This atmosphere of freedom is necessary for developing the morality of the mind. The government should assist with funds and provide general discipline and oversight, as through the UGC. Also, the central and provincial governments have a large place in agricultural education. Most research must be undertaken by the government.

The Kothari Commission (GOI 1966) emphasized introducing innovations and ensuring accountability in the higher education system. It highlighted the need to introduce autonomous colleges as a step to introduce innovations in higher education. The sphere of autonomy lies in selection of students, appointment and promotion of teachers, determination of courses of study, methods of teaching and selection of areas and problems of research. University autonomy functions at three levels:

1. Autonomy within a university, for example, autonomy of the departments, colleges, teachers and students in relation to the university as a whole;
2. Autonomy of a university in relation to the university system as a whole, for example, the autonomy of one university in relation to another, or in relation to the UGC and the Inter-University Board (IUB); and
3. Autonomy of the university system as a whole, including the UGC and the IUB, in relation to agencies and influences outside that system, the most important of which are the central and the state governments.

Central Advisory Board of Education Committee on Autonomy of Higher Education Institutions (CABE) (MHRD 2005) examined in-depth the various implications of academic, administrative and financial autonomy of higher education institutions. According to the committee, autonomy should necessarily lead to excellence in academics, governance and financial management of the institutions. Academic autonomy is the freedom to decide academic issues such as curriculum, instructional material, pedagogy and techniques of students' evaluation. Administrative autonomy is the freedom to the institution to manage its own affairs in regard to administration. Financial autonomy is the freedom to the institution to expend the financial resources at its disposal in a prudent way keeping in view its priorities. Accountability enables the institutions to regulate the freedom given to them by way of autonomy.

The Yashpal Committee (MHRD 2009) recommended that equally important to autonomy is the need for governance structures, which ensure the preservation of such autonomy under all circumstances. Accordingly, there is interference in the university functioning and loss of autonomy. Such interference touches all aspects of higher education and involves improper admission of students, pressures in selection of teachers, manipulation in the appointment of senior functionaries such as vice chancellors, registrars and deans, purchase of equipment and allotment of construction contracts. It also observed that blaming private initiative, political interference and other forces for the loss of autonomy of universities is not sufficient. There was no rigorous resistance from within the academic community to the role played by socio-political and market forces to manipulate and subvert the normative structures of the university system.

According to the National Knowledge Commission (GOI 2009) reform in the structures of governance of universities is needed to preserve autonomy and accountability. The appointments of vice chancellors must be freed from direct or indirect interventions on the part of governments, and should be based on search processes and peer judgment alone. The size and composition of academic councils and executive councils, which slows down decision-making processes and sometimes constitute an impediment to change, needs to be reconsidered on a priority basis.

The government has decided to introduce the Higher Education Commission of India (Repeal of University Grants Commission Act) Bill 2018 (Government of India 2018) that will do away with the UGC Act and set up the Higher Education Commission of India (HECI). The decision to set up HECI is the latest among reform measures for the overhaul of higher education regulatory bodies. The new commission will focus on improving academic standards and the quality of higher education. Most importantly, the grant functions would be carried out by the MHRD, unlike the UGC, thus allowing HECI to focus on academic matters only.

Let us examine the state–university relationship and decentralization within the university in the next two sections.

STATE–UNIVERSITY RELATIONSHIP

In India, the Ministry of Human Resource Development (MHRD), UGC, state departments of education and governing boards exercise direct control over universities. All decisions taken at the university level are prescribed by rules and regulations of the MHRD, UGC or sector-specific organizations such as AICTE (Chandra 2018). Thus, from faculty selection to conducting admissions to deciding curriculum, compensation of teachers and the number of hours teachers teach is decided by the government.

In the interviews with institutional leaders, it came out that while central universities are governed by rules, in the case of state universities, there is another layer of control exercised by the state government and state department of education. Thus, in relative terms, the control exercised is less for central universities as compared with state universities. Anandakrishnan (2010) also discusses how in case of centrally funded government institutions such as Indian Institutes of Technology (IITs), Indian Institutes of Management (IIMs), central universities, Indian Institutes of Science, Education and Research (IISERs) and National Institutes of Technology (NITs) the interference and control of the government is less and the boards and the heads of these institutions have the freedom to evolve their academic policies and strategies except in some critical areas such as reservations and pay commission norms. Thus, it is seen that the governing boards of these institutions include just one or two officials of the central government.

A comprehensive research study based on field visits, interaction with various stakeholders and review of literature in the subject was conducted at the CPRHE. The objective of the study was threefold— first, to investigate some policy considerations regarding governance; second, to analyse current practices; third, to recommend some 'best practices' to the universities' governance. The higher education system is facing difficult challenges, for example, inadequate funding, poor infrastructure, quality and standards, lack of autonomy and academic freedom, and a rapidly rising demand for higher education. The project is focusing on the issues and problems related to universities governance in India. The select universities, namely, Banaras Hindu University (BHU), Bharathiar University (BU), Savitribai Phule Pune University (SBPU) and University of Rajasthan (UOR) and their affiliated colleges were studied. An extensive field study was conducted to collect relevant data from the concerned stakeholders, namely, teachers, students and interviews were held with the institutional leaders. A structured questionnaire was prepared and administered to obtain required data and information. Separate questionnaires were prepared for different categories of stakeholders, that is, teachers and students.

Institutional Autonomy to Decide about Internal Governance and Organizational Structures

1. Freedom to set up internal governance structures including governing bodies and external members
2. Freedom to determine internal academic structures
3. Freedom to select institutional leadership (executive head)
4. Legal status of universities
5. Examples of university governance and organizational structures

The present research was undertaken to study the governance structures in the four case study universities and affiliated colleges. The central university (BHU) is characterized by having a BHU court which acts as an advisory body, and its functions are to advise the visitor in respect of matters which may be referred to it for advice.

In the case of the three state universities (Bharathiar, Pune University and UOR), there are a senate, syndicate and academic council (standing committee on academic affairs in the case of BU. The executive council in BHU is the executive body of the university and has charge of the management and administration of the revenue and property of the university and the conduct of all administrative affairs of the university. The academic council is the academic body of the university and, subject to the act, the statutes and ordinances, has charge of the organization of study and research in the university and the colleges, the courses of study and the examination of students and the conferment of ordinary and honorary degrees. In the case of UOR, there is an academic council as well as the senate and syndicate. The academic council has the control and regulation of and is responsible for the maintenance of the standards of teaching and examination in the university. It advises the syndicate regarding the institution of teaching posts, proposes to the syndicate ordinances regarding admission to the university and advises the syndicate regarding the institution of boards of studies.

As can be seen from Tables 8.1 and 8.2, many similarities exist in governance structures in the state universities. In the case of Pune University, there is a management council as well as the senate and syndicate, which is the principal executive authority to formulate statutes and forward the same to the senate for approval and make ordinances to administer the affairs of the university. Pune University additionally has the board of college and university development, which is responsible for the planning development of the university, both physical and academic, and conducts academic audit of the university departments, institutions, colleges and recognized institutions. It also plans, monitors, guides and coordinates undergraduate (UG) and postgraduate (PG) academic programme and development of affiliated colleges. It also has a board of examinations which conducts the examinations and makes policy decisions in regard to organizing and holding examinations, improving the system of examinations appointing the paper setters, examiners, moderators, and also prepares the schedule of dates of holding examinations and declaration of the results.

WITHIN-UNIVERSITY RELATIONSHIP

We need to also understand who this autonomy is going to really benefit? What we observe is greater centralization in offices of vice chancellors and lesser powers for the professoriate and for individual departments. Thus, we need to clearly understand the relationships within universities through various dimensions of autonomy.

Table 8.1 *Governing Bodies in Sample Universities*

University of Rajasthan	Savitribai Phule Pune University	Bharathiar University	Banaras Hindu University
			Visitor-President
Chancellor	Chancellor	Chancellor-Governor of Tamil Nadu	Chancellor-elected by BHU Court
Vice Chancellor	Vice Chancellor	Vice Chancellor	Vice Chancellor
			BHU Court-Advisory body
Senate	Senate	Executive Council- Senate	Executive Council
Syndicate	Syndicate	Academic Council- Syndicate	Academic Council
Academic Council			
	Management Council		
		Standing Committee on Academic Affairs-Advises Syndicate	
Board of Studies	Board of Studies	Board of Studies	Board of Studies
Board of Inspection	Board of Examination		
	Board of College and University Development		
Finance Committee	Finance Committee	Finance Committee	Finance Committee

Source: Malik (2018).

Table 8.2 *Governing Bodies in Sample Colleges*

Kanoria Mahila Mahavidyalaya (Private Unaided)	S.M. Joshi College (Private Aided)	Government Arts College (Autonomous)	Vasanta College for Women (Private Aided)
Management Committee	Management Committee	Governing Council	Management Committee
Manager		Academic Council	Manager
Principal	Principal	Principal	Principal
Finance Committee	Finance Committee	Finance Committee	Finance Committee
Staff Council	Staff Council		Staff Council

Source: Malik (2018).

1. Institutional autonomy to decide about curriculum, academic programmes and teaching method
   a. Capacity to design academic content
   b. Capacity to introduce new degree programmes
   c. Capacity to choose language of instruction
   d. Capacity to organize and take part in academic events
2. Institutional autonomy to decide about issues related to quality assurance
   a. Capacity to choose quality assurance mechanisms
   b. Capacity to select a quality assurance agency
3. Institutional autonomy to decide about issues related to research and freedom to publish
4. Institutional autonomy to decide about student-related issues
   a. Deciding on the overall student numbers
   b. Student selection process and admission
      In BHU, the admission to all the UG, PG and research programmes is through an all India entrance test (UG entrance test/PG entrance test/research entrance test). The merit of the candidate in the entrance test is the sole factor for admission, and there is full transparency in the admission process. Student admissions in the BU are conducted strictly on the basis of

government of Tamil Nadu regulations. UGC guidelines are followed when restricting/assigning a maximum number of research students to each faculty.

Admission in UG courses in UOR is on merit on the basis of percentile. The percentile formula was introduced in the academic session 2014–2015 by the government of Rajasthan. This ensures parity in the percentage secured among state board and central boards. In PG courses, admission is made through entrance examination. The entrance exam is of 70 marks, and 30 marks are given on the basis of academic merit.

5. Institutional autonomy to decide about staff employment issues (academic and non-academic staff)

   a. Staff recruitment

   BHU is the first university to adopt the system of recruitment that is being followed in the IITs. University recruitment is governed by the Statute and ordinances and the appointment to all teaching programmes, including new and emerging areas is governed by the same.

   The selection of faculty in BU is based on the UGC norms, government of Tamil Nadu regulations as well as the conditions stated in the board of studies minutes. According to the university act, the Syndicate is empowered to institute lectureships, readerships, professorships and any other teaching posts required by the university, appoint the university lecturers, university readers, university professors and the teachers of the university, fix their emoluments, define their duties and the conditions of their services and provide for filling up of temporary vacancies.

   The UOR follows the UGC prescribed norms for recruitment of teaching staff. The government of Rajasthan sanctions the teaching and non-teaching posts. According to an ordinance the selection committee for appointment of teaching staff consists of head of department, one chancellor's nominee, one government nominee, one member nominated by the syndicate, three subject experts (out of the panel approved by academic council), dean of faculty and senior most professor of the department while the vice chancellor chairs the selection committee. The quorum of the selection committee will be not less than five, out of which at least two would be subject experts in case of professor and one in case of assistant professor.

b. Capacity to decide on staff salaries

c. Capacity to decide on dismissals and promotions

BHU follows the rules, regulations and guidelines declared by the UGC for promotion of teachers under career advancement scheme (CAS). The recruitment and assessment cell of the university is given the responsibility of recruitment as well as promotion. The cell is headed by a joint/deputy registrar rank official. The promotion policy as declared by the UGC and approved by the executive council is enforced with the heads of departments, dean of faculties/directors of institutes and vice chancellor playing respective roles.

The promotions of teachers in the BU through CAS are done following the UGC norms. However, when teachers were interviewed they felt that there was not sufficient openness.

The UOR has adopted the UGC Regulations 2010 about minimum qualifications of teachers and has replaced its earlier ordinances with Ordinance 141–141F in January 2017 with effect from 18 September 2010. Ordinance 141F deals with rules and procedure of career advancement. Though the university is autonomous, permission has to be procured from the government before starting the process of interviews under CAS.

6. Institutional autonomy to decide about finances and administration

a. Allocation of public funding

b. The right to keep a surplus

c. Income-generating activities (diversification of income sources)

d. The right to charge tuition fees

e. The right to own buildings

f. The right to borrow money

We can understand this better using the examples of the UOR and BHU. The UOR enjoyed a lot of institutional autonomy in the beginning. It was promulgated by a joint action of a group of princely states and the states granted the university an annual grant of over ₹2.5 lakhs for first five years with the understanding that the acceptance of the grant will not impact the autonomy and its freedom to organize its teaching and administration. However, after a while, the government started interfering in the affairs of the UOR and curtailed the autonomy of UOR through curtailment of block grant. The government curtailed the autonomy of the state universities through RAPSAR (The Rajasthan Regulation of Appointments to Public Services and Rationalisation of Staff) Act.

The UOR has had a practice of hiring teachers on ad hoc basis under Section 3(3) of the University Ordinance. This ordinance gave power to the vice chancellor to appoint faculty on ad hoc basis for a period of one year. The appointments made under this section were then continued by the UOR by giving one day's technical break to the teachers and reappointing them for the next session and this practice continued for more than 25 years. It was repealed by the government of Rajasthan in 1999. While all these ad hoc teachers were finally absorbed in the university services through an ordinance in 2008, in 2003, the government introduced the RAPSAR Act, which forbade any public institution, including UOR, from making any appointments, taking any decision having financial implications without the concurrence of the state government. Every time the university tried to exercise its autonomy, the state government stopped the block grant of the university.

With the declining state grant, the university is not in a position to give pension to retiring teachers. The UOR has a history of not advertising posts and also not holding interviews for promotion. There are teachers at associate professor level for last 7 years who were promoted to associate professor level after serving for more than 17 years with retrospective benefits. Again, the same set of teachers has been asking for career advancement but it has not taken place. The university asked them to submit their forms for CAS in 2013/2015/2016 but the interviews have not taken place. UGC's CAS gives the academic performance criteria and service requirements for promotion. Many of the professors were also given the benefit of CAS many years after the UGC implemented the promotion scheme.

It was found in discussions that in UOR, all the positions are given to teachers on the basis of seniority. Whenever the department gets an opportunity to organize refresher course, the responsibility lies with Head of the department. It also came out in the interviews with dean, head of departments that the teacher is free to use any pedagogy in the classroom interaction but within the framework provided by the examination system of the university. The university teachers have a say in the framing of the syllabus since the curriculum revision is done at the university department level.

According to the interviews held with institutional leaders at BHU, sufficient autonomy is given to the departments in designing curricula, introducing courses and organizing different academic activities. The central administration under the overall guidance and direction of the vice chancellor manages the finance, general administration, examination and so on. The university ensures culture of participative management at all levels of its operations from top decision-making to the bottom level of execution. The vice chancellor and his/her team of officials (registrar, finance officer, joint registrars etc.) work with directors of institutes and deans of the faculties (directors are appointed from among the senior teachers of the institute by the executive committee on the recommendation of the vice chancellor, while deans are on the basis of seniority). Deans work in consultation with the Faculty Policy Planning Committee (PPC) in which all heads of departments and coordinators of centres are member. The faculty PPC frequently has invited members (from among the faculty members) in its meeting. Teachers are involved in the decision-making at the faculty level when the faculty needs their expertise in taking different decisions. Hence, all major decisions at the faculty level are taken by the dean after consulting HODs and other concerned senior faculty members. However, even though the situation seems quite favourable, there is scope for improvement. Decentralization at the faculty or department level varies with those at the leadership positions. Thus, the senior people do not allow the decentralized system to function and unfortunately the central administration does not take any active measures to correct this situation.

Financial management in the university departments of BU is based on the rules and recommendations of the government. The deans and heads have almost no role in the allocation of funds to the departments or respective school. The heads of the departments submit a budget; however, there are no specific norms that direct the allocation of funds to individual departments.

CONCLUSION

The chapter has examined the governance structures and processes in central universities, state universities and their affiliated colleges. The framework developed and relied on by the research was to analyse: (a) government–university relations and (b) within–university relations. The chapter shows that government–university relation has evolved over time from direct control and monitoring to steering from a distance and devolving authority to institutions. While central universities enjoy relatively more autonomy, state universities are subject to more control and enjoy less autonomy. Even the funding given to central universities is at a higher level as compared to the share of funding from state governments to state universities. Hence, state universities face more resource crunch than central universities do.

Further, the chapter finds that the universities, in general—central and state universities—enjoy more autonomy in academic matters and less of administrative and financial autonomy. Thus, design of academic programmes and curricula is done by the universities and approved by their board of studies.

Additionally, the governing bodies in the state universities have government officials and representatives from the Legislative Assembly and Legislative Council. For example, in the UOR, BU and SBPU, one finds these trends. However, central universities do not have as many representatives from political parties. This pattern of representation has important implications for the way control is exercised by these functionaries on the university.

Institutional autonomy is a necessary but not a sufficient condition for the decentralization of decision-making within the university. It is observed that in central and state universities, there is over-centralization of power and decision-making at the level of offices of vice chancellors. It shows that the autonomy enjoyed by the university has not necessarily translated into decentralized and participative decision-making process within the university.

It can be concluded that there is a decline in the bargaining power of the 'professoriate'. New governance arrangements have clearly reduced the collective influence of academics over decision-making in the institutions.

It is observed that a move to outcome-based measures from being purely input-based measures need to be strengthened. Internal quality assurance cells need to function effectively. Thus, quantitative metrics such as the academic performance index are being used extensively though many teachers expressed their dissatisfaction with the metric. Governance structures are in need of reform, and there is a sense that a form of 'managerialism' is gripping the institutions under study. Recruitment of teachers has not taken place for several years in some cases, so there is an excessive reliance on ad hoc and guest teachers.

The performance of educational institutions as measured on quality parameters will, in the future, determine the extent of autonomy and the level of regulatory scrutiny they will face. The government has also decided that top-ranking institutions will be exempt from the UGC's review mechanism. The draft UGC (Grant of Graded Autonomy to Institutions of Higher Education) Regulations 2017 is critical in this regard. These regulations aim to divide all UGC-recognized public, private and deemed universities into three categories, each of which will bestow different degrees of autonomy on the educational institutions.

One of the flagship projects of the MHRD for internationalization of Indian campuses and creating world-class universities is the establishment of 20 world-class institutions: 10 public and the rest private. The UGC has announced the initiation of the 90 days application process from public and private institutions for being recognized as institutes of eminence. The institutions which are shortlisted will be free from regulatory mechanism and can place an emphasis on multidisciplinary initiatives, high quality research, global best practices and international collaborations.

The government has also approved the setting up of a higher education financing agency (HEFA), which would be jointly promoted by the identified promoter and the MHRD with an authorized capital of ₹2,000 crore. The major objective of the HEFA is to leverage funds from the market and supplement them with donations and Corporate Social Responsibility (CSR) funds. These funds will be used to finance improvement in infrastructure in top educational institutions.

Thus, HEFA indicates a move towards greater financial autonomy for higher education institutions. However, autonomy (academic, administrative and financial) should be accompanied with retaining of core funding and capacity building efforts.

REFERENCES

Anandakrishnan, A. 2010. 'Accountability and Transparency in University Governance'. *University News* 8–14 November 48(45): 18–23.

Anderson, D., and R. Johnson. 1998. *University Autonomy in Twenty Countries.* Canberra: Department of Employment, Education, Training and Youth Affairs, Commonwealth of Australia.

Bhushan, S. 2016. 'Institutional Autonomy and Leadership'. In *India Higher Education Report 2015,* edited by N.V. Varghese and Garima Malik, 412–427. New Delhi: Routledge.

Chandra P. 2018. *Building Universities That Matter: Where Are Indian Institutions Going Wrong?* Delhi: Orient BlackSwan.

Chattopadhyay, S. 2012. *Education and Economics: Disciplinary Evolution and Policy Discourse.* New Delhi: Oxford University Press.

Estermann, T., T. Nokkala, and M. Steinel. 2011. 'University Autonomy in Europe II'. *The Scorecard.* Brussels: European University Association.

Eurydice. 2008. *Higher Education Governance in Europe: Policies, Structure, Funding and Academic Staff.* Brussels: European Commission.

Government of India (GOI). 1950. *Report of the University Education Commission 1948–1949* (Chairman Dr S. Radhakrishnan). New Delhi: Ministry of Education.

Government of India (GOI). 1966. *Education and National Development: Report of the Education Commission* (Kothari Commission 1964–1966). New Delhi: Education Commission.

Government of India (GOI). 2009. *National Knowledge Commission Report to the Nation 2006–2009.* New Delhi: GOI.

Government of India. 2018. *Higher Education Commission of India (Repeal of University Grants Commission Act) Bill 2018.* New Delhi: Government of India.

Huisman, J., ed. 2009. *International Perspectives on the Governance of Higher Education: Alternative Frameworks for Coordination.* New York and London: Routledge.

Lo, W. Y. 2010. 'Decentralization of Higher Education and Its Implications for Educational Autonomy in Taiwan'. *Asia Pacific Journal of Education* 30(2): 127–139.

Malik, G. 2017. *Governance and Management of Higher Education Institutions in India, CPRHE Research Paper 5.* New Delhi: Centre for Policy Research in Higher Education, National University of Educational Planning and Administration.

Malik, G. 2018. *Governance and Management of Higher Education in India.* Synthesis Report, Centre for Policy Research in Higher Education, NIEPA, New Delhi.

Mathur, K. 2017. Changing Perspectives: Neoliberal Policy Reforms and Education in India. Eleventh Foundation Day Lecture, NUEPA, New Delhi, August 11.

Ministry of Human Resource Development (MHRD). 2005. *Report of the Central Advisory Board of Education Committee on Autonomy of Higher Education Institution*. New Delhi: Government of India.

Ministry of Human Resource Development (MHRD). 2009. *Report of the Committee to Advise on Renovation and Rejuvenation of Higher Education* (Yashpal Committee). New Delhi: Government of India.

Neave, G. 2003. 'The Bologna Declaration: Some of the Historic Dilemmas Posed by the Reconstruction of the Community in Europe's System of Higher Education'. *Educational Policy* 17(1): 141–164.

Organisation for Economic Co-operation and Development (OECD). 2008. 'Tertiary Education for the Knowledge Society'. *OECD Thematic Review of Tertiary Education: Synthesis Report*. Paris: OECD.

Prakash, V. 2011. 'Concerns about Autonomy and Academic Freedom in Higher Education Institutions'. *Economic and Political Weekly* 46(16): 36–40.

Saint, W. 2009. 'Guiding Universities: Governance and Management Arrangements around the Globe'. Human Development Network, Working Paper, the World Bank, Washington, DC.

Scott, P. 2000. 'Globalization and Higher Education: Challenges for the Twenty First Century'. *Journal of Studies in International Education* 4(1): 3–10.

Tapper, E. R., and B. G. Salter. 1995. 'The Changing Idea of University Autonomy'. *Studies in Higher Education* 20(1): 59–71.

Turcan, R. V., J. Reilly, and L. Bugaian. 2016. *(Re)Discovering University Autonomy: The Global Market Paradox of Stakeholder and Educational Values in Higher Education*. New York: Palgrave Macmillan.

University Grants Commission. 2017. *UGC (Grant of Graded Autonomy to Institutions of Higher Education) Regulations 2017*. New Delhi: Ministry of Human Resource Development.

Varghese, N.V. 2008. *Globalization of Higher Education and Cross-border Student Mobility*. Paris: UNESCO, International Institute for Educational Planning.

Varghese, N.V., and M. Martin, eds. 2014. *Governance Reforms in Higher Education: A Study of Institutional Autonomy in Asian Countries*. Paris: International Institute of Educational Planning/UNESCO.

Varghese, N.V., and G. Malik. 2015. 'Institutional Autonomy in Higher Education in India'. *University News* 19–25 January; 53(3): 115–122.

Varghese, N.V., and G. Malik, eds. 2016. *India Higher Education Report 2015*. New Delhi: Routledge.

Varghese, N.V., and G. Malik. 2019. 'Institutional Autonomy and Governance of Higher Education in India'. In *Governance and Management of Universities in Asia: Global Influences and Local Responses*, edited by Chang D. Wang, M. N. N. Lee and H. Y. Locke, 43–55. London: Routledge.

Chapter 9

Governance and Management of Higher Education at the Institutional Level
Reality, Concerns and Transmutation

Rakesh Raman

As India embarks on an ambitious voyage of universalization of higher education in a federal, decentralized, neoliberal set-up and braces itself for the myriad of problems, the issue of evolving an efficient and effective governance and management model for higher educational institutions (HEI) gains crucial significance. The job is tough considering rapid massification of higher education (Trow 1973), increasing diversities among HEIs spread across the nation (Vught 2007), paradigm shift in stakeholders' approach towards education including the intention of the government to gradually withdraw financial support, increasing role of market in the field and global competition (Dobbins and Knill 2009), emerging challenges of equity, expansion and excellence and ever-increasing expectations of the recipients. At a time when the nation sees its population as its greatest strength and plans big to reap the demographic dividend for bolstering its position, it is imperative that we make genuine efforts to identify where do we stand and what concerns do we face in terms of evolving an apropos governance and management structure that could handle these complex issues and ensure quality output (Salmi 2009). It is sincerely believed that such an understanding will help us alchemize a better, robust and protean structure.

Governance and management of higher education in India works at three levels: At the top are the centre and state governments and buffer bodies (e.g. University Grants Commission [UGC] and All India Council for Technical Education), which create a macro structure of HEIs of different types, determine their hierarchy, give 'strategic direction' to the sector and frame rules and systems within which the institutions operate. The second tier consists of the universities (public and private, central and state) and autonomous institutions such as Indian Institutes of Technology (IITs), Indian Institute of Science (IISc) and the like, which, within the distinctive structure created for them by the tier I, produce and foster their own, often 'unique' governance framework, supervise and manage institutions coming under their purview. The lowermost tier consists of affiliated institutions (colleges) working under the tier II. These have their own internal management skeleton, shaped by college governing bodies and led by principals. They have rather circumscribed academic autonomy but enjoy varying degrees of financial and administrative freedom. Tier III also includes institutes (in some cases), faculties and departments within the university/institute system that have mainly managerial function but in a number of cases practically take most of the academic decisions and might have different degrees of intervention in administration. The nation has debated a lot about governance and management at the first tier contemplating alternative frameworks to the existing system. The issue at the institutional level, however, has received scant attention. This is a crucial omission as the same tier I structure has fostered a wide spectrum of HEIs with varying levels of efficiencies and performance; for example, despite having broadly the same system for all old central universities, there exist significant differences amongst them. This is also valid for old IITs. There exist differences, despite being governed by a uniform act, across new central universities and variations in performance between new central universities and new IITs. Similarly, there not only exist huge interstate variations among HEIs in different states but even within a particular state having the same system there exist wide variations.

A prominent factor that explains variation in performance of individual institutions in terms of approved parameters is their internal governance structure and the way overall administrative and managerial efficiency is ensured (Fielden 2008). Unfortunately, things have not gone that well on this front. The higher education system today is facing crisis of recognition and reverence. The HEIs are not unequivocally treated as the 'temple of knowledge', infallible and paragon that could do no wrong. The failure of governance and management system has turned things against them and allowed the vested interest of stakeholders to collectively impugn and besiege the citadel on which these institutions stand. Quality of education has nosedived, research has gone missing, academic standard has deteriorated and the like. What we have today are selected institutions with rather impeccable record surrounded by a vast sea of mediocre and poor ones. It is important to study the governance and management structure of HEIs spread across the nation in order to understand the flaws and capture the best practices adopted by the performers. This issue is the main focus of this chapter. Based on a research study conducted by the Centre for Policy Research in Higher Education (CPRHE), it attempts to study the governance and management structure of the HEIs. The chapter is structured into three sections. Sections I and II try to capture the reality, while Section III talks about the concerns and mentions transmutation required. Thus, while Section I provides a theoretical perspective of evolution of governance and management of HEIs, Section II briefly discusses the methodology and explains in detail how the existing governance system in reality performs and is able to achieve best governance practices. Section III talks about the major concerns and then attempts to come up with some broad suggestions for transmutation to a better system.

SECTION I. EVOLUTION OF GOVERNANCE AND MANAGEMENT SYSTEM: THEORETICAL PERSPECTIVE

Education being the principal means to build human capabilities (Sen 1999) and a chief driver of economic growth (Schultz 1961) has always encouraged nations to strive to create a vast network of educational institutions and consistently evolved and reform governance structure (Varghese and Martin 2014). The expansion of network of institutions has led to a vertical separation between governance and management functions. Higher education governance has been primarily concerned with creating hierarchy of institutions, mediating between the autonomy and accountability of these institutions/functionaries, giving strategic direction to them developing a system of control, audit and supervision so on and so forth. Management, on the other hand, is primarily seen to be restricted to implementing the strategic plan, coordinating the activities of the stakeholders at the institution level and bringing harmony between their goals, ensuring regulatory compliance within the system of rules and regulations developed by the governance so as to ensure quality, efficiency and excellence. Together governance and management are very crucial for the success and sustenance of higher education system (Fielden 2008, Kearney and Huisman 2007, Stensaker et al. 2007).

Governance and management structure, domain and roles have evolved with time, necessitated by changing circumstances. There are three phases with features clearly discernible with a very long phase of transition having mixed features in between them (Figure 9.1). We briefly mention these here:

Phase I

The first phase relates to governance in the ancient Indian and Roman systems continuing up to the modern Humboldtian education until the beginning of the 20th century. This was clearly the phase when universities were seen as a 'republic of scholars' and decision-making was consensus based and decentralized within a multitude of departmental, faculty, and institutional committees (Saint 2009). The phase could be largely theorized as 'collegial'. Universities though received some financial support from the rulers and the rich but enjoyed complete autonomy. Institutional leaders such as the president, rector or vice chancellor (VC) were elected from among the university's most esteemed scholars to fulfil administrative and managerial duties. There was shared understanding about the aims of the institution and as such the scholars set their own standards, enjoyed complete academic freedom and any effort to introduce accountability was treated as an effort to impugn academic freedom and was criticized and condemned strongly by the society.

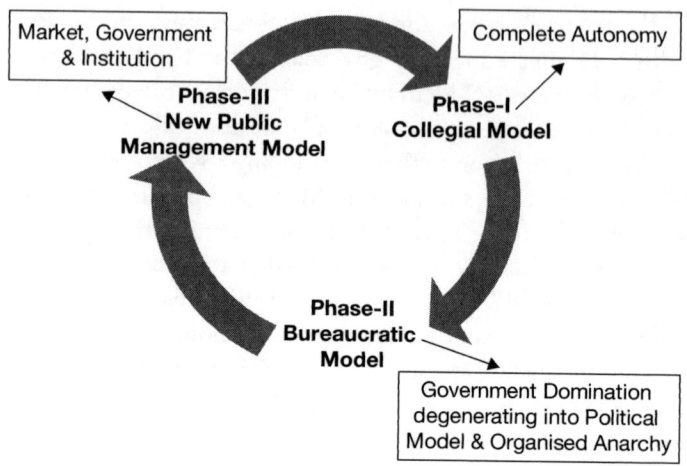

Figure 9.1 *Evolution of Governance and Management System*
Source: Raman et al. (2018).

Phase II

The growing realization of 'economic productivity' of higher education by the turn of 20th century changed the informal relationship between the teacher and the taught into a formal relationship of the seller and the buyer. The state became first a financier of higher education and subsequently a controlling shareholder. As the government emerged as a proprietor of public universities, it demanded loyalty, control and accountability from those who worked here. Thus, in this phase, a number of alternative theoretical models of governance such as administrative, bureaucratic and their variants began to appear. The government began creating and shaping institutions, building hierarchy and making rules and regulations. The head of the state served as chancellor to the public universities, appointed their senior officers, for example, VCs and rectors, and chose a significant portion of university council members (Ajayi et al. 1996). Through these appointments, state control was exercised even in the day-to-day functioning, and in the name of accountability, key affairs of the universities came to be controlled by ministries (Neave and van Vught 1994). Complete bureaucratization of university happened curbing creativity and doing a blow to excellence.

With time the state control and bureaucratic governance model degenerated into a political model as politicians came to play a direct role in educational management. Decisions were made based on bargaining among coalitions and not by applying existing standard operating procedures, programmes, and routines. Decision-making became a process of conflict resolution. The ultimate outcome of political intervention resulted into an organized anarchy model and converted universities into 'organized anarchies', that is, organizations characterized by multiple goals, unclear technology and fluid participation (Cohen et al. 1972). There was complete 'ambiguity of intention', confusion, chaos and absence of common purpose and goal.

Phase III

The final phase of evolution of governance emerged in the West in the 1980s with the adoption of the New Public Management approach (NPM). NPM puts emphasis on leadership principles, incentives and competition between public sector agencies and private entities to enhance the outcomes and cost efficiency of public services (Marginson and van der Wende 2007). This has been necessitated by growing realization of the governments across nations that the job of providing quality higher education to an increasing number is too demanding to be handled exclusively by the government. This has led to gradual withdrawal of the government and has paved way for the growth of the entrepreneurship model of governance and management. This indeed is a market share model that has promoted academic freedom, internal democracy and the organizing role of academic disciplines obviously to produce education that can be sold (Maassen 2007).

The Indian Scenario

For developing nations such as India, the governance and management system is in a phase of transition. Different reincarnations of the bureaucratic model are still prevalent with government attempting to bulldoze its way and dilute the autonomy of universities. This, at the same time, has been accompanied by the realization that the public

180 | Rakesh Raman

universities have to strive hard to improve quality, meet international standards, compete with private sector and generate sufficient internal resources to become self-sufficient. This realization has 'forced' the government to concede some authority at least in case of top HEIs such as IITs, IIMs and in a very limited way to central universities.

The fragmented vision could be seen in many forms, for example, for most universities, the acts and statutes are framed in a way that technically reflect adherence to the collegial model. VCs are though projected as the CEOs, yet there are bodies, viz. senates, syndicates and executive councils, that collectively help the CEO in taking decisions in a rather democratic frame. Theoretically speaking, substantial academic autonomy to the faculty is given by the acts, and within the umbrella of the acts and public accountability provisions, reasonable adminis-trative and financial autonomy, respectively, are made available to the HEIs. A decentralized and democratic decision-making system with participation of faculty is propagated in principle giving a free hand to the 'republic of scholars'. On the practical side, however, the state has attempted to dilute the 'theoretical autonomy' through two prominent ways. First, governments have used their authority to appoint VCs of universities/directors of top institutes and power to nominate members of senates/executive councils to indirectly control the functioning of the HEIs. Second, they have used their responsibility to fund HEIs as a bargaining tool, often forcing them to follow its dictates something that is in complete contrivance to the theoretically proposed autonomy.

It is therefore neither a typically bureaucratic model where the top bureaucracy owes responsibility for the performance of the system and definitely not a collegial model in our country. Today, we have a model the shape of which has depended on who is running the show—both at the government level and at the university level. For old universities/ institutes, there is a 'system' functioning, and the whims and policies of these leaders can only partially change the course of the system but in most state universities governance and management has changed significantly with 'who is running the show' at the government and at the university level. Thus, despite having same acts, there is no uniform system of governance and management. There are some broad similari-ties among the old central universities, among new central universities and also among universities within a particular state but otherwise they vary significantly in terms of the 'governance processes', 'degree of autonomy exercised', 'levels of participative decision–making practised' and in general best practices followed. This variation calls for a more decentralized study of the governance and management system of higher education in India.

SECTION II. METHODOLOGY AND GOVERNANCE AND MANAGEMENT SYSTEM IN SAMPLE INSTITUTIONS

Methodology

Wide diversities in HEIs and their governance and management require any study on them to collect first-hand information from representative institutions chosen from all quarters. The resource requirement for such a study is huge and normally beyond the reach of even institutional researchers. The present chapter uses information collected by a CPRHE/NIEPA-sponsored study through primary survey of three public sector state universities from different regions—Savitribai Phule Pune University (SBPU) from West, Bharathiar University (BU), Coimbatore from South and Rajasthan University (RU), Jaipur, from North and one central university, Banaras Hindu University (BHU), Varanasi. This was done to have representation from all regions and to compare the state universities with a central university. From each university, subject to their presence, five faculties were chosen with effort made to have representations from arts and humanities, social sciences, science, engineering and medicine. In some cases, where medicine or engineering was not present, these were substituted based on specific criteria. From each faculty, one department was chosen. Different departments were chosen to understand and capture specific needs, complexities and managerial issues involved therein.

A concurrent triangulation design (Creswell 2013) was used. Qualitative data were collected through interviews of top management, including VCs, registrars, deans of faculties, heads of department, chairperson of college governing council and principals and so on, and focus group discussions with faculty and students of chosen departments were conducted. The qualitative information was supplemented by quantitative data collected through administering semi-structured schedules over roughly 50 per cent of faculty members of chosen departments with at least five-year experience and 50 per cent students with at least one year in the institutions. The qualitative and quantitative data were analysed separately and then compared and combined to confirm, cross-validate and corroborate findings.

Governance and Management System in Sample Institutions

Governance as 'the structure and processes of decision-making' (Carnegie Commission 1973) could be seen to work in HEIs at three levels. At the top is the government–university (HEI) relationship that determines the way the state approaches university governance issue and builds its internal governance structure. The second tier is the university and its components, for example, institute, faculty, department relationship that primarily deals with the managerial role and determines the internal autonomy structure. Finally, the third is the university–college relationship, which is very crucial for affiliating universities with hundreds of affiliated colleges. The level and kind of decision taken, the parties involved and the perspective of autonomy and accountability differ significantly in these three cases. In this chapter, we concentrate only on the first two tiers.

The First Tier

There exists marked differences between a central and a state university in the way they are formed, funded, their top officials are appointed and faculty members are recruited and so on. State universities are established by the respective state university acts, for example, the BU Act 1981, the University of Rajasthan Act 1948 and the Poona University Act 1948. These acts lay clear-cut provisions for the constitution of different bodies such as syndicate and senate, appointment of pro-chancellors, VCs and so on, and powers and functions of these and other functionaries. The funding of the universities is primarily by the state governments. Department of the state government, such as directorate of higher education, intervene and guide the day-to-day functioning in a significant way. All the state universities taken up for the study are found to have more or less the same organizational structure with the governor of the state as chancellor, followed by the VC (appointed by the governor), senate and syndicate and then a number of other bodies such as academic councils, management councils and officials such as registrar, controller of examinations, directors of institutes/sports and so on. There are minor variations between universities, for example, SBP University Pune has management council in place of syndicate. The members of the policy-making bodies, such as senates and syndicates, though have representation from within the university, for example, deans of faculties, principals of colleges, representatives of teachers and so on, but they are normally dominated by nominees of the state government and directors of higher/technical education, finance department and so on of the government, and peoples representatives (MLAs). In BU, there is a hierarchy among members as class I members (comprising of state government officials) having more powers than class II members. There is very frequent intervention of the state through these that disrupt the normal functioning of these universities.

VCs are responsible for ensuring that the regulations, ordinances and statutes are observed and are vested with the powers to take actions on issues such as appointment, promotion, suspension and so on. Their powers are, however, effectively constrained by intervention of the state and syndicate. The general perception of the faculty and students was that in most cases the VCs are not appointed because of their academic credentials, administrative acumen or experience but for their connections and they become a tool for the state governments to manipulate activities in the universities. They come with an agenda in which giving right direction to the university is normally the least favoured item. In the past, there have been instances in these state universities where the weak and 'political' VCs have paved way for universities to be governed on the 'organized anarchy' model, thereby completely disrupting the academic environment. In a number of cases, VCs have not been able to complete their terms and have been removed because of serious allegations labelled against them. Even in cases where the VCs have tried to reform and create the right environment, they have received stiff resistance from pressure groups operating within the university with ulterior motives and supported by the political system. Frequent interventions by ministries from behind the curtain have left the top management demoralized and have derailed the university governance.

Since the state funds these public universities, it exercises control through its representation in the finance committee of the university that approves annual accounts and budget of the university and regulates the heads of expenditure. In most cases, after the approval of the finance committee, the annual accounts are placed before the syndicate for approval. The cases of not getting the minimum funds required for funding the universities or inordinate delay in sanctioning and disbursal of funds is pressure tactics used very frequently, causing chaos and stunting normal functioning. A very prominent governance issue is recruitment and selection of faculty. Though state university acts have clearly laid down procedures updated in conformity with the UGC guidelines related to appointments, yet the states normally on one pretext or the other delay filling up of vacancies, forcing these state universities to operate at very small percentage of the sanctioned posts filled. The case of RU was extreme where 54 per cent of the sanctioned posts of teachers were lying vacant at the time of the survey.

The situation of central university is radically different. The BHU was established in 1916 by an Act of Parliament (The Banaras Hindu University Act, Act No. XVI of 1915). As the largest residential university of Asia with five institutes, 16 faculties and 140 departments located in a huge campus, the university is managed by the BHU acts and statutes. The organizational structure of the university is different from the state universities. President of India is the visitor of the university and has the power to appoint the VC. Below him is the chancellor, who is elected by the members of BHU court. The court is an advisory body to the visitor and has chancellor and members of executive council as its ex-officio members. In addition, it has members nominated by the visitor and teachers' representative. The most powerful body of the university is its executive council (like syndicate in state universities). It has the VC as its chairman and eight members nominated by the visitor. The council appoints all important functionaries of the university

including faculty and in addition is also entrusted with the responsibility of managing and regulating the finances, accounts, investments,
property, business and all other administrative affairs of the university.
The university then has all other functionaries and committees which
are common in educational institutions with their role designated by
the BHU Act.

The major point of departure in central universities is president
as visitor and extent of intervention by the government. These have
important implications—First, there is relatively greater objectivity in
appointment of VC and stability in the term of appointment; second,
although the MHRD monitors the functioning of the VC there is
a relative absence of intervention of the ministry in the day-to-day
functioning; third, the executive council and BHU court consist of
members most of whom are educational administrators, statesmen and
men of eminence whose approach towards the university is construc-
tive, thereby giving the VC a free hand; fourth, there is an absence of
intervention of local politicians, and since last couple of decades staff
and student union are banned (BHU), internal pressure groups pose less
challenge in decision-making. Fifth, unlike state universities, the VC is
given enormous power as per the BHU Act that allows him to function
without intervention. There is a finance committee chaired by the VC
with two external members nominated by the visitor, representatives
of employees and deans of two faculties. The budget approved by the
finance committee is endorsed by EC and then sent to the UGC for
approval. Unlike state universities, there is minimum intervention by
the government. Sixth, in matters of appointment, the VC is given a
free hand and within the framework approved by the UGC, he is free
to fill the vacant positions.

The study encourages us to conclude that in case of the state universities at the first tier governance system is fractured and diluted and
the system is not allowed to function as per the spirit of the university
acts. The involvement of state often compromises the selection of
the VCs and even if correct choice is made, he/she is not allowed to
function smoothly. In central universities such as BHU, first devia-
tion is that a system based on acts and statutes normally functions, the
direct involvement of the government in the functioning is less and if

the choice of the VC is correct, the chances of the governance system working efficiently and properly remain very high.

The Second Tier

The second level consists of the way decision-making at the university level is carried out and the kind of relationship of top university administration with the faculty and other stakeholders, that is, the extent to which shared/collegial governance is adhered to. We approach to examine the universities studied based on the principled stand that the success of governance is to be evaluated based on the extent to which governance is able to achieve theoretically designed goals (Table 9.1). We have chosen to indicate these goals based on the performance of universities.

Table 9.1 *Criteria for Effective Governance and Management*

SN	Governance Goals	Variables
A.	Participatory	A.1. Leadership
		A.2. Participation in Decision Making
		A.3. Autonomy of different types
B.	Equitable & Inclusive	B.1. Admission Process
		B.2. Appointment & Promotion
		B.3. Grievance Redressal
C.	Transparent	Transparency in functioning of the administration
D.	Effective & Efficient	D.1. Examination & Evaluation
		D.2. Provision of Student/Staff Related Facilities
		D.3. Infrastructure
		D.4. Workload
E.	Accountable	Accountability of functionaries
F.	Follows Rules and is Responsive	Responsiveness to societal needs and commitment to implementation of rules

Source: Raman et al. (2018).

Participatory/Shared Leadership

Higher education must promote collegial/consensus-based governance. Unfortunately, the universities were found to follow the top-down approach with the top management taking decisions with involvement of powerful lobby of senior professors. Figure 9.2 shows that the general perception in all universities is that it is a handful and handpicked who have say in decision-making. Young teachers remain a disenchanted lot, feeling that they are purposefully kept out of the decision process. They are not part of important committees, allegedly not heard and not represented. A sizeable section of teachers (including even senior members) believes that there is bias in nomination for important committees. Teachers are not asked to work in committees of their ability and choice, rather it is bureaucratically imposed on them (BHU, 76.7%; SBPU, 56.4%; RU, 88.8%; BU, 42.1%). For a large university (BHU), to some extent, it can be attributed to authorities not having information about interest of young teachers, but for state universities it seems deliberate. This creates distrust and inhibits involvement of a sizeable number. Ideally, the administration should seek information as regards their area of interest and expertise.

Autonomy

Internal autonomy is considered a must for HEIs (Carnegie Foundation 1982, Duderstadt 2000, Fielden 2008). The academic autonomy was captured by faculty perception on autonomy in designing academic programmes and curriculum, teaching style and pedagogy, control over

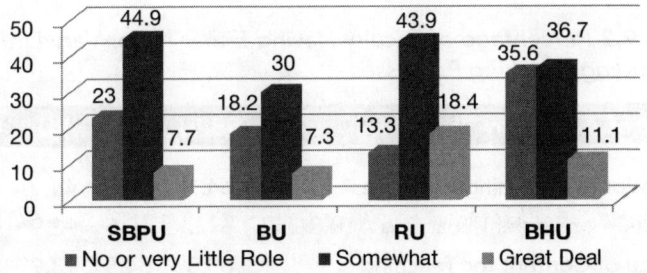

Figure 9.2 *Faculty Perception of Its Participation in Decision-Making*
Source: Raman et al. (2018).

time, determination of workload, choice of doing research, collaboration and twining and so on while administrative autonomy on the basis of involvement in governance processes, committees and so on, shared governance at the department/faculty/institute level, existence of grievance redress system and so on.

The study found that more than 85 per cent of the faculty members in both the central and state universities were happy with the autonomy in pursuing research, collaboration, carrying out innovation and attending seminars and conferences. There were some reservations relating to the biased attitude of heads and principals in granting leave for seminars. Surprisingly, autonomy in adopting teaching practices was found to be very low (Table 9.2). Teachers were found to have little say in deciding the content to be taught. Only 5 per cent of teachers in RU believed that they have significant say in deciding the content. The percentage for other universities varied between 31 and 44 per cent. A more disaggregated analysis found that the senior faculty enjoyed more autonomy in this regard while the young assistant professors despite having innovative ideas and exposure to the latest development in their field found their voice going unheard in board of studies meetings. They had little freedom in designing the teaching process and selecting student learning activities due to non-availability of support infrastructure. In BHU, the situation was better. Overall, on the academic autonomy front, there is very little autonomy given at the department level, and the situation is discouraging improvement in quality of teaching.

For a creative work like teaching, teachers should have control over their time and workload. This was surprisingly found missing as on an

Table 9.2 *Percentage of Faculty Having Either No or Very Little Say in Deciding Teaching Processes*

Kinds of Autonomy	SBPU	BU	RU	BHU
Adoption of Teaching Processes	64.1	50.0	44.9	41.1
Selection of Student Learning Activities	61.5	60.0	92.9	66.7
Choice of Content for Teaching	60.3	54.5	93.9	68.9
Scheduling Time	71.8	64.6	96.9	73

Source: Raman et al. (2018).

average more than 70% of the teachers believed that they have either no or little control over their productive time (97% in case of RU). There was a marked difference among the central and state universities as regards who controls the work time of teachers—for state universities it was the UGC (69.4% for RU and 43.6% for SBPU), while for BHU, it was head of the department (71.1%). This clearly reflects more decentralization of authority in BHU (Raman et al. 2018).

Judged from the perspective of involvement of faculty in decision-making, the governance system looks completely heavy with the bulk of teachers having strong feeling that they have to work under bureaucratic control of the university and have very little administrative, financial or academic autonomy. In most cases, there was clear division with senior teachers having the say. Low financial autonomy is understandable as it is warranted by strict 'government financial rules'; what is shocking is that a very high percentage of faculty felt that they do have either no or only partial academic autonomy. It shows that the governance model is primarily 'bureaucratic', and decision-making is hardly consensus based.

Transparency

Transparency could be reflected in the extent to which decisions are based on declared principles and approved rules with free flow of

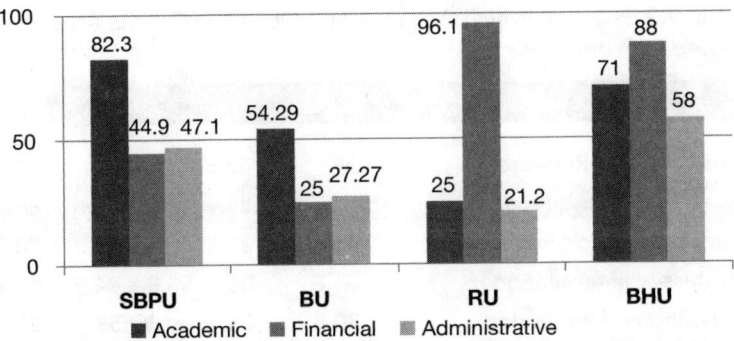

Figure 9.3 *Proportion of Faculty Believing That It Has 'No or Only Partial Autonomy in Academic, Financial and Administrative Matters'*

Source: Raman et al. (2018).

information to the concerned parties. In general, students in all the universities found the admission and examination system very efficient and transparent. The teachers, on the other hand, had a lot of dissatisfaction for the appointment and promotion procedures. They felt that rules are ambiguous and interpretation is always biased. Promotion criteria are not transparent, and weightage given to research, teaching and so on changes from case to case depending on who the person is. Table 9.3 shows that barring research, there are no other criteria that more than 50 per cent teachers found important, reflecting thereby lack of clarity bred through lack of transparency in the system.

Effective and Efficient

The governance system has to be effective and efficient in managing admission, teaching, examination and other processes. Though students and teachers found the system transparent and applauded the introduction of online system yet, there were some concerns. First, a sizeable section of teachers found admission and examination process very lengthy, resulting in waste of time in non-academic work (teachers in BHU and SBPU felt that this unnecessarily increases workload). Second, despite rating examination system as fair and transparent, teachers believed that it is stereotypical, does not give sufficient scope to test the real worth of students on a continuous basis and relies more on rote

Table 9.3 *Extent to Which the Important Objective Criteria Are Heavily Valued in Promotions*

	SBPU	BU	RU	BHU
Research and Publications	59	42.6	94.73	70
Teaching contribution	51.3	34.9	1.32	41.1
Service (e.g. committee work)	41	34.3	1.32	28.9
Professional reputation	34.6	30.6	3.94	36.7
Advising and mentoring	30.8	25.9	10.52	22.2
Refresher Courses	44.9	56.9	76.31	54.4

Source: Raman et al. (2018).

learning. Young teachers wanted more autonomy in testing students and felt that there is considerable scope for examination reforms. Third, a general concern of students was lack of timely, clear and sufficient information relating to admissions and examinations.

Teachers working in universities in general were satisfied with the overall efficiency of the system as regards general service condition (salary, medical facilities etc.), leadership at the department level, prospects for career development and so on. In general, more than 75 per cent of them across universities expressed satisfaction about the professional relationship with other faculties and above 80 per cent have job satisfaction. There is some dissatisfaction about the prospects for career development. Teachers strongly feel that those at the top are not very supportive in this regard. They deliberately delay promotion interviews, come out with highly subjective and clumsy criteria, create an environment not friendly for career growth and lamented that in many cases this is done without the knowledge of the VC.

Overall, teachers appeared to be not so happy and satisfied with different components of governance structure like openness, accountability, communication, coherence, participation and so on. Hardly 20 to 25 per cent said that they are satisfied or very satisfied. A very high percentage preferred to remain neutral while around 30 to 40 per cent said they are dissatisfied or very dissatisfied. Thus, the situation overall looks poor.

Accountability

A very disheartening reality in higher education is complete absence of a system of accountability either for the top management or for the faculty. VCs are not held responsible for the performance of the university and teachers similarly have no performance yardstick. Table 9.4 clearly shows that a sizeable percentage of teachers (between 30 and 50%) believed that the university does not have any system for evaluating and rewarding teaching and research. Another 20 to 30 per cent felt that the system is in a very nascent stage. Absence of a mechanism of reward and punishment has discouraged better performers and increased the proportion of shirkers and underperformers.

Table 9.4 *Percentage of Teachers Who Felt That the System of Evaluation and Reward Is Either Not Developed or Is Underdeveloped*

Governance Structures	SBPU	BU	RU	BHU
Evaluating Teaching and Learning	39.2	47.0	23.68	35.6
Evaluating Research	51.0	44.1	24.9	50.0
Rewarding Teaching Performance	47.0	51.6	93.4	40.0
Rewarding Research Performance	51.0	55.9	96.1	38.9

Source: Raman et al. (2018).

SECTION III. THE CONCERNS AND SUGGESTIONS FOR TRANSMUTATION

The higher education governance system in India in the transition phase has attempted to have a hybrid of collegial and bureaucratic models—in principle the former has been propagated and in practice the latter has been enforced. The attempt to have a government-regulated system having an ideal blend of autonomy and self-imposed accountability has met with limited success and the desired impact on quality and robustness of the system has eluded us. There are three main issues of concern. The first issue is the failure of a 'shared governance (autonomy)' model that has resulted in the bureaucratization of management and disillusionment of the stakeholders regarding functioning of the system. The second concern is the inability of the system to come up with a model of 'accountability', thereby allowing the institutions to develop into an asylum of nonperformers and shirkers. The third problem is the failure of the governance and management system to deliver quality and result to the satisfaction of stakeholders, principally the teachers and students. We briefly turn our attention to these. For brevity, along with the concerns we also suggest measures to handle these so as to facilitate transformation.

Shared Governance/Autonomy

The system of appointment of the VCs and members of syndicate/senate by the government has resulted into political interference and seriously diluted the professional management of the HEIs. The VCs often do not have the right credentials and are forced to carry forward the political agenda of the government. The worst part is that the government does not make the top officials accountable in any respect. There are no declared, clearly articulated goals for VCs on the basis of which their performance could be evaluated and fate could be decided. The qualification for the post of VCs should be made more stringent and should give importance to academic achievement, exposure and capability. The appointment should be made by the chancellor but on the basis of search committees consisting of scholars of repute. There should be objective criteria for the evaluation of their performance, such as university ranking, level of satisfaction of stakeholders, regularity of session/examinations and so on, and based only on successful performance, next term should be given. Government's representation in the senate/syndicate and day-to-day functioning should be reduced. An inter-university board consisting of VCs of central university, scholars of repute and civil society might be given the responsibility to monitor the functioning of VCs.

The much talked about 'shared governance model' has not worked. While in administrative and financial matters the system continues to be bureaucratic, in academic matters it is at the most 'hierarchical collegial', that is dominated by senior faculty. The problem is at three levels.

- First, there is reluctance in the top administration to share decision-making authority in administrative and financial matters. The VCs have compromised loyalty. (a) They often forge an unholy alliance with the university bureaucracy and together attempt to centralize decision-making process and minimize the role of teachers in the same. (b) They in most cases create their own coterie of senior faculty members, their 'yes men' who are put in all important committees whose principal task is to endorse the decisions of the VC. Thus, faculty committees do not have the true representation of teachers and as such do not reflect the consensus. (c) They promote a system in which rules are vague (so that they can be interpreted as per the need and preference of the administration), are changed as per their desire and these changes in rules are not put in public domain and conveyed to teachers and students. The teachers feel that the policies are sound but the administrators make use of the loopholes to circumvent the procedures to suit them. (d) They foster a system in which the decisions are taken as per the bargaining strength of the affected person. (e) They promote only top-down communication and that too in a selective fashion and there is no bottom-up communication. The combined effort of all these is confusion and mistrust of faculty members about the intentions of the administration.

- Second, there is reluctance among senior members of the faculty to share decision-making authority with younger colleagues. The internal democracy within the faculty is missing. There is clear hierarchy within faculty members, and there are divisions based on cadre and whether they are insiders (alumnus of the university) or outsiders and so on. A common reservation of young teachers across universities is that they are deliberately kept out of the decision-making process, their voice is unheard and unrepresented and they are often demoralized and threatened by people from their own fraternity. Almost all the committees (especially the important ones) have members based on seniority, and there is no place for young teachers. The young teachers are not only not involved in taking any administrative or financial decision they are kept out in taking academic decision. Their suggestions to improve course content is not paid heed to, endeavour to reform pedagogy is discouraged and the like. Although they are part of the departmental committees, the study found that in most cases they do not have a voice or their voice goes unheard.

The sorry state of affairs calls for significant change in the system, just improving the system of appointing VCs would not help. First and most important one is clarity about rules and regulations and putting the same on the university website for their reach. The rules should clearly articulate broad-based representation of senior and junior teachers in different decision-making bodies and committees. The administration should use the data relating to teachers' ability and field of exposure to involve them in the decision-making process. The university administration should ensure that different bodies in place are working. The faculty committees, departmental councils and other such bodies need to be activated. These should meet regularly and should function the way they are designed to. It is noticed that the communication channel between the top administration and faculty is not working and more often than not the mistrust and bad blood is on account of insufficient and incorrect information. The University website should be used to handle this issue. In order to have faith in the system, it is important that the grievance committees are made more efficient with broad-based representation and a mechanism for quick disposal of complaints.

Accountability

A major concern of governance is its failure to evolve any system of accountability for the functionaries—VCs, deans and heads, adminis-tration and more importantly teachers. Deans and heads are appointed on the basis of seniority and there is no system of evaluation of their performance. It all depends on personal interest and drive of the person concerned whether he chooses to be an administrative head trying to dominate the members of the faculty or academic head encouraging academic reforms. Absence of a system of accountability for teachers has had catastrophic effect. Teaching has suffered—while students bunk classes as they find that the curriculum does not guarantee employment/ quality of teaching is poor; teachers miss classes as there is no system to acknowledge, evaluate and reward teaching. Research and publications are considered important but again the system has not been able to display the commitment to evolve a foolproof system to evaluate their quality. The teachers have a lot of complaints about the importance given to research and publication at the time of promotion and the way the research work has been graded. The internal quality assessment system has collapsed in most universities and the quality of PhD being produced has touched the bottom. The involvement in administrative and supportive activities is again not considered as there is no system of giving these responsibilities, and no objective criteria put in place to acknowledge the same.

The need for the hour is to come out with a system of account-ability to continuously assess the performance of teachers. Teaching performance could be monitored through (a) monitoring attendance, (b) introducing a mandatory transparent online student feedback system,

(c) giving weightage to student performance in external examination, (d) involving third-party agencies in the process and (e) evaluating innovations in teaching method and pedagogy brought about by the teacher. A system of rewarding better performers must be incorporated. As far as accountability with regard to research is concerned, we already have a global system in place. The system needs to be modelled and adopted to suit Indian conditions and standards.

Delivery

The failure to promote a shared governance model and develop a system of accountability ultimately has resulted in poor quality of education and discontent and disillusionment of the two main stake-holders, viz. teachers and students. The lack of a system of incentives and rewards has significantly affected the quality and resulted into poor ranking of the universities in global perspective. The recruitment and promotion system has failed to attract quality students to the teaching profession and failed to enthuse the qualified faculty to work with zeal respectively. Apathy of government has resulted in significant propor-tion of teaching positions lying vacant, and lack of clarity in eligibility and scrutiny processes and transparency in appointment process has discouraged talented youth from joining the profession. In all the uni-versities surveyed including the central university BHU, inbreeding is considerable, clearly highlighting the failure to attract quality stuff from outside. Promotion policy lacks clarity, and teachers strongly feel that this is highly subjective, giving undue scope to the heads and deans to manipulate things and maintain their upper hand on juniors. This has, on the one hand, created a feeling of mistrust among teachers and adversely affected the internal dynamics of the department and, on the other hand, created a feeling among the juniors that more than their teaching and research performances, their proximity with the high ups and connections clinches issue for them.

Students have been at the receiving end. They are getting poor-quality output—outdated curriculum, unscientific teaching methods and teachers who are not committed to their profession. They are made to believe that most important things in universities are the admission and examination processes—curriculum, quality of teaching, training and practical exposure are issues they have stopped complaining about.

National Assessment and Accreditation Council (NAAC) is already working in the direction of evaluating the delivery system. The system has to be modified a bit to make it broad based and apropos for continuous assessment of delivery system and give feedback to the university. In addition, an internal feedback mechanism involving all stakeholders should be promoted.

Final Words

Governance and management of higher education in a world where knowledge is not a monolithic and tangible entity produced by standardized process by institutions having uniform structure is becoming increasingly complex and difficult. The wide diversities make it aptly clear that there can be no 'unique', 'ideal' and 'dream' system that is appropriate for all kinds of institutions in all circumstances. Our effort to build one has resulted in failure and started the blame game with every stakeholder attacking the other for the sordid state of affairs. A deeper look would reveal that all stakeholders have to take responsibility—government for its inability to create governance models apropos for specific kinds of institutions in specific settings and also for having too much intervention and infringement in the autonomy of universities; the 'republic of scholars' for misuse of autonomy and freedom given in specific situations and failure to create trust and faith in the market that it stands for quality and can ensure the same given suitable environment; the recipients for their inability to appreciate quality and sacrifice individual gains for important long-term goals of education system; and market for deliberately creating information asymmetry and playing spoilsport by promoting institutions that do not stand for quality.

There are few major issues that need to be debated and governed properly. These include, among other things, coming up with a transparent, apolitical and fair system of appointment of competent, capable and dedicated top leadership with established academic credentials and exposure and giving it a free hand to run the show, development of a robust system of faculty recruitment, training and promotion that encourages efficiency and is based on a system of reward and in extreme cases punishment, evolving a system of accountability and internal quality control embedded in the system and regulated by the faculty themselves, allowing a designated role to the market and above all charting out long-term development goals for higher education arrived at after sufficient debate and inputs from all stakeholders. Best practices of governance and management followed by different universities have to be studied, acknowledged and propagated but not forced. We need to value the way successful universities and institutions in our country despite all handicaps have been able to come out with commendable performances in specific fields. Lessons have to be learnt from them.

REFERENCES

Ajayi, J. F. A., G. K. Lameck, and A. G. Johnson. 1996. *The African Experience with Higher Education*. London: James Currey.

Carnegie Commission on Higher Education. 1973. *Governance of Higher Education: Six Priority Problems: A Report and Recommendations*. New York: McGraw-Hill Companies.

Carnegie Foundation for the Advancement of Teaching. 1982. *The Control of the Campus: A Report on the Governance of Higher Education*. Princeton, NJ: Princeton University Press.

Cohen, M. D., J. G. March, and J. P. Olsen. 1972. 'A Garbage Can Model of Organizational Choice'. *Administrative Science Quarterly* 17(1): 1–25.

Creswell, J. W. 2013. *Educational Research: Planning, Conducting, and Evaluating*. Brantford: W. Ross MacDonald School Resource Services Library.

Dobbins, M., and C. Knill. 2009. 'Higher Education Policies in Central and Eastern Europe: Convergence toward a Common Model?' *Governance* 22(3): 397–430.

Duderstadt, J. J. 2000. 'A Choice of Transformations for the 21st-century University'. *Chronicle of Higher Education* 46(22): B6.

Fielden, J. 2008. 'Global Trends in University Governance'. Education Working Paper Series No. 9, the World Bank, Washington, DC.

Kearney, M. L., and J. Huisman. 2007. 'Main Transformations, Challenges and Emerging Patterns in Higher Education Systems'. *Higher Education Policy* 20(4): 361–363.

Maassen, P. 2007. 'Europe: Governance, Expectations, and Reform'. *International Higher Education* (49): 13–14.

Marginson, S., and M. van der Wende. 2007. 'Globalisation and Higher Education'. OECD Education Working Papers Series No. 8, OECD, Paris. Available at: www.oecd.org/edu/workingpapers.

Neave, G., and F. van Vught. 1994. *Government and Higher Education Relationships across Three Continents: The Winds of Change.* Oxford: Pergamon Press.

Raman, R., S. Singh, and S. Kumar. 2018. *Governance and Management of Higher Education in Uttar Pradesh.* CPRHE/NIEPA Research Report, New Delhi.

Saint, W. October 2009. 'Guiding Universities: Governance and Management Arrangements around the Globe'. Human Development Network, Working Paper, the World Bank, Washington, DC.

Salmi, J. 2009. *The Challenge of Establishing World-class Universities.* Washington, DC: World Bank.

Schultz, T. W. 1961. 'Investment in Human Capital'. *American Economic Review* 51(1): 1–15.

Sen, A. 1999. *Development as Freedom.* New Delhi: Oxford University Press.

Stensaker, B., J. Enders, and H. de Boer. 2007. *Comparative analysis on Governance reform in European higher education. The extent and impact of higher education governance reform across Europe. Final report to the Directorate-General for Education and Culture of the European Commission.* Enschede, the Netherlands: Center for Higher Education Policy Studies, University of Twente.

Trow, M. 1973. *Problems in the Transition from Elite to Mass Higher Education.* Berkeley, CA: Carnegie Commission on Higher Education.

Varghese, N.V., and M. Martin. 2014. *Governance Reforms in Higher Education: A Study of Institutional Autonomy in Asian Countries.* Paris: International Institute of Educational Planning/UNESCO.

Vught, F. V. 2007. *Towards a Cartography of Higher Education Policy Change.* Enschede: CHEPS, University of Twente.

Chapter 10

Managing Transition from 'State' to 'Central' University in the University of Allahabad

Issues and Challenges

Rajen Harshe

My basic training has been in the area of political science and international relations studies. At the same time, I have had an experience of administering and managing one of India's most difficult central universities, namely, University of Allahabad (UoA) as its first vice chancellor (VC; 2005–2010) after the central status was accorded to it in July 2005. I have expressed ideas and thoughts through my answers to the questions that are being raised related to the functioning of the university system in India, in general and UoA in particular. Thus, this chapter is an exercise in reflection. It is neither an attempt to assess oneself nor sit on a judgement on others but present a narrative analysis of things as they were to get a better understanding of public institutions. Keeping this in view, let me proceed to handle a range of questions.

WHAT IS A UNIVERSITY?

A university is an institution that imparts training in practically all the branches, including natural and social sciences, medicine as well as engineering and so on of higher education. Such education eventually leads to award of degrees and diplomas in various fields of study. By definition, a university is an inclusive institution. It offers a space where cultured individuals who are fired by intellectual imagination pursue their studies. Obviously, teaching, research, training and consultancy are integral parts of the functioning of any university. Besides, universities are meant to absorb and even encourage religious, cultural, ethnic, race, class and caste diversities of all kinds. Such diversities should be reflected in the composition of students, faculties as well as non-teaching staff. More significantly, universities have to encourage diversities of views and dissenting views from governing orthodoxies. Through constant dialogues between diversities of perspectives universities contribute to knowledge building exercises. Freedom of intellectual expression has to be a nonnegotiable condition of the functioning of any university. Paradoxically, although universities are not supposed to discriminate on the basis of caste, class, creed, race and religion, they are supposed to discriminate with reference to quality of work and grade students as well as faculty members.

HOW DO YOU PLACE UOA AMONG UNIVERSITIES IN INDIA?

The UoA is the fourth oldest university in India, established in 1887. In independent India it was run by the state of UP till it obtained central status in 2005. The UoA has had a glorious past. Owing to its outstanding faculty, it was able to produce extraordinary alumni in all the walks of life. For instance, its alumni include former president and vice president of the Republic of India, former prime ministers, and cabinet ministers in the central government, chief ministers, governors, and a large number of bureaucrats, scholars, scientists, artists and distinguished literary figures. Even though the past has been glorious, the UoA had deteriorated quite steeply after the 1960s. There could be several reasons that cumulatively caused this deterioration. To start with, the student–faculty ratio has always left much to be desired in the

UoA. Almost half of the sanctioned faculty positions had to be filled. Paucity of faculty appeared acute when there was sudden increase in the strength of the students in various programmes of study after reservations for other backward classes (OBCs) were introduced in 2006. Thus, roughly there were over 120 students per faculty in the UoA. The central government sanctioned new faculty positions in the departments that were supposed to be established and additional positions were also given under expansion due to OBC quota. But filling up the faculty positions with appropriate personnel was and is an extremely difficult task. Initially, it could not be done for the want of ordinances under central status of the UoA. The ordinances required careful drafting and consequent approval from the government of India (GOI). Besides, there were immense possibilities of litigations while filling up vacancies because Allahabad has been a seat of the largest high court in India. That is why filling up of vacancies had to be done very systematically. Due to a backlog in the filling up of faculty positions, the university was working almost with half of its strength.

Certain typical problems of a conventional state university such as growing student indiscipline due to politicization, the paucity of funds, in breeding in faculty recruitments, admission of students predominantly from only adjacent districts of the Hindi belt, lack of proficiency in English among students as well as faculty, and noticeable lack of competence regarding computer skills could also be picked up instantly and cited among the few causes of the UoA's constant deterioration. Indeed, Allahabad has been a major bastion of Hindi literature and no one can deny Hindi has its premier place in Allahabad. It is quite necessary and even normal to learn in one's own mother tongue in any part of India but proficiency over English is equally essential for higher education since it is an international language. In retrospect, it could be argued that movements like *Angreji Hatao* (remove English) of the 1960s have cut off students from abundant literature on all subjects that is available in English and thereby done damage to higher education in different parts of India. In India's context, every student necessarily has to be multilingual.

At this stage, some distinction between 'state' universities (SUs) and 'central' universities (CUs) is essential to come to terms with the process of transition from state to central university as far as UoA was concerned. While the former are funded by the respective states, the latter are funded directly by the central government through the University Grants Commission (UGC). Centrally funded universities are better funded with more emoluments, autonomy and facilities than the state-funded universities. The character of CUs is also supposed to be more cosmopolitan than SUs. However, neither all the CUs are cosmopolitan nor do they necessarily have high standards of academic excellence. On the contrary, SUs such as SBPU, University of Madras and Jadavpur were among the first to be chosen under the University with Potential of Excellence (UPE) during 2001. The UoA remained somewhere in the middle of the spectrum with B++ grade from National Assessment and Accreditation (NAAC) by 2004.

WHAT WERE THE INITIAL CHALLENGES THAT YOU PERCEIVED WHEN YOU TOOK OVER?

At the outset, let me admit with all humility and look at my own minus and plus points. I have been a quintessential academic all my life. I did shoulder different administrative responsibilities at my parent institution, namely, University of Hyderabad (UoH), before going to Allahabad such as head of the department (1989–1992) and Coordinator of the Special Assistance Programme (DSA; 1991–2003). But I had never managed a large university, and I am not an instinctive admin-istrator. I certainly have had a vision and capacity to lead, deal with all kinds of people including top class intellectuals and politicians, give public speeches and even lead mass movements. Nevertheless, I had to constantly train myself to become an effective administrator. It was constant learning by doing. Since I am aware of my own limitations in the realm of law, accounts and audit, I was always ready to take help, learn and delegate responsibilities.

When I met the faculty I could realize that the UoA indeed had a number of excellent faculty members, albeit thinly spread out in sci-ences, arts and commerce and law faculties. As far as social and human sciences are concerned, it is well known that UoA has been primarily a teaching university and research culture had really never caught on with the faculty. More often students too were primarily interested in appearing for Civil Services Examinations (CSE). Also, there were faculty from 11 constituent colleges (UoA Act 2005). Colleges in general were a much-neglected lot, and there was underlying hierarchy because the college teachers felt that university teachers perceived themselves as faculty that taught PG courses and they looked down on degree-college teachers. The UoA lacked work culture and an academic atmosphere. Classes were not conducted regularly in several places; a few teachers were spending time in coaching classes, a few of them were working full time for their respective political parties and some of them were campus politicians. Notwithstanding these limitations, the faculty expected a great deal from its central status in terms of pecuniary gains and privileges such as medical facilities and leave travel concessions (LTC) and so on. They almost had lost sight of the fact that they had to prove themselves in their subjects to be worthy of faculty in a good central university by consistently working hard.

As far as the non-teaching employees were concerned, there were more than 1,000 and most were computer illiterate. They were highly politicized. Students within the campus were roughly 25,000. A number of students for the want of jobs had a habit of staying on in the university by enrolling themselves in one course or the other. In fact, one of the important preoccupations of such senior students was to eventually join politics to lead society. The UoA provided years of apprenticeship in this regard.

I think that literature politics can be a creative activity if it is used for positive purposes and betterment of the nation. However, as an activity it can degenerate into the 'last resort of the scoundrels'. Being an intensely political city, it is believed that people breathe politics in Allahabad. Any issue can get politicized, and to my dismay I could learn that politics was possible over the dead as well.

HOW GOOD WERE OTHER IMPORTANT BODIES SUCH AS ACADEMIC COUNCIL (AC), EXECUTIVE COUNCIL (EC) AND THE COURT?

All these bodies in the initial phase were not regular and in transitional mould for initial three years. The AC was full of celebrities from all over India during the first three years. Even though all of them could not attend meetings regularly, those who attended the meetings provided useful inputs and the meetings with large agendas also used to get over within two to three hours. The EC has had all the nominated members by the ministry of human resources development (MHRD) with strong local connections, and out of 15 at least 7 had a direct link with a particular political party and some of them only thrived on politics. Even though there were members from academic community of the UoA in the EC, they were reticent and scared to deal with politicians. Personally, it was excruciatingly painful to sit through the meetings of the EC, constituted by the MHRD, as some members failed to observe even basic decorum and decency in the house. The second EC that came into being after July 2008 was quite good, and we could take a lot of decisions due to harmony of views among all the members. By any standards, the EC is the most powerful body as far as the governance of the university is concerned. The court too had academics and public figures as members. The annual budget and annual report of the university are submitted for the approval of the court. I have had smooth sailing in the AC and court all the way and but for the first EC (2005–2008); the second EC too was fine.

With regard to the functioning of the first EC, I would like to state that since most of the members were local, they had too many vested interests. Apart from this, too many people such as from student leaders, faculty and non-teaching employees used to approach them to get undue favours through the EC. Being politicians, they never liked to turn such requests down by themselves but preferred such requests to be turned down by the EC so that VC and administration could be conveniently blamed for not doing a particular work well outside the rules. I also could not appreciate the fact that issues related to Allahabad University Students Union (AUSU) were regularly discussed in the EC meetings.

Moreover, the first EC was also capable of taking populist decisions without caring for the long-term consequences. I recall in 2006, as a result of the high court order, the EC members enthusiastically integrated Motilal Nehru Medical College (MLNC) and Swaroop Rani Nehru Hospital (SRNH) within the fold of the UoA without properly thinking through how the funds could be obtained to run those institutions. Unfortunately, it was left to the VC to negotiate with the funding agency like the UGC to obtain such funds. Similarly, in an unprecedented move the EC, held on 4 February 2007, chose to promote 18 associate professors of MLNC to professorship on the basis of a UGC letter. The underlying reason for this was support mustered by one of the influential politicians for this from a few EC members. The court order in this regard had insisted that such promotions could be allowed only through the statutes of the central university alone because the UoA was no longer a state university. It was ignored by the members even if the registrar had read the order out twice in the EC meeting. The members passed almost a unanimous resolution to promote 18 faculty members of the MLNC to the post of professor. Unfortunately, even seven senior academics who were members of the EC were party to it. Only one of them resisted the resolution on such lines but eventually restrained from recording dissent note formally. A few others murmured against it but failed to record their disapproval. Perhaps such a resolution was being carried only by vociferous minority by browbeating the rest. In spite of such resolution, the VC refused to implement the orders, in the ultimate analysis. It is common sense that the EC is not an appointing authority, and it only has powers to ratify minutes and recommendations of the selection committees before the appointment orders are issued. And yet the resolution itself had led to contempt of court. The VC personally had to apprise the then HRD Minister late Shri Arjun Singh about what had happened in the EC meeting. He took an unorthodox step and called for an informal EC meeting in his own office by taking VC's consent in June 2007. After hearing the EC members and VC's version, he interrogated the EC members stating that there are so many central universities in the country but no EC had committed contempt of court. He was in a mood to dissolve the EC if the members did not behave themselves. His unusual support gave the VC immense strength to function in days ahead. Subsequently, the university was able to hold regular selection committee by nominating appropriate experts to ensure promotions of those 18 faculty members of the MLNC.

The narration of these episodes only raises one pertinent question. Must regular politicians or individuals associated with political parties be made members of the apex bodies such as the EC? By and large, I have seen from my experience that politicians are indifferent to academic concerns such as quality, maintaining excellent standards, attracting sound faculty and building institutions of academic excellence. Narrow, petty and marginal interests overpower their imagination. This is not to state that all of them have questionable credentials. Indeed, there have been decent individuals among the politicians too. However, while choosing them for responsible bodies, due consideration has to be given to their academic interests/credibility before they become a part of decision-making bodies such as the EC. I would also like to add that even several academicians too are, quite surprisingly, uncon-cerned about academic norms and standards. This means there cannot be a hard and fast rule about who should be members of EC. The only viable argument that could be advanced is that the members have to be chosen carefully because they must have integrity.

HOW COULD YOU GET COOPERATION FROM FACULTY WHICH IS SO POLITICIZED?

As far as the faculty of the university was concerned, I could seek cooperation from practically all the quarters and they came forward to extend it. They were ready for conducting all India entrance tests, organize national and international seminars and sign memorandum of understanding (MoU) with other major universities. We were also able to work out a 20-year academic vision plan after organizing sev-eral meetings. One of the faculty members did a tremendous job by organizing events such as campus recruitment and almost four thousand students got employment as soon as they passed out.

However, the faculty had to change its mind-set. They were still used to the state university system where accountability was absent. They were not used to submitting annual reports of the university to Parliament of India for approval when UoA was a state university. That is why we were slow in preparing our report. In spite of repeated requests from the administration, faculty was slow in giving required data and later preparing and processing the data that they had gathered to finalize the reports. It did cause considerable embarrassment for the VC in the gatherings of central university VCs. Besides, faculty expected advantages without working for it on several instances. And to earn such advantages they could resort to pressure tactics including sitting on relay hunger strikes. This, to me, is a normal problem in public universities where everyone is more conscious of rights without thinking about corresponding responsibilities that come with any job.

Nevertheless, I would certainly like to raise one larger issue at this stage. A number of faculty members in different times from the UoA have been active members and even office bearers in leading political parties of India. While doing full-time party work they have often neglected their primary duties. I think their involvement in active politics has taken toll on academic ambience within the university. Imagine for a minute what would happen if like these faculty members all the remaining faculty members choose to join different political parties and work for them and treat university job as a part-time job. There will be havoc in the university and it will become dysfunctional in no time. I have often felt that faculty that is working for their university never gets adequately recognized for their services while those who shirk university work get attention, public status and other rewards just because they are in active politics. If anyone wants to join politics as citizens they are free to do it. However, let a public institution and its work not suffer because of their extra-curricular activities. I personally am of the view that there have to be some regulations that prevent faculty members from playing any active role as members of political parties. They can be neutral or even committed intellectuals who express themselves through reading, speaking and writing but they need not abdicate academic responsibilities and join full-time politics. This issue needs larger debate and thinking. Similarly, the individuals who hold VC's posts have to be politically neutral and apolitical. They must not yield to any political pressures to ensure fair selections and general working of the university. Unfortunately, the VCs are also picked up on political basis and canvassing. Thus, there is always a gap between 'what is' and what 'ought to be'. To bridge it carefully appears to be a major challenge in contemporary times.

HOW COULD YOU HANDLE STUDENT INDISCIPLINE IN THE UOA?

It depends on how we define indiscipline. University is space where all controversial ideas need a continuous debate and contestation.

Especially, governing orthodoxies have to be challenged in any domain. If the students are intellectually demanding and rebellious they have to be encouraged. For any teacher it is always a challenge to satisfy intellectually young and at times intolerant students. I suppose universities must provide appropriate ambience for intellectual dialogue (Harshe 2012).

However, in a university like the UoA, the main source of indiscipline always had been activities of the student union (AUSU) and the manner in which it functioned. Admittedly, the same AUSU in the past have thrown up future leaders who have led India and the AUSU too had a glorious past. Somehow things had deteriorated steeply over the years. Actually if anyone entered the portals of the UoA in 2005, they would be struck by the presence of the wheeler-dealers. There were alleged student leaders behaving like agents to give mark sheets or even change the mark sheets, get the required NOCs and so on by getting commission and doing many such petty jobs by forming the link between clerical staff and officials. These things appeared strange.

Moreover, since the previous VC had already committed to conduct elections, there was no choice but to honour his commitment. The administration scheduled elections in November 2005. During the time of elections, however, the students dirtied walls all over the campus as well as the city. It was observed that they forced owners of the coaching classes, shopkeepers, doctors, and independent professionals to give contributions towards their election funds apart from squeezing funds from political parties. During those days, top office bearers of the AUSU used to come with security guards and expensive cars. As the elections were announced the university was a witness to a strange sight. An old man in the late 40s had enrolled himself as a regular student just to get elected as president of the AUSU that year. He was meeting his constituency and along with him his son who was also a student in graduate programme was campaigning for his father.

HOW WAS THE COURSE OF ELECTION?

The elections were conducted smoothly. However, before the process of counting began, one of the candidates for president's post had allegedly shot a candidate, contesting for the post of vice president, dead. The incident occurred when the AIU had organized an all India conference of VCs in Allahabad. As a delegate, the VC had to suffer embarrassment as a large number of VCs publicly condemned the incident and raised doubts about the viability of student unions. Since it was reported that the caste affinity of the victim had something to do with the caste base of the then political regime, the murder had led to chaos in the entire city. Ironically, the police forces were being beaten up by the mobs and they were on the retreat. Nuisance caused by the elections had become so serious that the VC was summoned by the Allahabad high court. The high court gave orders to clean up walls in the entire city before the election results were announced.

HOW DID THE AUSU FUNCTION LATER?

As the AUSU office bearers were sworn in, the VC's trial began. The so-called student leaders with the support from their parties and tacit support from forces within the university were perennially involved in organizing anarchy on the campus. The description 'organized anarchy' sounds self-contradictory but that is how it was! Somehow politics of teachers, non-teaching staff and students were interlinked and all other groups other than students were indirectly involved in AUSU politics. Since the VC had just begun his innings they were working to desta-bilize him so that by building pressures they could get acceptance for their various unreasonable demands. On every other day mobs would *gherao* VC office and shout slogans to a point that he had to come out to talk to them. After he used to come out they immediately would take pictures and videos to made public through the media. AUSU leaders were building their careers and such publicity was essential for them. The misbehaviour of student leaders crossed all limits when they disrupted a selection committee meeting meant to select architect for the university and ill-treated the external experts. Their contention was that entrance tests had to be conducted once more as the entrance tests papers were leaked. Actually, there just was no truth in such allegation as was found out later. As a response, the VC appealed to all the decent elements of the university community to join him in a peace March on 4 July 2006. It was a historic march where an unprecedented number of people marched from the Senate Hall campus to Gandhi Bhavan to work towards peaceful campus and fight hooliganism. This trial of strength was so successful that the AUSU went on a back foot.

Before that march in May 2006, the VC and his administration had deposed before the Lyngdoh committee and briefed the members about the plight of the university. The committee report observed the similar plight of universities in the state of UP, thanks to functioning of student bodies. They also condoned if the universities in UP avoided conduct of elections for three years. Such elections too had to be held according to the recommendations of the Lyngdoh committee (MHRD 2006). On the whole, the recommendations of the commission had strengthened the VC's hands. However, AUSU was intermittently causing nuisance in regular functioning of the university. Subsequently, the Allahabad high court gave a judgment that the student who was elected as president of the AUSU was not a bona fide student of the UoA. Obviously, pressures were exerted on the VC to select a new president as his replacement on the basis of election results that were held earlier. The VC refused to nominate anyone after taking advice from additional solicitor general. The lack of a students' union offered the university a breathing space to clean up the campus.

Further, the university hostels were almost functioning without any rule of law. There were illegal residents and antisocial elements that were staying by threatening the university officials. They also indulged in excessive drinking, extortion, smuggling and other criminal activities. Cleansing hostels of unauthorized occupants has remained a perennial challenge in the UoA. Even if they are taken out, they try to enter through the back door. Each year the administration ensured that bona fide students are able to occupy the rooms and illegal inmates are thrown out of the hostels.

Each year as soon as the New Year began the students used to pressurize to hold the AUSU elections. Their agitation intermittently would disturb peace on campus from August until November and then they would give up. However, in 2008 the agitation was fairly virulent. On 23 August 2008, a large number of outsiders entered the campus on a Saturday to pressurize the VC to hold elections. A few in front had flowers in their hands, behind them there were individuals with bar in hand with attached national flag. There were a large number of them who were carrying stones. The agitators pelted stones for half an hour, broke pots and became unusually rowdy in their behaviour. There was no way out and police help had to be taken. This agitation was launched by the then alliance of the students belonging to the youth wings of the Congress and the Samajwadi Party (SP) to warm up the pitch before an important leader was scheduled to visit Allahabad by the end of the month. The police arrested a number of agitators. The VC was pressurized to release them from Delhi. Besides, local Congress and SP leaders tried to bail the agitators out. The VC did not yield to pressure and remained neutral. Some of those hard-core activists were kept behind bars for almost three weeks.

From 8 September until 14 November 14, HRD pursued the matter of AUSU elections with the VC informally. Eventually, the VC was summoned by the then HRD minister on 15 November at his residence. He repeatedly pressured to hold the AUSU elections and the VC kept telling him that they are busy in drawing rules for the new students' representative body in light of the recommendations of the Lyngdoh Committee Guidelines. The stubborn attitude of VC disappointed him and an unpleasant meeting ended. The VC was also ready to tender resignation on the issue of indiscipline but not lose the gains that we had during initial three years. It must be added here that in spite of the differences expressed in an informal meeting between the VC and the HRD minister, the minister chose to defend VC's position in public. The administration successfully avoided the AUSU elections throughout the remaining term of the VC that led to a lot of progress in the university. It was as if the administration had struck at the roots of the tree and branches were falling by themselves. However, VC in his tenure until 2010 October was not able to install new students' representative body as per the recommendations of the Lyngdoh Committee Guidelines.

CAN YOU GENERALIZE FROM YOUR EXPERIENCE ABOUT THE FUNCTIONING OF STUDENTS UNIONS ACROSS INDIA?

It is not appropriate to make generalizations because each of them will meet exceptions and exceptions only improve the rules. For instance,

SBPU/University of Poona had no tradition of students union. The university has not merely been a major centre of academic excellence but it always has had a history of disciplined and peaceful campus. In contrast, Jawaharlal Nehru University campus got totally politicized in the 1970s itself. Debates among students in those days were interesting, lively and educative. But the student body was getting polarized on ideological grounds. Subsequently, class and caste backgrounds of students also began to polarize students. Arguments could always be made for and against the existence of student bodies. Such bodies can become a medium to sort out conflicts, raise voices against injustice and process legitimate demands from the students. At the same time, they open up universities to the interference of all kinds of outside forces. Particularly, as student groupings get linked up to political parties, regional or national politics starts influencing university life. They also aggravate divisions among students. In the northern parts of the country, criminal elements too are a part of student politics. They not just cause a lot of nuisance but make routine functioning of universities almost impossible.

IS IT THEN POSSIBLE TO DEPOLITICIZE UNIVERSITIES?

Strangely, bodies like a students' union have provided a cradle for future politicians, at least in North India. Politics has also been criminalized and there is also politicization of crimes. Admittedly students have a great deal of energy and they need to be engaged creatively. In that case, so many other ways of engaging them creatively have to be explored. For instance, universities can run fortnightly magazines and allow students to express their ideas. Students could be involved in healthy debates, fine arts and diverse annual social events. Under any condition this problem needs to be addressed effectively and immediately in public universities, which are deteriorating in their academic standards.

HOW WERE YOU ABLE TO MANAGE NON-TEACHING STAFF?

The non-teaching staff had so many accumulated problems including a large army of daily wagers doing different forms of manual work, stagnation for the want of promotion-related rules and policies, required fitment into central university scales and the system and so on. They agitated to get their demands processed in July–August 2008. The university was never closed but they held demonstrations in front of the VC office. Most of these demands were met. In fact, regularizing over 120 personnel was the boldest step that the administration took against the existing vacancies. Most of those employees were working for more than 10 to 15 years on those very manual jobs and they felt gratified. A section of teachers and students leaders was supporting their agitations. A few members of the non-teaching association were not conducting themselves properly. When the problems were resolved and everyone resumed work the VC had told their president, who was particularly rude, that if such things happen again, the administration will be constrained to initiate strict punitive action. In spite of this understanding, just three months before the tenure of VC was about to end, they went on a path of agitation again. The administration chose to wait and watch. By and large, the president and his comrades were feeling complacent and triumphant. Somehow, on the last working day of the president of non-teaching union, just before an hour before he was about to retire and enjoy his send-off party, the administration initiated a strong action. He was suspended pending due enquiry and all his benefits were being suspended till the result of the enquiry. Suddenly, the focus of the agitation shifted from demands of various groups of employees to giving fair treatment to president of the union before he retired. They were all keen to revoke his suspension and restore his service benefits. It gave administration leverage to bargain and the matters related to staff were amicably settled.

WHAT WAS ACHIEVED DURING YOUR TERM?

There were several noteworthy achievements and they could be attributed to collective work done on a sustained basis by faculty, students and non-teaching staff. The VC is just a facilitator. The campus was peaceful and had turned academic throughout the tenure (Harshe 2017). The UoA was not closed down even for a day. There were plenty of national and international seminars in each department that led to exchange of ideas among scholars and scientists. Just as the university was turning academic in its orientation, we were able to succeed in getting ordinances of the central university approved and they were promulgated on 8 February 2008. Getting the ordinances prepared was an uphill task. However, there was a professor who had most thorough knowledge of the history of university and its governance. He also had a wider vision and capacity to address minute details within a grand scheme of ordinances. The MHRD cooperated with the university by deputing one of their officers to Allahabad and the ordinances were collectively read before they were finalized. Even if the VC had to run around for their approval from officials to the then MHRD minister; it was all worth it. As the ordinances were being prepared, a stalwart professor from history along with a team nominated by the VC worked out academic vision plan of the university. Similarly, Allahabad became the first university to draw a master plan prepared by one young architect. Amidst these positive developments, a number of enthusiastic teachers organized UoA's alumni meet in February 2008. It was an unprecedented gathering of political leaders, including Mr Arjun Singh, the then HRD minister, five former chief justices of the Supreme Court, judges of the high court, top echelons of bureaucracy, outstanding scholars and scientists. The event brought back life to UoA and inspired everyone to work towards recapturing the lost glory of the UoA. To add to everyone's joy the honourable minister announced grant worth ₹10 crores for the development of the library.

As the ambience was turning academic, new books and journals were getting added to the library. Science labs were replete with new machines and equipment. In general, infrastructure facilities including furniture, computers and items required for experiments were in abundance. Such facilities demonstrated a perceptive rise in quality and quantity of publications in academic year during each passing year. In addition to this, the construction work was done at an unbelievable speed as incomplete works were completed and new constructions were undertaken and completed. The new ones included hostels, faculty quarters, grand building opposite the Senate Hall campus, building for the department of home science, e-learning centre and so on. Besides, one floor was added to guesthouse; Gandhi Bhavan was renovated along with most of the old hostel buildings. It would be necessary to add that it was difficult to build some of these buildings due to several irritants. However, through patience and perseverance, the task was achieved. Arrangements were being made to ensure 24-hour power supply through 33/11 KV power station within the campus.

The UoA had already recruited administrative officers including the registrar, finance officer, controller of examinations and several deputy and assistant registrars to function more efficiently. Team of over one dozen officials proved capable of moving the files promptly. With the new ordinances new faculty members were recruited in all the newly sanctioned departments such as centre for cognitive and behavioural sciences, globalization and development, sociology, material sciences, biotechnology, atmospheric and oceanic sciences, and food and technology. Similarly, traditional departments such as philosophy, law, English and so on also had a new faculty. On the whole, due to entry of bright, young and creative faculty academic environment improved perceptibly. Centre of Women Studies and Film and Theatre Institute were also made functional. Jawaharlal Nehru Centre for differently abled was established to ensure that visually challenged students are able to read with the help of computer.

In the cultural world, there were several noteworthy activities that warrant a mention. Every year Kala Mela was organized. Besides, students periodically brought out a monthly called 'Bargad'. We were able to stage a play called 'Mistaken Annie Besant in India', which was watched by over 1,200 students. It had a playwright from Pakistan, an Indian storyteller and the rest of the actors and actresses were British.

A few words regarding student progression would be in order. The campus recruitment cell, as noted earlier, was able to recruit over 4,000 students. The UoA students began to do extremely well in national tests like Junior Research Fellowships, National Eligibility Test (NET) and the entire gamut of CSE.

At the end, it also needs to be noted that so long as the medical college (MNMC) and hospital (SRNH) were under the UoA, their functioning had improved remarkably. Umpteen numbers of new facilities were introduced and the institutions catered to the entire district as far as health care was concerned. However, since the successive state government regimes wanted to get hold over those institutions, eventually the president chose to delink them from the UoA by amending the statute, a right that she held till the first three years after they came into existence in 2005.

WHAT DO YOU THINK WAS LEFT UNDONE?

The UoA was able to recruit only 50 faculty members because ordinances were not ready for almost two and half years. If there was more time left in the tenure, there could have been at least hundred more faculty members and the face of the university would have transformed. It is difficult to get quality personnel to man faculty and before I became a VC, I can state with pardonable pride that I was instrumental in choosing some of the best faculty members all over India in my own field. I also feel that it is difficult to lead a life of an honest person when you are VC. I did not compromise on my values any time but I do remember being a bit less strict when merit promotions were being decided. I could not have been able to recruit bright academic without satisfying the existing faculty. Promotion added to their self-esteem and made them feel less stagnant. I would have been happier had I completed the grand building that I began in front of the campus during my tenure. On the whole, I did my best during the period of transition.

WHAT COULD BE THE LESSONS THAT PUBLIC INSTITUTIONS IN INDIA CAN DRAW FROM YOUR EXPERIENCES?

I seriously feel that public universities have to rethink about the role of student unions and avoid politicization of campuses and all forms of external interferences that disrupt smooth functioning of the universities. Further, teachers must be assessed more strictly. Indeed, they must have all the academic freedom. They must be free to critique official policies. However, they should be more committed to universities. Teachers need not join political parties and if they want to, they should resign. Similarly, a large number of teachers have behaved like nonperforming assets and find all kinds of excuses to avoid work. Let them be judged by their work. The day students agitate in central universities against substandard teaching, I believe, India would progress. By and large, in universities good work goes unrewarded and underappreciated people who do not work are equated with those who work and this needs to change.

REFERENCES

Harshe, R. October 2012. 'Handling Student Indiscipline'. *Seminar No. 638*, pp. 97–102.

Harshe, R. 2017. 'Life and Times as Vice Chancellor in Allahabad'. In *Governance in Action: Reminiscences of the Vice Chancellors*, edited by F. Qamar and S. R. D. Pani, 209–232. New Delhi: Association of Indian Universities.

Ministry of Human Resources Development (MHRD). 2006. The Lyngdoh Committee Guidelines. Department of Higher Education, Government of India, New Delhi. Available at: http://mhrd.gov.in/report-committee-frame-guidelines-students-union-elections-collegesuniversities-lyngdoh-committee (Accessed on 28 November 2018).

The University of Allahabad Act 2005. Available at: https://indiacode.nic.in/bitstream/123456789/2019/1/200526.pdf.

PART III

Managing Quality at the Institutional Level

Chapter 11

Managing Quality and Excellence
Conceptual and Institutional Factors

Supriya Chaudhuri

This brief study outlines the theoretical debates, worldwide, surrounding the measuring of quality and excellence in higher education. It will then go on to consider the situation at the institutional level in India, drawing upon the author's own experience at a relatively small and poorly funded state university in India that has nevertheless achieved a high reputation nationally, as well as a degree of international recognition, for its academic excellence. It will end by asking how far this reflects real possibilities within our much-criticized public university system, and is replicable as a model by other institutions—especially the many new universities, both public and private, that are being created today.

THE HIGHER EDUCATION LANDSCAPE

The very idea of 'managing quality and excellence at the institutional level' draws upon a number of presuppositions regarding higher education as an organizational field, where the relatively abstract and indefinable notions of *quality* and *excellence* can be associated with specific indicators or parameters, and employed to accredit, assess, or rank institutions. The use of the verb 'managing' also suggests the operation of market ideologies governing the performance of the higher education sector, that must measure up to standards set within a competitive and ever-developing field. The emergence of this discourse in India followed on from worldwide developments in the higher education sector: indeed, the formation of the National Assessment and Accreditation Council of India (NAAC: motto, 'NAAC for Quality and Excellence in Higher Education') in 1994, and the current focus on institutional rankings, cemented by the launching of the National Institutional Ranking Framework (NIRF) by the ministry of human resource development (MHRD) in 2015, suggest a conscious adoption of the evaluation apparatus required by a modern knowledge economy. Over a decade ago, the National Knowledge Commission (NKC) of India, charged with bringing about major changes in the Indian higher education landscape to create such a 'knowledge economy', did not hesitate to identify a real crisis in terms of both quality and excellence:

> There is in fact a quiet crisis in higher education in India that runs deep. It is not yet discernible simply because there are pockets of excellence, an enormous reservoir of talented young people and an intense competition in the admissions process. And, in some important spheres, we continue to reap the benefits of what was sown in higher education fifty years ago by the founding fathers of the Republic. The reality is that we have miles to go (GOI 2006: 1).

Over the past 13 years, there have been quantifiable changes in the higher education landscape, from 345 universities in 2005–2006 to a figure of 903 listed in MHRD's (2018) All India Survey of Higher Education (AISHE) for 2017–2018. Of these, 147 are central universities or Institutes of National Importance that would also receive central funds; 380 are state public universities (including open universities); and 343 are private universities (including institutions deemed to be universities); additionally, there are a number of government and government-aided 'deemed' universities (GOI 2018: 5). The gross enrolment ratio (GER), calculated for persons in the age group 18 to 23, has gone up from 11.6 in 2005–2006 to 25.8 in the most recent figures (GOI 2018: 19). Additionally, the task of increasing the provision of online resources for higher education—already underway through the National Platform for Technology Enabled Learning (NPTEL, mainly run by the IITs), the University Grants Commission (UGC)'s e-Pathshala, and other providers—was energetically taken up by the National Mission on Education through Information and Communication Technology (NME-ICT), with its drive for Massive Online Open Courses (MOOCs), as created by six national coordinators including NPTEL, UGC, Indira Gandhi National Open University (IGNOU), National Council for Educational Research and Training (NCERT), and others, to be made available on MHRD's web portal SWAYAM (Study Webs of Active Learning for Young Aspiring Minds). Does this increase in student and faculty numbers in higher education translate into better quality?

Despite the initiatives towards 'massification' in higher education (Varghese 2015), quality and excellence are also very much at the forefront of national concern, as suggested by anxiety about institutional rankings and the identification of 'Institutions of Eminence' (see https://www.ugc.ac.in/ioe/about.aspx). But it is important to understand the issues involved here. First, how do we define quality and excellence? Are these to be understood *extrinsically*, as a set of parameters to be satisfied before an institution can claim 'quality' or 'excellence'? What role does accreditation play in the process? If, by contrast, there are *internal or intrinsic* criteria governing an institution's aspiration for excellence, how are these internal motivators defined and incorporated? How, at the institutional level, are targets set, motivation inculcated, work done, and self-assessments imposed within teaching–learning and research environments? On the one hand, we have regulatory or assessment bodies and national and international ranking exercises. On the other hand, we have a steady process of institution-building that involves research, teaching and the discharging of social responsibilities. Higher education in India today presents a complex and uneven picture. 'Quality' and 'excellence' are still aspirational categories, not simple terms of description (*Mint Budget Report* 2018).

THE CONCEPT OF INSTITUTIONAL QUALITY

Internationally, the concept of institutional quality, together with ancillary notions such as quality assessment, quality assurance, and quality indicators or parameters, entered the discourses surrounding higher education in the 1980s, and in the subsequent decades, the idea of *quality* engendered intense public engagement, involving both institutional and state actors. The debate around quality was seen as linked to a need to overhaul and reform higher education in the interests of what has been described as the 'structuration of an organizational field', where higher education institutions are seen as a field constituted by numerous stakeholders and actors with collective and connected roles (DiMaggio and Powell 1991, Scott 1995, Scott and Meyer 1991). The term 'structuration', borrowed from Anthony Giddens, is used to define 'the process of institutional elaboration, building and definition of an organizational field' (Giddens 1984, Vaira 2007). In Europe, during the decades of the 1980s and 1990s, the restructuring of the higher education sector came in the wake of new management ideologies, viewing higher education as a type of enterprise admitting entrepreneurs and answerable to an emerging market, as well as to the state and society as a whole. This view, influenced by neoliberal economic theories and the example of higher education in the USA, was at odds with the European Union's commitment to higher education as a public good, and a certain degree of strain and tension between differing perceptions was evident in the 'structuration' process.

The process of restructuring was materially advanced by the issuing of the *Magna Charta Universitatum* at Bologna, Italy, in 1988, and the signing of the Bologna Accord by education ministers of 29 European countries in 1998. During this period, we witness the emergence of quality assurance agencies, independent or state-appointed evaluators or quality assessment bodies, the growth of literature on quality indicators and assessment practices, national and international accreditation or certification for institutions and programmes, and research journals such as *Quality in Higher Education* (Taylor and Francis), which commenced publication in 1995. If the initial efforts were largely nation-based, various international bodes such as the Organisation for Economic Co-operation and Development (OECD) soon turned their attention to the higher education sector, and national quality assurance agencies formed transnational networks. The International Network for Quality Assurance Agencies in Higher Education (INQAAHE) was established in 1991 with only eight members: the total membership now exceeds 200. A 'new infrastructure' was being generated for the mapping of quality in higher education, so that 'while in the 1980s no industrialized country had a higher education quality assessment system and policy and almost none had any kind of accreditation scheme, in 2003 almost all have both, yet still with some differences in their scope, arrangements and practices' (Vaira 2007). Meanwhile, 'excellence', a term more difficult to pin down to 'indicators', was generally associated with ranking processes, or the publication of a 'league table' of leading institutions, such as *THE* World University Rankings (founded in 2004), or the Quacquarelli Symonds (QS) World University Rankings, originally associated with *THE* but operating independently from 2010. Thus, the formation of NAAC in India in 1994 puts it only slightly behind international developments in this direction, and international rankings have been at the forefront of higher education debates for the past decade at least.

REGULATING AND ASSESSING INSTITUTIONAL QUALITY IN INDIA

The notion of quality, with respect to any single higher education institution (HEI), might be invoked in a number of separate contexts: firstly, for the purpose of approval, affiliation, recognition and accreditation, that is, the right to operate as an HEI, admit students and run programmes; secondly, for the purpose of assessment or grading, compared with other HEIs; thirdly, in terms of the satisfaction of stakeholders, including students, faculty, staff, funders (who may be taxpayers) and employers; fourthly, with regard to knowledge contribution through research, teaching and outreach; and finally, in the context of funding, from the state or private capital, higher quality outputs supposedly attracting more resources. In India, long before the formation of NAAC, the quality of higher education institutions was under the care of the UGC, which came into existence on 28 December 1953 and became a statutory organization of the government of India by an Act of Parliament in 1956. Its website declares that it 'has the unique distinction of being the only grant-giving agency in the country which has been vested with two responsibilities: that of providing funds and that of coordination, determination and maintenance of standards in institutions of higher education'. Additionally, its mandate includes

> monitoring developments in the field of collegiate and university edu-
> cation; disbursing grants to the universities and colleges; serving as a
> vital link between the Union and state governments and institutions of
> higher learning; {and} advising the Central and State governments on
> the measures necessary for improvement of university education (UGC
> 1956; see also UGC Act 1956).

In the case of institutes of technology, or programmes of technical education, accreditation was given by the All India Council of Technical Education (AICTE), and for medical colleges, by the Medical Council of India (MCI); other councils, such as the Bar Council of India (BCI), Council of Architecture (COA), Indian Nursing Council (INC), National Council on Teacher Education (NCTE), Pharmacy Council of India (PCI), or the Distance Education Council (DEC), were responsible for other branches of tertiary education. Thus, together with the UGC, several councils functioned as regulatory bodies for higher education in India.

It may be noted that the UGC, in its dual capacity, together with other official funding bodies, did conduct periodic assessments of institutions, departments and programmes, disbursing research and infrastructural assistance according to performance, or quality. Thus, the UGC's *SAP*, for university departments deemed to be of exceptional merit, was instituted as long ago as 1963, and science and engineering departments (or institutes) of proven research excellence received assistance from the government's Department of Science and Technology (DST), or the Department of Atomic Energy (DAE), or from the Council of Scientific and Industrial Research (CSIR), and other such bodies. These schemes were subject to initial assessment and periodic review, exercises viewed with great seriousness by both the granting bodies and the beneficiaries, since funding was involved. Thus, it would be completely wrong to assume that questions of academic quality and research performance, or educational standards, had no part to play in the higher education landscape prior to the 1990s in India. The task assigned to the NAAC was not that of 'affiliating' or 'granting recognition' to a new university, or derecognizing an existing one, functions still reserved for the UGC. Nor could NAAC conduct the kind of rigorous academic audit (with corresponding financial scrutiny) that was regularly undertaken, both for individual departments and for faculties or institutions as a whole, by the UGC under its various schemes for research and infrastructural assistance. These include the departmental Special Assistance Programme (SAP), the UPE scheme, the Centre with Potential for Excellence in Particular Areas (CPEPA) programme, or schemes under Assistance for Strengthening of Infrastructure for Science and Technology (ASIST) and Assistance for Strengthening of Infrastructure for Humanities and Social Sciences (ASIHSS). Additionally, individual researchers could apply for a range of UGC or DST fellowships (such as the INSPIRE fellowship) or for minor or major research projects, all of which would enhance the research profiles of their institutions.

Post-1994 and after the creation of NAAC, a new discourse emerged around quality indicators and assessment. This led to internal quality assurance cells being formed in higher education institutions, as well as fairly intensive record-keeping exercises for the preparation of institutional self-study reports, as required by the periodic NAAC assessments, and some soul-searching and publicity over the award of grades. But these grades, though indirectly (and belatedly) linked to UGC funding, and thought to improve peer perception and societal recognition, cannot be interpreted as the only markers of institutional quality and excellence. Rather, what we find is that the country's funding bodies continued to use their own criteria for assessing and rewarding performance, while NAAC promoted a debate around quality, focusing on a variety of markers and indicators, partly adopted from international agencies and partly devised for Indian conditions. Meanwhile, the MHRD's NIRF, having invited institutions to submit data annually, which it evaluated according to its own parameters, began listing the best universities in the country, thus inviting attention to excellence, as reflected in competitive rankings. We will look at NAAC's criteria of quality, and the NIRF's criteria of excellence, more closely in a later section of this chapter. The fact that no Indian university has figured among the top 100 institutions in the world was a point repeatedly stressed in meetings with VCs by the former President of India, Shri Pranab Mukherjee. In 2017, the third year of NIRF, the minister for human resource development, Shri Prakash Javadekar, announced that the 20 best higher education institutions in the country (10 public and 10 private) would be granted the status of 'Institution of Eminence' and be allowed greater freedom of operation to enable them to match the best in the world. The public institutions would each receive state funding of ₹1,000 crore over five years (IoE Guidelines MHRD, 2017). One hundred and fourteen applications were received under this scheme (74 from public, 40 from private HEIs), and on 9 July 2018, the MHRD minister announced that only six, three from the public sector (IITs Bombay and Delhi, and the Indian Institute of Science Bangalore), and three from the private sector (BITS Pilani, Manipal Academy of Higher Education and Jio Institute), were to be awarded this status. Of the six named institutions, one in the private sector (Jio Institute) did not yet exist, and had apparently been included under the 'greenfield' category (IoE Press Release 9 July 2018). This controversial selection did not increase public confidence in the government's commitment to excellence in higher education. In fact, the Empowered Experts Committee (EEC) overseeing the process had originally recommended eight public HEIs, the five inexplicably omitted from the first announcement being IITs Kharagpur and Madras, Jadavpur University, Delhi University and Anna University. In December 2018, the EEC forwarded these five names, in addition to those of a further 19 institutions (12 private and 7 public) to the government for their inclusion in the list (making a total of 15 private and 15 public institutions if all 30 recommendations were accepted). Up until the end of January 2019, there was no indication whether the government, which had originally mooted a total of 20, would agree.

FUNDING FOR QUALITY IMPROVEMENT

Efforts to determine higher education quality at the highest level in India today, then, remain controversial. For institutions themselves, there is a need to decide what the most effective determinants of quality and excellence might be, and how they can be managed. For the past two decades at least, questions of HE quality, and increased access to it, have been at the forefront of national policy pronouncements. In his Union Budget speech on 1 February 2018, the finance minister had reiterated India's commitment to education as a priority area. On 2 February 2019, presenting the Interim Budget, Finance Minister Piyush Goyal did not repeat this, making a somewhat vaguer mention of artificial intelligence as a focus area. Rupees 93,848 crore (3.3 per cent of the total budget expenditure) was allocated for the education sector (over ₹10,000 crore more than the revised estimate of ₹83,626 last year). However, the actual spend last year, at ₹80,215 crore, was less than the allocated sum. In 2018–2019, 3.48 per cent of the total budget was allocated for education, with less than half, or ₹35,010 crore, for higher education. So despite the hike, the share of expenses on the education sector has actually declined. Last year, the finance minister presented a new scheme called 'Revitalizing Infrastructure and Systems in Higher Education or RISE', to be financed through a restructured HEFA that will give loans to centrally funded HEIs, such as IITs, IIMs, IISERs, central universities and so on. The allocation for HEFA has been reduced from ₹2,750 crore last year to ₹2,100 crore this year. The actual spending by HEFA last year was just ₹250 crore.

Questions surrounding expenditure on higher education are especially urgent at a time when the Higher Education Commission of India (HECI) Bill is still pending in Parliament. This bill, which has replaced earlier suggestions for a common regulator (HEERA) to take the place of both the UGC and the AICTE, proposes to take away the UGC's fund-dispensing powers and turn them over to the MHRD directly. It has been repeatedly emphasized that the existence of multiple regulators, with varying financial powers, has led to a state of disorder in the higher education landscape, and has blocked the road to institutional excellence (Malik 2018) In May 2017, the UGC announced a scheme granting 'graded autonomy' to highly ranked institutions, with those in the top rank having the power to confer degrees, start their own courses, and establish off-campus centres abroad (UGC Graded Autonomy Regulations, 2018). We should note that even during the term of the previous UPA government, five bills proposing a sweeping restructuring of higher education were drawn up. These were the National Commission for Higher Education and

Research (NCHER) Bill, seeking to replace the UGC; the National Accreditation Regulatory Authority for Higher Educational Institutions Bill seeking to replace NAAC; the Prohibition of Unfair Practices in Medical Educational Institutions, Technical Educational Institutions and Universities Bill (against capitation fees); the Educational Tribunals Bill; and the Foreign Educational Institutions (Regulation of Entry and Operations) Bill (Nos. 54–57 of 2010). The confusion created by multiple regulators, accompanied by a proposal to replace the UGC with the NCHER, was first noted by the Yashpal Committee in 2009, on the grounds that:

> The regulatory provisions of the various Acts are substantially different from each other since they were created at different periods by different legislations. The overall responsibilities for the entire higher education system assigned to the UGC are not validated in the provisions of other Acts. There is very little co-ordination among the statutory bodies in respect of degree durations, approval mechanisms, accreditation processes, etc. It sometimes leads to very embarrassing situations in which we find two regulatory agencies at loggerheads and fighting legal cases against each other. (MHRD 2009: 52)

Additionally, the UPA government also wished to create world-class universities or universities of innovation (UGC Guidelines for Innovation Universities 2012), and several policy pronouncements to that effect were made, echoes of which are audible even today in the rhetoric around institutions of eminence. As a salutary reminder, let us note, however, that the University of Pittsburgh, ranked 100th by THE in 2018, had an operating budget of ₹1,400 crore, and assets worth ₹2,000 crores in 2017. It also had an endowment fund of ₹22,500 crores in 2017, which is well over 60 per cent of India's 'entire' outlay on higher education in any financial year. India has a long way to go before it can match the kind of funding available to institutions in the West.

The ground reality is that while the number of universities and colleges has grown exponentially in the past decade, the quality remains uneven, campuses are in disarray, and academic issues are often overshadowed by political interests. This malaise affects centrally funded institutions as well as those under the control of the states, though the former are better equipped and have more resources to devote to infrastructure, equipment, teaching–learning and research. UGC funding, received by both central and state HEIs (though not by the IITs) is often delayed, or held up in bureaucratic red tape; research fellowships and scholarships are particularly badly affected. Through a gradual and momentous shift in the higher education terrain, more than 60 per cent of students now study in privately managed institutions (including colleges), since while private universities number only 343, 78 per cent of colleges are privately managed. India's GER for tertiary education, at around 25 per cent, is extremely low compared to the USA's 86.7 per cent, the UK's 79.94 per cent, Germany's 65.5 per cent, France's 64.4 per cent, Japan's 62.2 per cent, and even China's 39.4 per cent and Brazil's 46.4 per cent (2014 figures). The fact that India has very large student numbers, and may have the largest in the world by 2025, is simply a reflection of its large population. Seventy-nine per cent of the student population are in UG education, and only around 0.45 per cent are enrolled in PhD programmes (GOI 2018: 10): According to OECD figures from 2016, India produces 24,000 PhDs annually, the fourth largest number in the world but still far behind the United States, which produces 68,000 (OECD 2016: 147). Again, the large number reflects India's population, but as a percentage of that population it is infinitesimal. Moreover, the quality of these PhDs is generally unsatisfactory except in the country's top institutions, and a substantial proportion of the best PhDs produced annually in the United States are actually earned by Indian doctoral students, indicating a continuing and unchecked brain drain.

QUALITY AND EXCELLENCE IN INDIAN HEIS

Let us now look at some of the indicators for quality and excellence in Indian higher education. NAAC was set up in 1994 with the specific mission of improving the quality of higher education institutions. Its stated vision is

To make quality the defining element of higher education in India through a combination of self and external quality evaluation, promotion and sustenance initiatives (NAAC 2018b: 5).

This vision is to be executed through a number of action plans, in which the word 'quality' occurs at least thrice. Further, it is stated that 'the NAAC methodology for Assessment and Accreditation is very much similar to that followed by Quality Assurance (QA) agencies across the world and consists of self-assessment by the institution along with external peer assessment organized by NAAC' (NAAC 2018b: 5). NAAC quality assessments look at seven criteria, with a number of key indicators for each. In the case of universities, they carry the following weightages (NAAC 2018b: 9–25):

1. Curricular aspects   150
2. Teaching–Learning and evaluation   200
3. Research, innovations and extension   250
4. Infrastructure and learning resources   100
5. Student support and progression   100
6. Governance, leadership and management   100
7. Institutional values and best practices   100

The criteria are the same for autonomous and affiliated colleges, but the weightages differ. Moreover, the provision of key indicators, as sub-categories within each criterion, each with its specific weightage (also varying with the type of institution) apparently makes for ease of assessment, and a 'transparent' system, since the criteria and indicators are shared as public information. Checking the NAAC criteria against, for example, the Standards and Guidelines for Quality Assurance in the European Higher Education Area (ESG) published in 2015, we find some similarities, though not a complete overlap. The ESG are declaredly based on the following four principles:

- Higher education institutions have primary responsibility for the quality of their provision and its assurance;
- Quality assurance responds to the diversity of higher education systems, institutions, programmes and students;
- Quality assurance supports the development of a quality culture;
- Quality assurance takes into account the needs and expectations of students, all other stakeholders and society (ESG 2015: 6).

Interestingly, the ESG focus almost exclusively on teaching and learning, and do not take research into consideration. Much of the debate around quality in higher education has indeed focused on the quality of programmes and outcomes, such as student and employer satisfaction, rather than research quality. The problem of defining quality in higher education has been repeatedly addressed, notably in a celebrated paper by Harvey and Green (1993), which states the following five alternatives: quality as *exceptional*, quality as *perfection* or consistency, quality as *fitness for purpose*, quality as *value for money*, and quality as *transformation* or value enhancement. Arguably, NAAC needs to look for all these types of quality in higher education institutions, but much more importantly, it needs to promote and encourage qualitative improvement across the board.

Statistics released on 16 August 2018 indicate that, so far, 323 universities and 7,473 colleges have been graded by NAAC, a total of 7,796 institutions: of these, some have gone through the accreditation process more than once. The grades awarded are as shown in Table 11.1 (NAAC 2018a).

Thus, the picture of higher education institutions presented by NAAC is relatively reassuring, with around two-thirds of the accredited universities (but only one-fifth of the colleges) being awarded the A grade. It was from among this group of 203 universities that 62 were singled out by the UGC for 'graded autonomy' on the basis of their NAAC scores, though considerable anxiety has subsequently been expressed by the universities so favoured as to whether this may imply

Table 11.1 *Grade Break Up of Institutions Accredited (As on 16 August 2018)*

	A	B	C	Total
Universities	203	116	4	**323**
Colleges	1622	5051	800	**7473**
Total	**1825**	**5167**	**804**	**7796**

Source: NAAC (2018a).

that they will in the future be required to generate a larger proportion of their own funding through 'autonomous' financial operations. While some institutions have registered complaints against 'unfair' NAAC assessments, the more common perception is that NAAC assessments are on the whole generous rather than strict, and that close analysis of institutional strengths and weaknesses is not permitted by the relatively mechanical system of 'indicators'. In fact, much more rigorous self-analysis and intellectual effort are required by a grant or project application on the part of the HEI as a whole or by a single department.

How far has NAAC, in its 24 years of operation, promoted quality in Indian higher education? While it is undoubtedly the case that a relatively uncritical and even moribund higher education system was compelled to undergo extensive stock-taking, documentation, self-examination, face-lifting (in terms of physical infrastructure), and self-education as to what 'quality' and 'assessment' might mean, it remains unclear as to whether institutions have actually been motivated to improve—that is, to transform themselves in a positive way—through participation in NAAC accreditation. Educational quality depends on many factors, notably the unbiased appointment of highly qualified faculty, the devising of appropriate curricula, the mentoring of students, the promotion of a research culture, adequate infrastructure, and smooth, honest, and principled administration. All of these are included among the NAAC criteria for assessment: but has NAAC actively intervened in the higher educational landscape to make these the focus of internal quality improvement efforts, by the HEIs themselves, and more importantly the centre and state governments, or the private bodies which fund these institutions and (despite their ostensible autonomy) control them to all intents and purposes? On the whole, NAAC has been absent from policy discussions at centre or state level, and has had little to contribute to a national debate on university development in all its aspects. While the MHRD and, on occasions, the UGC are very much at the forefront of policy pronouncements, the role of NAAC appears to be limited to assessment.

Meanwhile, the national debate on quality has focused, in recent years, on excellence at the top, rather than uniform quality through the system (a concern that NAAC has undoubtedly acknowledged, and could have done more to publicize). The MHRD's NIRF exercise was, like the Shanghai rankings initiated by China, intended to provide a better method of ranking HEIs based on more accurate indicators suited to the country of origin (though the Shanghai list is international). The NIRF emphasizes the learning environment, research culture, the impact made by graduates, social inclusivity and, finally, reputation among the public, peers and employers. Its rankings give 40 per cent weightage to 'Research Productivity, Impact and IPR', 30 per cent weightage to 'Teaching, Learning and Resources', 5 per cent weightage to 'graduation outcomes', 5 per cent weightage to 'outreach and inclusivity' and lastly 10 per cent weightage to 'Perception'. Clearly, these criteria—and especially the weightages attached to them—are somewhat different from those employed by NAAC. In fact, they are similar to those used by international agencies, though with adjustments for Indian conditions. For example, the QS rankings are based on the following five criteria: academic reputation (40%), employer reputation (10%), student–faculty ratio (20%), citations per faculty (20%), and internationalization (5% each) for faculty and students. Data for the first two criteria are compiled from large international surveys of academics that QS conducts every year. Citations are calculated from the SCOPUS database. The emphasis is, as we can see, on 'reputation', in respect of both employers' perceptions and international visibility, research expertise as measured by citations and PhDs, and internationalization in respect of students, projects and faculty. Slightly differently, the *THE* criteria stand as given in Table 11.2.

Indian universities fare poorly in respect of international reputation, since Indian HEIs, especially the top publicly funded research institutions, do not have many international faculty or students (in fact, until very recently, they were not permitted to hire foreign faculty using taxpayers' money, nor could they offer seats to foreign students given the demand from Indian students whose education was being subsidized). In the QS rankings last year, the top Indian institution, Indian Institute of Science, Bangalore, had no scores for employer reputation, international faculty or international students.

Table 11.2 *Times Higher Education Criteria*

Criterion	Indicator	Weight
Citations – research influence	1. Citations impact (normalized average citations per paper) (Database: Thomson Reuter's Web of Science)	30%
Teaching – the learning environment	1. Income per academic 2. Reputational survey – teaching 3. PhD awards per academic year 4. PhD awards / bachelor's awards 5. Undergraduates admitted per academic year	30%
Research – volume, income and reputation	1. Papers academic and research staff 2. Research income (scaled) 3. Reputation survey – research	30%
International mix – staff and students	1. Ratio of international to domestic students 2. Ratio of international to domestic staff 3. Proportion of internationally co-authored research papers	7.5%
Industry income – innovation	1. Research income from industry (per academic staff)	2.5%

Source: Times Higher Education.

Given these disparities, how reasonable would it be to measure excellence using the NIRF criteria, or the international criteria laid down by QS or *THE*, and attempt to match peers in China, Korea, the USA, the UK or Europe? How should the task of fostering excellence at all levels be undertaken? Or should there be another definition of excellence, more sensitive to Indian conditions and the gross disparities and inequalities in our social and economic landscape? Most important, how should the 'quality' criteria be linked to the notion of 'excellence' and made part of the very large task of 'developing' higher education, not just assessing its successes or failures?

An Institutional Example

The modern university is not a monolith. It is a highly complex organization whose smooth functioning depends on the cooperation of many individual units, that are linked together by an understanding of the university's role in society and in the production of knowledge. An impartial review of the growth and development of the best higher education institutions in India will reveal that their achievements depended upon a combination of many factors: the vision of the founders and first stakeholders, the provisions of the act of incorporation, reputation among students and society, faculty recruitment, innovative curricula and teaching, funding for new programmes, research and projects from state, UGC or other central bodies, infrastructure development, outreach and partnerships and good governance. In the chaotic conditions within which public higher education has to operate, several of these factors might have been adversely affected at different points of time, but the institution might still have retained the momentum to enable it to progress in other areas. Nevertheless, there is no doubt that all the factors mentioned above, and possibly several more, would have been essential to build up an institution of excellence and provide education of high quality to students (Wooten and Hoffman 2008).

The example I will discuss, Jadavpur University, is a state university located in the city of Kolkata, West Bengal. It was established as a university post-Independence, in 1955, but traces its origins to the Swadeshi movement and the foundation of the National Council of Education, Bengal, in 1906, to impart technological education to young Indians in opposition to colonial educational policy. Its largest faculty remains the faculty of engineering and technology, but it also has excellent faculties of arts and sciences, and its unique interdisciplinary schools have now been placed within the faculty of interdisciplinary studies, law and management. In the last NAAC accreditation in 2014 (as well as in all previous ones), Jadavpur was placed in the highest grade, grade A, with a CGPA of 3.68 on a scale of 4. Jadavpur was ranked 5th among all Indian universities in NIRF 2017 and 6th in NIRF 2018; among engineering universities, it was 9th in 2017, 12th in 2018; overall, it was 12th in 2017, 13th in 2018. In the *THE* World Rankings, 2018 and 2019, it has been placed in the 601 to 800 bracket (though it was in the 501–600 bracket in 2017). It applied successfully to be recognized as an Institution of Eminence in 2018 (it was one of the eight public universities originally recommended by the EEC for this status, but was not mentioned in the first notification; it appears now to be set for recognition, though the situation is still fluid).

As a state university (in a less well-off state like West Bengal), Jadavpur receives significantly less funding than central universities such as Delhi, JNU or Hyderabad, and certainly much less than the IITs. However, it has always positioned itself as a leading research university, a vision aided by two important factors: that it was primarily a non-affiliating institution (that is, without affiliated colleges), admitting students to graduate and PG programmes through rigorous admission procedures (such as the WB-JEE, departmental admission tests, GATE, and so on), and it had a high degree of internal cohesion in terms of administrative structures and academic interaction in what was initially a single campus but has now grown to three (of which two are adjacent to each other). A major feature of the university has been its consistent pursuit of interdisciplinary research areas as well as disciplinary innovation, so that it now has a separate faculty to house its interdisciplinary schools, while innovative centres are attached to individual departments in the traditional faculties of engineering, arts (humanities), and science. Jadavpur has consistently been able to attract highly qualified faculty, and its research output is among the best in the country, but it should be noted that the disparity in salary and benefits with central or private universities, the lack of university fellowships for doctoral students, limited research/travel funds for faculty, poorly maintained infrastructure, inadequate hostel facilities, insufficient faculty housing, and lack of provision for international students and faculty were undeniable constraints.

As against these problems, some of which Jadavpur shares with other state universities, there has, over several decades, been a real drive to tap into the schemes through which national bodies such as the UGC, DST, DAE, and so on have sought to promote research and academic excellence in our public universities. Over half of the university's 37 departments receive special assistance through programmes such as

DST–FIST, UGC–SAP: several are designated as Centres of Advanced Study. The university provides inputs to critical sectors such as defence and atomic energy, and played a pivotal role in the Integrated Guided Missile Development Programme, which led to the establishment of a dedicated Advanced Technology Cell (ATC) for coordinating DRDO projects at Jadavpur, a continuing relationship that has culminated in an agreement to set up a larger centre, funded by the DRDO, to be housed in the West Annexe of the Jadavpur Main Campus. It is identified as a knowledge partner by the NITI Aayog and as a nodal centre for syllabus creation by the RUSA secretariat. It has recently been awarded funds to the sum of 100 crores under RUSA 2.0 for research and academic development, infrastructure improvement, modernizing laboratories and other facilities and buying equipment. Jadavpur is also a mentoring institute in the TEQIP–III programme of the MHRD, and a member of the Confederation of Indian Industries. The French multinational group AREVA sponsors PhD scholars carrying out research in nuclear and renewable energy. Additionally, the university has consistently engaged in internationally funded collaborative research programmes, as well as dual-degree or joint academic courses with universities abroad, undertaken consultancy through its industry–institute partnership cell, attracted international scholars for short visits to its departments, carried out MHRD Global Initiative for Academic Networks (GIAN) programmes, built up academic links and exchanges with leading global universities, initiated innovative research projects globally (e.g. in climate change), fostered a culture of research leadership and exchange from the student level upwards through programmes such as Sasakawa Young Leaders Fellowship Fund (SYLFF) and EU–Erasmus Mundus/Erasmus Plus schemes and connected to the community through social outreach.

The point to be made here relates not to a record of achievement, but to the fact that this pursuit of research and academic excellence can only be sustained (a) through the support obtained from national and international bodies—from the UGC and DST to the EU—and (b) through the efforts made by the university, a community made up of students, teachers, non-teaching staff, administrators and alumni, to compete and qualify for these opportunities (which are by no means easy to get). In fact, the case of Jadavpur University is worth serious consideration precisely because it offers an example of the good utilization of available resources by a public, 'state', as opposed to 'central' university in a climate of declining confidence in the public university system.

In the first place, this success—though much remains to be done by way of global competitiveness—confirms that despite severe constraints, the public higher education system in India can encourage and reward academic quality and excellence, and that our better HEIs have availed of the schemes on offer, in addition to seeking international collaborations. Given that our public universities have very little by way of corpus funds and have been actively prevented by state and central legislation, over the past decades, from (a) raising money through higher fees; (b) augmenting their finances by setting aside some of their sanctioned places for international students; and (c) adding to their profile by hiring foreign faculty, it is necessary to emphasize the role played by government agencies in ensuring their academic development. And it is important to see this role also in a larger developmental context, that is, in the context of a grossly unequal nation where economic and social deprivation is still a widespread reality. For this reason, the periodic pronouncements by government that universities should become self-financing, that graded autonomy, or even the Institution of Eminence scheme, should end by making universities capable of surviving on their own, appear to be grossly premature in the Indian context. Not until individual universities can draw upon a really substantial corpus fund and can improve their international profiles by diversifying both faculty and student bodies, 'while at the same time honouring their commitment to the poor and disadvantaged citizens of India', can government funding, and assistance for research and development to public HEIs, be reduced. It is worth recalling that even in the USA or the UK, the major part of funding for higher education still comes from the government, that is, from taxes paid by ordinary citizens.

Secondly, however, the drive for quality and excellence is not a gift from above; it originates within the university itself and is given concrete embodiment by the various stakeholders of the university. Like many state universities, Jadavpur University is governed by the provisions of an act of the state legislature. Its internal constitution, its administrative structure from departmental boards of studies through faculty councils to the executive council and the court may not be very different from that of other HEIs, though the involvement of teachers in every stage of the decision-making process is an important and perhaps distinctive feature. Much more than the statutory provision of an internal quality assurance cell (IQAC) according to NAAC guidelines, the university's research and teaching excellence is made possible by commitment of faculty and students at departmental level and cooperation at every stage of administrative support. Rather than a simply anecdotal account of this, let us look briefly at Jadavpur's participation in Enhancing Quality Assurance Management and Benchmarking Strategies in Indian Universities (EQUAM-BI), a prestigious Erasmus+ project coordinated by the University of Barcelona (UB) and ANECA, Spain, and NAAC, India. This project seeks to identify the internal systems and markers for quality enhancement and management in Indian universities. One of the tools for this is a questionnaire, similar to others produced by NAAC, but more condensed and focused. While it is not possible to reproduce the full questionnaire here, I am offering a sample of two sections, with the university's responses:

EQUAM-BI QUESTIONNAIRE (RESPONSES FROM JADAVPUR), SECTIONS III AND IV

III. Research

1. Which of the following processes or tools are used to monitor/ measure enhancement of research in your HEI?

Processes/Tools	Yes	No	I Do Not Know
Internal review of research proposals	✓		
Internal peer review of ongoing research projects		✓	
Review of current research by external peers invited by your HEI	✓		

Processes/Tools	Yes	No	I Do Not Know
Monitoring research productivity/impact based on indicators	✓		
Facilitation, granting monitoring of research project funding	✓		
Reward and recognition of research outcomes of faculty members	✓		
Establishment of research clusters (specialized and interdisciplinary)	✓		
Mentoring for research	✓		
Research relevant training and Development programmes	✓		

Other (please specify) _____

_____

IV. Innovation

2. Which are the following support systems made available for identifying and nurturing innovation in your HEI?

Support Systems	Yes	No	I Do Not Know
Establishment of research centres/think tanks	✓		
Collaboration with national/international centres of excellence (QA agencies, specialized institutions)	✓		
Establishment of centres of excellence in areas of futuristic relevance	✓		
Establishment of research and development centres/labs	✓		
Entrepreneurial development centres/cells/incubation centres at university/faculty/constituent levels	✓		

Support Systems	Yes	No	I Do Not Know
Consulting centres for intellectual property protection for innovation (patents, trademarks, copyrights, logos, know-how and so on)	✓		

CONCLUSIONS

Jadavpur University's dedication to managing quality and excellence, as exemplified in the responses above, arises from its founding commitment to a model of nationalist education and self-improvement (through the National Council of Education). It has been furthered by a combination of internal and external factors: from within the university and from the higher education infrastructure outside it. Such histories are not unique in India: They can be matched in other state and central universities, including heritage institutions. However, questions of quality and excellence need to be detached from the rhetoric around 'quality assurance' and quality indicators', or from 'rankings', to be reinstated in their proper developmental context. Without wishing to downplay the many agents that keep the university running, let us focus on two major elements, the students, who are at the core of the teaching–learning process, and the faculty, who not only teach but also contribute to knowledge through research. Indian universities have for too long treated students merely as passive consumers of a predetermined set of courses which they are required to consume or pass. Even the 'cafeteria' analogy used by the UGC in its efforts to impose a 'choice-based credit system', or CBCS, is uncomfortably close to the idea of consumption. Meanwhile, students often contrast the relative rigidity of courses, syllabi and examinations in most Indian HEIs with a measure of freedom they experience in other systems, especially abroad. If quality is to be promoted, or developed, at the institutional level, it has in some sense to be created, and students must learn to be innovators and researchers. The restructuring of the learning environment requires autonomy for the institution, respect for students as young adult citizens with a real responsibility for the future, and respect for faculty as mentors, interlocutors, and educational thinkers. It is from a learning environment of this kind that the university can play a role in bringing about social change. This is what might make the 'quality' of Indian higher education distinctive.

Secondly, faculty are at the centre of the university's contribution to learning through their pedagogy and research. They, too, are not in the university simply to implement a predetermined curriculum. As it stands, research incentives are scarce, and mainly visible in the urge to notch up academic performance index (API) points by younger scholars, and in the occasional conference invitation. Few, if any, Indian universities have fully functional research (or research and innovation) wings that (a) maintain a full database of funding sources, project bids, possible research partners and MoUs with other universities, with staff who can help draw up a project proposal or grant application and (b) possess complete records of all the research being undertaken by the university at any given time, whether on an individual or collective basis, across departments and faculties. Given the now unending series of requests for information that come to each HEI for the purpose of NIRF data collection, NAAC self-study reports, ministry requirements and so on, it is amazing that universities do not set up such research wings, which would serve two purposes: first, data collection and research audit; and second, research facilitation and management. Most foreign universities (with which we are compared) have research development wings that not only manage and coordinate research but also help to obtain or manage funds. Indian universities actually do get research funds from many sources. It needs to be remembered that the research excellence of top institutions was brought about not by IQACs but by the commitment of dedicated faculty and the provision of funds from various agencies, including international funding bodies. This aspect of faculty work is often hidden from view and involves solitary paperwork or small research clusters engaged in project liaison. But unless research and innovation are given a central, and publicly acknowledged, place at the heart of the university's organizational structure, excellence cannot be achieved.

Finally, despite the genuine reservations of principle about how taxpayers' money should be spent in an unequal society where public universities cannot accommodate all aspirants, some degree of internationalization is needed. Only through student and faculty mobility, in India and abroad, can national and international integration be achieved. Internationalization is not simply a means of ensuring 'reputation' as the international rankings might suggest. It is a genuine means of promoting global awareness and exchange. Such internationalization should not be a privilege enjoyed only by institutions of eminence. Unless the conditions for quality enhancement are made generally available, and supported by energetic public action, quality will not improve, and excellence will remain a privilege reserved for a very few.

REFERENCES

DiMaggio, P. J., and W. W. Powell. 1991. 'The Iron Cage Revisited: Institutional Isomorphism and Collective Rationality in the Organizational Fields'. In *The New Institutionalism in Organizational Analysis*, edited by W. W. Powell and P. J. DiMaggio, 41–82. Chicago, IL: University of Chicago Press.

ESG. 2015. *ESG Standards and Guidelines for Quality Assurance in the European Higher Education Area*. Brussels: EQUIP.

Giddens, A. 1984. *The Constitution of Society*. Berkeley, CA: University of California Press.

Government of India. November 2006. *Note on Higher Education, National Knowledge Commission*. GOI, New Delhi.

Harvey, L., and D. Green. 1993. 'Defining Quality'. *Assessment and Evaluation in Higher Education* 18(1): 9–34.

Malik, G. 2018. *Governance and Management of Higher Education in India*. Synthesis Report, Centre for Policy Research in Higher Education, New Delhi.

Ministry of Human Resource Development. 2009. *Report on the Committee to Advise on Renovation and Rejuvenation of Higher Education* (Yashpal Committee Report). New Delhi: Government of India.

Ministry of Human Resource Development. 2017. Institutes of Eminence Guidelines. New Delhi: Government of India.

Ministry of Human Resource Development. 2018. *All India Survey of Higher Education 2017–18*. New Delhi: Department of Higher Education, Government of India.

Mint Budget Report. 2018, 2 February. Available at: https://www.livemint.com/Politics/DR0A4NOQgu1fZwdGzHwugO/Budget-2018-Govt-to-spend-₹1-trillion-to-on-school-infrast.html

National Assessment and Accreditation Council. 2018a. *NAAC Statistics 2018*. New Delhi: Government of India. Available at: http://www.naac.gov.in/docs/EC/52EC.pdf (Accessed on 23 September 2018).

National Assessment and Accreditation Council. 2018b. *NAAC University Manual 2018*. New Delhi: Government of India. Retrieved from http://www.naac. gov.in/images/docs/Manuals/University%20Manual%20Amended-%20 20th%20June%202018n.pdf (Accessed on 23 September 2018).

Organisation for Economic Co-operation and Development. 2016. *OECD Science, Technology and Innovation Outlook*. Paris: OECD. Available at: http://dx.doi. org/10.1787/sti_in_outlook-2016-en.

Organisation for Economic Co-operation and Development. 2018. *Education at a Glance*. Paris: OECD. Available at: http://www.oecd.org/education/ education-at-a-glance/.

Scott, W. R. 1995. *Institutions and Organization*. London: SAGE Publications.

Scott, W. R., and J. W. Meyer. 1991. 'The Organization of Societal Sectors: Propositions and Early Evidence'. In *The New Institutionalism in Organizational Analysis*, edited by W. W. Powell and P. J. DiMaggio, 108–140. Chicago, IL: University of Chicago Press.

University Grants Commission. 1956. *UGC Mandate*. New Delhi: Government of India. Available at: https://www.ugc.ac.in/page/Mandate.aspx.

University Grants Commission. 2012. *Guidelines for Innovation Universities, 2012*. New Delhi: Government of India. Available at: http://www.prsindia.org/ uploads/media/Universities%20for%20Research%20and%20Innovation/ Guidelines%20for%20Innovation%20University_UGC.pdf.

University Grants Commission. 2018a. *UGC (Categorisation of Universities (Only) for Grant of Graded Autonomy) Regulations, 2018*. New Delhi: Government of India. Available at: https://www.ugc.ac.in/pdfnews/1435338_182728.pdf (Accessed on 23 September 2018).

University Grants Commission. 2018b. *Union Budget 2018*. New Delhi: Government of India. Available at: https://www.indiabudget.gov.in/ (Accessed on 23 September 2018).

Vaira, M. 2007. 'Quality Assessment in Higher Education: An Overview of Institutionalization, Practices, Problems and Conflicts'. In *Quality Assessment for Higher Education in Europe*, edited by C. Alessandro, 135–146. London: Portland Press.

Varghese, N.V. 2015. *Challenges of Massification of Higher Education in India. Research Paper Series, 1*. New Delhi: Centre for Policy Research in Higher Education.

Wooten, M., and A. J. Hoffman. 2008. 'Organizational Fields: Past, Present and Future'. In *The SAGE Handbook of Organizational Institutionalism*, edited by R. Greenwood, C. Oliver, R. Suddaby and K. Sahlin, 54–74. London: SAGE Publications.

Chapter 12

Managing Quality and Excellence at the Institutional Level
A Study of Bharathiar University

Narayanan Annalakshmi,
Rajalakshmi Bhavana and Bhuvana Esther

The vision of all higher education institutions essentially includes achieving 'excellence'. Parameters such as global university ranking and quality assurance are often recognized as indices of excellence. Excellence in various contexts of the institution, such as management, research, teaching, and student performance, is considered for such evaluations. The vision of the university is to provide internationally comparable higher education to people. The aim is not only to impart knowledge and skills but also to nurture a holistic development of the students with a focus on building their character. The university is committed to educating students who develop as a valuable human resource of the country contributing to national development. The university strives to realize the vision of India and excel in protecting and promoting the rich heritage and secular ideals of the country. The college works with the vision of providing quality higher education to all sections of society.

There may be numerous challenges ingrained in the system that thwart the attainment of excellence in these areas in any institution. The nature of these challenges and responses of institutions vary with the type of institutions.

Quality and excellence in higher education are reflected in several domains, namely, curricular aspect; teaching, learning, and evaluation; research, consultancy, and extension; infrastructure and learning resources; student support and progression; governance, leadership and management; and innovations and best practices. The National Institutional Ranking Framework published by the Ministry of Human Resource Development of Government of India identifies four domains, namely, teaching, learning and resources; research and professional practice; graduation outcomes; outreach and inclusivity; and perception (public and peer) as reflecting quality and excellence. The present study delimits itself to governance, leadership and management aspect of quality and excellence. Specifically, the study attempts to understand how quality and excellence in higher education can be achieved via governance, leadership and management.

The present chapter systematically examines the challenges to quality and excellence that confront the state university and the institutional responses taking the case of one state university and an autonomous government college affiliated to the state university (Narayanan et al. 2018).

DATABASE AND METHODOLOGY

The study is a descriptive research that employed cross-sectional research design to analyse the governance and management of Tamil Nadu using primary and secondary data. Tamil Nadu has both central and state universities. The public universities mostly consist of affiliated colleges that are both private and government aided. The research includes a study on state university and affiliated college in Tamil Nadu to understand the higher education in Tamil Nadu. Survey, interviews, focus groups, and secondary data analysis have been carried out to understand the governance structure and processes in Tamil Nadu. The study also includes an analysis of the relationship between the Ministry of Education, Directorate of College Education, Tamil Nadu Councils of Higher Education and higher education institutions.

Primary data have been collected from state decision–makers, decision–makers at the institutional level (e.g. chairperson of the governing board of the university), management team of the university (vice chancellor), the head of administration (registrar), and deans of selected faculties and heads of selected departments. The survey was conducted using self-report questionnaires to collect data from academic and administrative staff.

Data on policies and legislation, autonomy, state control and management, devolution of responsibility to universities, committee creation, funding models, accountability, performance and outcomes, the role of a university board, and intensity of the state in the appointment of the chair of the board were also collected.

MIXED-METHOD APPROACH

A concurrent triangulation design (Creswell 2013) was used to examine the research objectives. The qualitative (interview and focus group data) and quantitative data (survey data) were collected concurrently in one phase; the data were analysed separately and then compared and combined to confirm, cross-validate or corroborate findings.

THE SAMPLE

The present study employed collecting primary data from different sources, viz. institutional leaders, teachers and students. The details of the sampling design are presented as follows.

Sampling the University and College

One of the state universities located in South India that works only with the arts and science colleges was chosen as the sample. Also, one of the colleges affiliated to this university was also selected to participate in this study. The college selected is unique in that it is the only autonomous government college that is affiliated with the university. The university has 123 colleges, 29 autonomous colleges and 5 constituent colleges under its administrative purview.

Sampling the Departments

The inclusion criteria for the selection of departments include (a) avail-ability of that department both in the university and in the college and (b) one department from humanities, two from social sciences and two from sciences. A total of five departments were selected for the study, one department from the arts, humanities, social sciences, and sciences. The departments that were finally selected to participate based on the above criteria were department of English, physics, zoology, economics and management.

Sampling the Teachers

Teachers with more than five years of experience in the institution from each of the departments selected for the study were identified for administering the questionnaire. For the focus group in the university, the teachers nominated by the registrar were selected. For the focus group discussions in the college, teachers who were nominated by head of the departments (HODs) selected for the study were recruited as a sample.

Sampling the Students

The university offers only master's level programmes and research programmes. Hence, students in the second year of the master's programme in the university were recruited in the sample. In the college, students in the third year of bachelor's programme were recruited in the sample. Samples were drawn from students in the final year of their study programme in the university and college because they would be able to discuss their experience in the system better than those who spent a lesser number of years in the institutions. All the students in the classes and departments mentioned above served as a sample in this study.

MEASURES

The research instruments used to collect the primary data in this study include a faculty questionnaire, student questionnaire, semi-structured interview schedule for institutional leaders (vice chancellor, registrar, controller of examinations, dean, finance officer, department heads, college principal), interview schedule for administration, interview schedule for state bodies (state councils of higher education), and focus group discussion guide for faculty and students.

THE PROCEDURE OF DATA COLLECTION

Data were collected from administrators, faculty and students. A face-to-face interview was conducted to collect data from administrators/leaders of the institution. The interviews were audio recorded, transcribed and analysed. Focus group interviews were conducted on both faculty members and students. Field notes and audio recordings of these discussions formed a part of qualitative data for analysis. The survey was conducted on both faculty and students using the questionnaires prepared exclusively for this study. The faculty members completed the questionnaires at their convenient time and space. For surveying students, the questionnaires were administered to groups of students assembled in classrooms, with each group not exceeding 30 students. The same procedure of data collection was followed in the university and the college sampled.

Dataset

The interview data collected using interview schedule (appended) resulted in rich information from leaders of the institution on governance and management. Similarly, the focus group interview also yielded quality data on the issues discussed. The survey conducted using questionnaires yielded data on various aspects listed under 'Measures' section of this chapter.

Analysis of Data

The quantitative data collected in this study via survey were analysed using descriptive statistics. Using a grounded theory approach, we analysed the qualitative data gathered.

Findings

The revised accreditation framework of National Assessment and Accreditation Council (NAAC) launched in July 2017 represents an explicit paradigm shift, making it Information and Communications Technology (ICT) enabled, objective, transparent, scalable and robust. The distribution of weight is across seven criteria and 34 key indicators. The curricular aspect, which is one of the seven criteria, has direct implication for the quality of higher education. The university departments offer only PG courses largely while the autonomous college under the university considered for this study offers both undergraduate and postgraduate programmes. A brief comparison of the structure of the curriculum of selected disciplines such as psychology showed that there are significant differences in course structure but no significant differences in the overall credits or evaluation pattern.

COMPARISON ON INSTITUTIONAL AUTONOMY AND DECISION-MAKING PROCESS

The university and college are compared with regard to institutional autonomy and decision-making process. Autonomy in three areas, namely, academics, finances and administration, in university and college is being included. Academic autonomy is ensured through Board of Studies (BOS) and Standing Committee on Academic Affairs (SCAA) in the university, which is constituted by teachers. The university has the autonomy to introduce new courses. For admitting students and appointing faculty to the college, strict adherence is given to government norms. It is the government which appoints the teachers. The fund is allotted to the university and autonomy is given for utilization. Full autonomy is exercised in the conduct of examination and declaration of the results. The controller of examinations has the autonomy to bring in changes in the system as needed and implement it with prior approval of the VC. Autonomy of faculty members is reflected in ease of getting leave requests approved, and support received for academic activities like establishing research collaborations, participation in conferences and offering new courses. The finance committee, the senate and the syndicate play a significant role in the administration of the university. The dean of faculty and head of the department are part of the selection/scrutiny committee that is involved in faculty recruitment and promotions. The heads of the department have the autonomy to make necessary changes within the department and ensure the smooth functioning of the department. They are responsible for monitoring the attendance and day-to-day activities of teaching faculty, non-teaching staff, and students of the department. Faculty members are involved in a number of committees and participate in governance. Nevertheless, their role is not active, and the decisions are made at the apex in most of the cases. The role of students in governance is negligible.

The college being an autonomous institution enjoys full autonomy in framing the syllabus, conducting examination and publishing the results. It depends on the government for financial support. The admission committee and the principal carry out the student admission process. The faculty appointment to the college is done directly by the government through the Teachers Recruitment Board (TRB). Faculty promotions are purely based on years of service. The fund is allotted to the college by the government and autonomy is given for utilization. For example, no budget is allocated for maintenance, and hence the college does not have funds for attending to issues of maintenance in the college. The governing council allocates the budget for each department. The individual faculty members are not provided with travel grants. The academic council and governing council, both made up of heads of departments play a significant role in the administration. The governing council has adequate freedom to decide the functions of the college.

There is no students union in the college as in the case of the university, and hence students have no role to play in governance.

GOVERNANCE AND MANAGEMENT PROCESSES

The data on the perception of institutional leaders, faculty and students on governance and management process in the university and college revealed interesting findings. In the university, the senate and the syndicate play a prominent role in governance. Several other committees with specific focus are also involved in the governance process. Various aspects of internal governance structures like openness, accountability, policy effectiveness, communication and research are discussed in this chapter.

From the survey, focus groups and interviews conducted in the university, it is evident that a majority of the faculty and students are satisfied with the governance structure but are not happy with the way it is managed. While the rules and procedures are communicated as per university acts and statute guidelines, the implementation is not perceived to be effective. Top-down communication is effective while bottom-up is not as effective as that, though mechanisms are practically available. Accountability is moderately present, though no evaluation of the quality of teaching is available in the university. The Internal Quality Assurance Cell (IQAC) is present, and external audits are done before NAAC but not on a regular basis. Rules governing recruitment and promotions are communicated to the faculty members with a certain degree of clarity. There are policies in place for various aspects related to management, yet they are not followed in letter and spirit. Teachers report that the management process is individualized such that the rules are interpreted differently for different cases having the same issue.

The college teachers report satisfaction with openness and transparency. They prefer to be neutral concerning yardstick adopted for recruitment and promotion, and indicate that improvement on the existing governing mechanism is necessary. Teachers are satisfied with the fact that there is no formal monitoring system in the college and call monitoring 'dangerous'. They show a strong preference for a humanitarian and social approach to accountability where each teacher is individually responsible for his/her contributions. Communication is top-down and is done by the institutional leaders via HODs.

Students' accountability is well defined in terms of attendance and 'passing minimum' required to get the degree, in both the university and college. Both in the university and in college, students report dissatisfaction with communication. They state that the circulars do not reach them in time, and not all information is circulated. Research is considered a priority only in the university and not for the teachers in the college. The encouragement, facilities, and priority given to research in the university are, hence, significantly higher in the university than in college. Such differences in priorities are reflected in the research contributions made by the teachers in the two different institutions studied herein.

TOOLS AND CHALLENGES FOR ACHIEVING QUALITY AND EXCELLENCE

Good governance has direct implications for ensuring quality and excellence in higher education. Good governance in universities in India may also be seen as essentially involving several specific parameters. Good governance could be plausible with changes implemented at all levels of management. Clarity of rules and regulations are foremost important. Ambiguity in rules and regulations and expectations can thwart objectivity in interpretations, thereby creating chances for subjective bias in decision-making.

Further, transparency in the procedures adopted by the management can be instrumental in boosting the morale of the people involved. Two-way communication systems with equal attention to the upward and downward movement of communication can enhance the perception of inclusiveness. The organization should ensure that equity and inclusiveness are guaranteed in every procedure followed. Participatory management that involves every individual in the organization to be involved in decision-making could add strength to governance in universities. Nurturing participatory management would not only serve to create a sense of belongingness among the faculty members and students but will also be an aid in the effective management of knowledge systems available at all levels. Autonomy sanctioned to the people at different levels is essential for installing a sense of job satisfaction among them. The syndicate, senate, standing committee of academic affairs and board of studies are directly involved in facilitating the process of good governance. An administration that is sensitive to the sentiments of the people in the organization would also be responsive. A sound formal grievance redressal mechanism should be available to ensure this.

In the state, all the parameters of good governance are partially achieved. The tools of good governance and challenges for good governance are briefly discussed next.

BHARATHIAR UNIVERSITY

Accountability

Career Advancement Scheme (CAS) regulations govern promotions, and accountability is only implicit. No external monitoring process is present. Teachers are apprehensive and resistant towards strengthening measures of accountability. HODs monitor the attendance of faculty members. However, in reality, a lot of flexibility and subjectivity is involved in this. Getting regular feedback from students on faculty performance is present at the university, though such feedbacks have no serious implications for the teachers. There are no effective and tangible mechanisms in place to recognize the contribution to teaching since it is merely perceived to be the primary responsibility of the teachers. The completion of coursework is the sole responsibility of the faculty, which is seldom monitored by the institution. However, the onus is on the department to ensure that the programme is run satisfactorily. No reward system exists in the university to recognize the teaching services of faculty members. There is no monetary incentive for faculty running funded projects. Neither is the social reach of these projects evaluated.

Research contributions like supervising PhDs, publications and so on are also not given any particular reward. Reward for research where faculty members who have funded projects can claim 25 per cent of the overhead charges given by the funding agency for purposes like building infrastructure, purchasing assets for use at the department, travel and so on is suggested at the policy level but has not yet been implemented.

The infrastructure and facilities for teaching are adequate. Upgradation, however, takes a long time with the process being very elaborate.

Accountability of both teaching staff and students, besides that of the non-teaching, has to be ascertained. Though a structured regimen for academics is imparted through the state and University Grants Commission (UGC), flexibility requisites as per individual subjects can be given a better elbow room through the Board of Studies and Academic Council.

Transparency

Agenda are circulated before the meeting, and the minutes are also circulated. Clear communication of the proceedings of the meetings is also done. Administrative transparency in academic matters and admissions is appreciable. However, the criteria for allotment of funds to each department are not transparent.

With regard to appointments and promotions, there is moderate level of transparency. The stakeholders are kept guessing about their impending promotions. Guidelines and regulations are in place, and access to them is never restricted. Nevertheless, the chances of ambiguity do prevail due to the misinterpretation or misrepresentation of rules and regulations by the administration. Corruption, personal network, and political network play a role in promotions where the rules are violated in some cases. This is mainly in taking past service into account.

The acts and statutes of the university provide guidelines on the regulations governing the university. A copy of the acts and statutes are provided to all the heads of the department, and a softcopy of the same is uploaded on the university's official website. Most of the practical guidelines for procedures are circulated after approval of the syndicate to the heads of the departments. However, not all these guidelines get circulated to the faculty members, and hence many faculty members state that they are not aware of the rules. The discord between the regulations of the central government or UGC and those of the state government appears to be a challenge to good and concrete awareness creation and implementation of these regulations. To add to this, while the acts and statutes do cover most of the relevant areas, at the point of implementation a very objective approach is not always adhered to.

Benefits do not get extended to all eligible players in equal proportion. Prejudice or bias is found to prevail. Delay in decisions, prevention of the inevitable recognition and procrastination are some of the challenges. Consistency in interpretation of rules and regulations, irrespective of change of guard, is the need of the hour.

Responsiveness

Response to claims is always delayed. Financial support for conferences, getting advance of project funds, payments to project assistants or hiring services is delayed. Response to enquiries related to the evaluation of PhD thesis is not satisfactory. In the name of confidentiality, the office does not provide even routine information to people concerned. Requests for on-duty leave and applications for forwarding grant projects are quickly processed, and approval is accorded promptly. However, when people apply for no objection certificate to apply for positions outside the institution, the response is delayed. Even reimbursement of claims for contingency is delayed. Sometimes the delay is seen in granting permissions to carry out project-related activities. HODs have problems in claiming contingency funds. There is a scope for improvement in the area of response in terms of justified and speedier implementation. There is a need for an objective approach to the requests made. Justified flexibility to the rules and regulations needs to be made on a case-by-case basis at the discretion of the university. Such flexibility would help in a performance-based recognition that would become an impetus for innovations. Implementation of rules with flexibility in terms of respective cases can prevent a draconian approach by the administration.

Faculty members in positions such as 'academic deputy registrar' or 'academic assistant registrar' since they can understand the nuances of the credentials presented by the members of faculty better. Head of Departments (HODs) and Principal Investigators (PIs) desire to have an exclusive office to look after the projects and contingency issues.

Equity/Fairness

The university also addresses issues of equity/inclusion adequately. The norms of the state government for reservation are adhered to without prejudice.

Diversity is valued during admissions. Government communal roster is followed in appointments in most of the cases. People from other states are also provided appointments. Free education schemes are provided to students in the PG programme. Charity schemes are also available from donors to provide financial support for financially backward students. The evaluation process is appreciable, as it is also challenging to the stakeholder. The absence of impartiality is visible in the system. Chronological importance is compromised with, which gives room for circumventing the regulations. However, some faculty members perceive that there is no fairness in promotions, particularly regarding taking past service into account for promotion via the CAS. Calling for CAS applications have to be more frequent. There is no policy in place that ensures a regular call for applications for promotion via CAS. Hence, people have to wait for CAS promotions.

The university should attract students from all over India with the help of a legitimate branding exercise. This would rope in better levels of competition and would aid the university to compete globally by raising its bar periodically.

Participation/Shared Governance

Students' participation is nil. No students union is present in the institution. Students are not involved in meetings related to developments in the departmental or Choice Based Credit System (CBCS) meeting. There is no tutorial system.

Participation of faculty in governance is substantive. Opportunities in bodies such as syndicate, senate, and academic council, besides positions of faculty heads (deans), directors, and co-coordinators, are available. Some believe that the 'seniority' of the faculty member chosen is the eligibility. However, there is a lack of uniformity in its implementation. There is no equal chance for all to participate in the governance, for norms are not well defined and implemented. Challenges to shared governance include lack of uniformity in the implementation of rules across all sections of the staff, the chances of adhering to 'favouritism' prevail and adversity like influencing decision-making may occur.

A democratic approach to governance demands sharing of responsibilities that in turn results in accountability. Moreover, it is elemental to build the necessary trust among working groups. Areas of improvement include the need for an institutional-level database accessible to all in order to prevent repetitive generation of the same, which affects productivity. Impulsive transfer of section staff slows down progress. Ensure strong bonding between the teaching and non-teaching staff to avoid administrative hurdles. Since institutional responsibilities are part of the criteria for an individual's upgradation, an opportunity for all is imperative. The assurance of consensus needs to be put in place rather than the implementation of authority-driven decisions.

Communication

The 'top-down' approach is the constantly used channel of communication, though a 'bottom-up' approach is not negated. Most of the faculty members receive all communications effected by the university via circulars. Faculty members communicate with higher authorities through the HODs. Informal communication channels with higher authorities are present. No formal communication between faculty members and dean of the school is present. At times 'grapevine' shapes decisions, but the need for forestalling 'rumour' in a proactive manner may be ensured.

Open circulars reach in the form of hard copies and intranet. Personal or confidential notices are issued in sealed covers. Also, emails and phone messages are provided simultaneously. Most often multiple channels are used. Delay in the communication of payment of fees (semester as well as the exam) to students is often seen. When ICT (email, SMS and intranet) is an effective channel, it can replace hard copies, unless legally essential. Maintenance of a university nodal database would help in avoiding repetitive generation of data from individual departments.

Autonomy

Academic autonomy is present for faculty. They can introduce new courses and for designing course materials (e-content). No one interferes with the faculty within the classroom. They have the autonomy to seek funds from other funding agencies for running projects. However, they have no autonomy to spend such a grant. Prior approval from the university authorities is required which is an elaborate procedure. Autonomy is ensured in the present system to faculty members in institutions of higher education. Nevertheless, there appears to be little awareness among individuals involved regarding the authority vested with them.

Faculty members have autonomy in selecting students for PhD research. Students have autonomy to choose supportive courses but not for elective. Provision for proper implementation of the choice-based credit system, where students have a choice to pick the elective courses of their choice, is required. Every subject needs an intrinsic approach. This can be ensured when academic autonomy is provided to the board of studies and the academic council, which can be allowed to admit measures that may relax the regulations of the UGC and the Tamil Nadu State Council of Higher Education (TANSCHE). Though ample freedom is in place, there is a scope for betterment.

Financial autonomy is restricted. The approval of the finance committee is needed before making any expenditure on salary, infrastructure and so on. At the department level, processing of department budgetary requirements needs to be undertaken speedily.

Provision for proper implementation of the choice-based credit system needs betterment. The course teacher can be the best evaluator of his/her students, provided factors such as favouritism and victimization can be avoided. Hence, they should be given autonomy to function as an evaluator of the students at every stage. The orientation and refresher courses are offered as mandatory training for the teaching faculty. This needs to be critically reviewed. Instead of the orientation and refresher courses, imparting of industry- and society-based training would help in the improvement of skills, knowledge and exposure.

Policy Effectiveness

The flow of authority is based on acts and statutes and government of Tamil Nadu regulation. Admissions in Bharathiar School of
Management and Entrepreneurial Development are entirely made by
the state government. Admissions to other programmes are also made
as per government reservation norms. A streamlined admission process
for School of Distance Education programmes, including BEd, is available. Procedures related to examinations are streamlined, and schedule
and results are published on the university website. Mark statements
are provided on time. All academic activities are planned by BOS and
SCAA. According to the administration, following the rules and regulations amount to accountability. The role of the dean is minimal with
being a part of selection committees and scrutiny committees. Dean
should be given a significant role in both the academic and administrative aspects of governance. Several committees are constituted to look
into varied aspects of the university functioning. Policies that govern
the constitution of such committees are not in place.

In the university, the finance committee approves the new proposals
related to financial expenditure, and the syndicate later approves it. The
policies governing financial expenditures are laid down. The individual
departments have autonomy to carry out the expenses of the departmental budget as per the policies that are in place. Similarly, individual
faculty members who run grant projects also have the autonomy to
make expenses related to the project as per the financial policies that
exist. Claims submitted are reimbursed as per the regulations. However,
this is unduly delayed in many cases, and there is abundant scope for
improvement in having policies in place that ensure quick processing
of the claims. Faculty members are reasonably aware of all the policies
related to research and development. However, these are not officially
circulated widely to all the members of the faculty, and being aware
of the policies related to research and development is based on an
individual's interest. Policies related to research and development are
not implemented consistently. Besides, an air of ambiguity exists in the
understanding of the policies. The students who are the primary stakeholders of the institution can be supported better at both the academic
and administrative levels.

GOVERNMENT ARTS COLLEGE

Accountability

Government Arts College being a college, places priority on teaching rather than research. There is no assessment of the quality of teaching. Importance is not given to research and projects since teaching is the primary focus in colleges. The only criterion for promotion is years of service. Hence, features of accountability are missing in the system. Accountability in teaching is purely a matter of integrity of the faculty.

Students' feedback is not taken into consideration for teacher evaluation. Even though student feedbacks are obtained for submitting NAAC, they are often not used in any way other than submitting it for NAAC records. The feedbacks received are not monitored by the head of the departments. No policy related to disciplinary action against teaching staff is available. At the least, such a practice is not prevalent in the college. The leadership style of principal appears to play a critical role. Only informal control over the faculty and students is prevalent in the college. Students state that there is a delay in getting Transfer Certificate (TC) and mark sheet, and also state that the teaching staff is not friendly and non-teaching staff is not cooperative. No process can check the accountability of the offices and faculty/staff.

Transparency

Complete transparency in recruitment and promotions of teachers is present. The recruitment is done by the government and so is transparent. Promotion is based on seniority based on the seniority list published by the Teacher Recruitment Board. Similarly, students' admission is also transparent. Single window system is followed in students' admission.

Responsiveness

Limited budget is allocated to the college by the government, resulting in financial constraints almost at all times. This limits the budget available for each department. Processing budgetary requirements of each department needs to be considered and responded positively. No TA/DA is provided to teachers for attending conferences. Providing financial support to faculty for such academic assignments should be considered by the state government to encourage participation of teachers in research since it has direct implications for improving the quality of teaching.

Equity/Fairness

Since there is no evaluation system, total equity is maintained among faculty. Students state that teachers hurt students those who get low marks, and do not treat all students fairly. However, overall, both teachers and students are treated fairly with no specific factor on which they are discriminated.

Participation/Shared Governance

Principal, Controller of Examination (COE), librarian and the heads of departments play a prime role in governance by being part of the governing council. In departmental meetings, the heads communicate council meetings' decisions to teachers. The students' council that was once present was derecognized due to the interference of political parties and subsequent violence among students. Presently, there is no students' council for the past ten years, and so students' participation in governance is nil.

Communication

Top-down communication is present while bottom-up communication is absent. Nevertheless, the staff has never expressed any resentment regarding this. All the information is circulated to staff and students and is put on the notice board. For teachers, the circular is kept in the department attendance register that they sign. Also, then the notice is put on the notice board that is exclusive to teachers. Information relevant to students is published in the calendar and also posted in the notice board. However, students report that communication is often delayed. The teachers state that students do not have the habit of seeing the notice board and hence miss reading important information.

Autonomy

Academic autonomy is absolute. The college does the framing of the syllabus once in every three years. Financial autonomy is also adequate. The funds received from government and UGC are equally shared among the departments. As per the government policy, these funds are restricted to purchase and maintenance, which must be spent through PWD and to purchase of books. No contingency or travel funds are available. A maximum of ₹20,000 per year is allocated to departments as department budget, which is insufficient to meet even the basic needs of the departments. Administrative autonomy is minimal since the college functions strictly by the rules laid down by the state government. The government provides scholarships for students. However, these scholarships are inordinately delayed. It is so delayed that some of the students receive the scholarship for the first year during their final year of studies.

Policy Effectiveness

The policy of the state government is followed strictly as per norms. Monthly health insurance for staff is available. However, no provision for TA or DA is provided to faculty members or students to participate in conferences. Teachers state that financial support for such academic activities must be initiated.

In the university, infrastructure and other facilities such as internet, personal computers and access to research journals in the library are adequate. Minimal secretarial assistance is provided for individual faculty members. Toilet facilities are adequate, but the drinking water facility is satisfactory. Students in the college are satisfied with facilities available for teaching, campus support services, library services and campus environment. College students are not satisfied with infrastructure, including the availability of drinking water and toilets. University administration affirms that the infrastructure available is adequate; however, the staff strength is minimal that adversely affects the service they can provide to the faculty as well as students.

Best Practices to Support Quality and Excellence

Best practices in the university and college include the provision of autonomy to individual teachers for issues related to academics. The budget allocation is done across departments and not schools. Hence, the need of each department is given adequate attention when allocating the budget for the year. The policies related to academic, administration and finance are communicated to the teachers. The university teachers have equal opportunity for them to participate in committees in the university. To improve the quality of teachers, the university adopts good standards of recruitment as per UGC's guidelines and also encourages the teachers to participate in faculty exchange programmes and other Faculty Development programmes (FDPs).

The advertisements for appointing new faculty are provided in both English and vernacular languages. The selection committee has members representing minorities such as scheduled castes/scheduled tribes, women, physically challenged, in addition to the subject experts, government nominee and governor nominee to ensure that the procedure specified in the acts and statutes is followed.

The examination procedure in the university is streamlined so that the exact schedule of exams and announcement of results is made available to the students in the academic calendar. The schedule is meticulously followed except in case of events such as government strike or a natural disaster such as floods. Presently, all applications are downloadable from the university website for the benefits of all candidates. All details relating to the examinations such as instruction to issue of provisional certificate, degree certificate, duplicate certificate, migration certificate and so on are available on the university website. Online verification for degree certificates is provided, and this scheme is beneficial for foreign candidates, and as to the status of PhD, the thesis is available on the university website.

A grievance redressal mechanism is in place at the university as well as in the college, and there are provisions for faculty and students to post their grievances by email. In the university, the students' records are maintained for ten years and can be accessed by anyone with appropriate authorization.

Most often, intradepartmental activities are assigned to and informally completed by teachers. This is seen in case of a few departments where most of the teachers are in the same cadre, and so they do not have a definite hierarchy. The supporting staff in specific university departments are also given much exposure, completely informally, to enrich their skills. For example, the supporting staff in the English department are encouraged to speak in English and are provided adequate opportunity to hone their spoken English.

The students are offered a need-based and skill-based curriculum. To improve the employability of the students, the university employs several strategies. The affiliated colleges offering UG courses are encouraged to start bachelor of vocational courses under KAUSHAL funded by the UGC and the Ministry of Human Resource Development. Our university is annually conducting several placement camps for finding suitable job opportunities for the university/affiliated college students. Certain MoUs have been signed (e.g. UTL Technologies, TCS-BPO, Telecom Sector Skill Council—TSSC, TCS iON, Infosys BPO) for giving short training to the students after completing their courses, like finishing school method. The Centre for Collaboration of Industry and Institutions of the university is offering regular certificate/diploma/PG diploma/degree courses with the more practical part than theory. These courses are offered at the industrial place by providing real-time environment experience to the students. Community College Consultancy Centre (CCCC) of the university is offering skill-based unconventional certificate/diploma courses through the organized as well as unorganized industries to train the students with suitable employable skills.

Constant expansion in academics with founding of new departments, MoUs with national and international universities, fee concessions to the wards of the staff pursuing degree programmes through distance education, initiation of e-governance, expansion and upgradation of infrastructure (laboratories, buildings and roads), establishment of a health centre, green campus, new bus facilities, world-class indoor stadium, well-equipped sports complex, CCTV surveillance in women's hostel, and construction of check dam, percolation pond and farm pond to conserve rainwater are ways in which the university has ensured providing support to all its stakeholders.

CHALLENGES TO QUALITY AND EXCELLENCE IN HIGHER EDUCATION

The interview with institutional leaders, teachers and students revealed interesting insights into the challenges to good governance in the university and college. Both administrators and teachers believe that policies related to governance are available and are sound. Though sound administrative policies are in place for every issue concerning administration, following them 100 per cent in word and spirit is not always witnessed. In some cases, the administrators experience pressure from their higher-ups to circumvent specific procedures. The leaders of the institution are well aware of their roles and responsibilities and are sensitive to these. However, the subordinates are usually not sensitive to their responsibilities. Interference from the government, political party, public, parents and students poses challenges to the administrators to follow the procedures laid down in the acts and statutes of the university. The interference from employees (employee association) can also pressurize the administration and influence the decisions made in the university. Teachers state that a lack of clarity with regard to specific criteria for promotion (e.g. the inclusion of past service) exists. The acts and statutes do cover most of the principal and relevant areas. Their implementation is not always objectively done. The teachers state that the policies are sound but the administrators make use of the loopholes to circumvent the procedures to suit them.

Further, implementation of the policies is also slow and delayed. Benefits do not get extended to all eligible players with equal proportion. Prejudice or bias is found to prevail. Delay in decisions, prevention of the inevitable recognition, procrastination, and so on and so forth are some of the challenges.

Teachers are represented in the syndicate, and as HODs in the senate. Individual teachers are also involved in various committees at the university level by which they participate in the governance. Mostly the decisions made at these committees agree with the stand taken by the administration. Though teachers are provided an opportunity to voice their concerns in the decision-making process, more often than not they are complacent in going along with the administration. The assurance of consensus needs to be put in place rather than the implementation of authority-driven decisions.

Another issue that thwarts diversity is that in most of the committees only, heads of the departments and deans are involved, which again challenges equal participation of all teachers in similar committees. Participation of teachers of all cadre in committees and rotation of headship may be introduced to strengthen equal opportunity for teachers to participate in the governance process. Often, in reality, it is the same set of people who serve on various committees. Clear policies must be laid down to guide this constitution of committees so that each teacher has equal opportunity to serve these committees. Lack of uniformity in the implementation of rules across all sections of the staff is witnessed.

In some cases, 'seniority' of the faculty member is taken into consideration, which is not uniformly followed. The chances of adhering to 'favouritism' prevail. Since institutional responsibilities are part of the criteria for an individual's upgradation, the opportunity for all is imperative. Another challenge that prevails in the system for establishing shared governance is the integrity of the individual teacher who will be playing an active part in the governance process. Building the necessary trust among working groups becomes inevitable. The role of the dean is restricted to serving in selection and scrutiny committees during recruitment and promotion of teachers. Limiting the role of dean impedes the scope of their involvement in promoting innovations for academic excellence in the school.

Top-down communication is done via circulars in the form of letters, SMS, phone calls and emails. Nevertheless, only information that is directly relevant to an individual faculty is sent to them. Posting of all policy information on the university website may be done to make it publicly available. The rules and regulations prescribed in the acts and statutes of the university are made available to all through the university website. However, other than that there are so many rules, amendments, financial rules, ad hoc regulations framed and formed by the university, policy decisions made by the syndicate are not available online, and the faculty members are forced to know only when they face any difficult or challenging situation. Bottom–up communication is also present. HODs are provided an opportunity to voice their concerns in HOD meetings and in senate. Individual faculty members may individually represent their case in the form of a letter to the administration. The overall objective of faculty meeting in each department is disseminating information received from the top rather than to represent the issues of the department to the top collectively. Even in cases where issues are represented by faculty via departmental faculty meeting minutes, there is no guarantee that the administration will address them. Sometimes the issues remain, and no response is received in return. At times 'grapevine' shapes decisions, which heightens the need for forestalling 'rumour' in a proactive manner.

There is no clear yardstick to measure accountability in the university. Academic Performance Indicator (API) of the teachers is perhaps the only way by which the accountability of teachers is ensured. There is no means of measuring accountability of supporting staff. This lack of accountability measures is reflected in a delay in movement of files, delay in response from the administration for the requests sent by the faculty and delay in disposal of claims. There is no system in place that enables a teacher or a student to track his/her file once it is submitted. Implementing e-governance will enable quick processing and communication. Lack of adequate personnel to support administration is a massive impediment to the governance process. Recruitment of people at different cadre, both teaching and supporting staff, must be made to ensure the smooth running of the governance process.

Some of the challenges that prevail in the university are raising funds for future sustainability and development of the university, clearing the audit objections to regularly receive grants from state government, establishing interdisciplinary, multidisciplinary and vocational departments, monitoring and improving the services of distance education centres, industry collaboration centres, and community colleges, preparing the teachers and students to adopt with modern teaching–learning environment in addition to the traditional methods, encouraging the teachers to undertake more research projects and involve equally in extension activities, and managing the research (MPhil/PhD) guides of self-financing colleges as the teachers regularly move to other colleges. Limited funds, lack of autonomy, lack of accountability of teachers as promotions are based on years of service and not their academic contribution, and lack of opportunity for individual teachers to participate in the governance are among the challenges confronting the governance in college.

It must be noted that the college sampled for the present study is an autonomous government college, and the model of governance will differ if the college were an affiliated college or a constituent college.

The style of the influence of the administration on the individual teachers is also individualized and not very rigidly influenced by regulations. Individual discretions and flexibility are a witness in the style of functioning of the administration, both at the university level and within the individual department.

POLICY MESSAGES AND ROAD MAP FOR ENSURING QUALITY AND EXCELLENCE IN HIGHER EDUCATION

New policies on higher education must address the issues highlighted above to maintain quality and nurture excellence in state HEIs. To address the challenges that thwart good governance and management in higher education, there is a need to bring in new policies for higher education institutions in addition to refining the existing one. They are briefly discussed hereunder.

Academic

Though a structured regimen for academics is imparted through the state and UGC, flexibility requisites as per individual subjects can be given better elbow room through the Board of Studies and Academic Council.

There are no effective and tangible incentives in place to recognize the contribution to teaching, for, it is merely perceived to be the primary responsibility of the teaching faculty. As for research, the number of research scholars supervised and the allocation of funding for projects are alone considered relevant. However, the social reach of the projects is not evaluated judiciously.

The dean must be provided with a more elaborate role in both academic and administrative domains to effect improvement in academics and administration in the university. Provision of an individual cell for dean's office will bring in significant improvement towards achieving excellence in higher education.

In the university, recognition of activities done by teachers, even if they are not listed in the UGC's criteria for API scores, may be provided. Sometimes quantity and not the quality of research is given priority. The orientation and refresher courses offered as mandatory training for the teaching faculty requires a critical review. Instead, imparting industry- and society-based training would help in the improvement of skills, knowledge and exposure. In college, contribution to research concerning publication by faculty in peer-reviewed journals and participation in conferences must be encouraged since a strong base in research is imperative for effective teaching.

Administrative

The current lengthy and cumbersome administrative procedures need to be simplified to avoid delay in the processing of requests by students and faculty. Processing of department budgetary requirements and processing of claims by individual faculty need to be undertaken speedily. E-governance must be encouraged, which will enable timely reimbursement or claims and speedy processing of files placed for approval. When ICT (email, SMS and intranet) is an effective channel, it can replace hardcopies, unless legally essential. Maintenance of a university nodal database would help in avoiding repetitive generation of data from individual departments for various purposes such as NAAC and the national institutional ranking framework. Enterprise Resource

Planning software should be implemented in the campus, where so many activities of the faculty can be minimized, such as letter writing, submitting these reports and valuation reports.

Ambiguity exists in the understanding of the policies. Consistency in interpretation of rules and regulations, irrespective of change of guard, should be encouraged through well-trained staff. Specifying a well-thought-out eligibility criterion for each staff position to aid recruitment of qualified staff and offering them orientation and training to the administrative staff is needed to ensure that the rules and regulations are understood without ambiguity.

Policies must be framed to streamline the calling for CAS applications more frequently and regularly as a matter of routine administrative procedure, and the process should be completed within a specified time frame.

Shared Governance

Procedures should be established to ensure that the same set of people are not repeatedly nominated to participate in governance while several others do not get a chance. An institutional-level database accessible to all can help prevent repetitive generation of the database from individual departments. Since institutional responsibilities are part of the criteria for the promotion of individual faculty, all must be provided with the opportunity to participate in governance. Opportunity for every teacher and student to participate in governance must be ensured through clear policies in the university. The assurance of consensus needs to be put in place rather than the implementation of authority-driven decisions.

Transparency

Even national institutions, such as the UGC, National Council for Educational Research and Training, and National Council for Teacher Education, upload the information about the decisions taken in their meetings on their official websites. However, this practice is not available at the university. This may also be adopted at the university level. Recruitment of teachers should also include job talks in the presence of all members of the department. Further, recruitment of institutional leaders must also be made transparent. Selection of administrators such as VCs, registrars and CEOs, must be transparent, and people with more integrity should be selected, other than considering their intellectual capability.

Accountability

Provision of effective and tangible incentives for contribution in research and teaching, providing material productions relevant to the coursework to support learning and an external monitoring system can contribute to better accountability. Teachers are sometimes assigned roles that are not prescribed in the acts and statutes to support the administrative process. The teachers are also willingly participating in those assignments. However, this affects their availability to carry out teaching and research as required by the UGC for their API. The university also does not acknowledge this to give it due consideration for promotion purpose. Besides accountability of both faculty and students, the accountability of non-teaching has to be ascertained.

In the colleges, students feedback may be given due weight for teachers' evaluation. Procedures that check accountability of faculty and staff are non-existing and hence need to be established. Providing financial support to faculty to participate in conferences, seminars and FDPs will be useful in encouraging them to participate in them.

In addition to the above, policies to nurture diversity must be framed. The state government policy specifies the community-wise distribution. Representation of religious minorities and women must be encouraged through policies. The university should attract students from all over India with the help of a legitimate branding exercise. This would be instrumental in bringing in better levels of competition and would aid the university to compete globally by raising its bar periodically.

REFERENCES

Creswell, J. W. 2013. *Qualitative Inquiry and Research Design: Choosing among Five Approaches*. 3rd ed. Thousand Oaks, CA: SAGE Publications.

Narayanan, Annalakshmi, Rajalakshmi Bhavana, and Bhuvana Esther. 2018. *Governance and Management of Higher Education in Tamil Nadu*. New Delhi: CPRHE/NIEPA Research Report.

Chapter 13

The Political Economy of Governance in Higher Education
Temporary Teachers Phenomenon

Sudhanshu Bhushan

INTRODUCTION

Managing human resource, particularly, teachers, to teach 36 million students in universities, colleges and institutes is a gigantic task. The complexity of the situation arises because the teaching cadre is controlled by various agencies. For example, the teaching cadre in centrally and state-funded institutes and universities is controlled by the central government and state governments, respectively. Teachers employed in private and aided colleges are controlled by the privately managed bodies as well as the government. All the teachers in the universities and colleges are also regulated with respect to the maintenance of standards by the University Grants Commission (UGC) and the respective professional bodies at the apex level. An important aspect of the management of teaching cadre is to attract good faculty and in right numbers. Over the years, the management has failed, as with the rising demand for higher education and increase in the enrolment of students, almost all institutions of higher education have failed to recruit teachers in adequate numbers. There is an acute shortage of teachers and in the last three years, the number of teachers has been declining in absolute terms. There is growing casualization of teachers. Temporary teachers phenomenon is a reality and is guided by the objective conditions expressed through the political and economic forces—overt or covert.

The statistics on temporary teachers at macro level conveys very little as temporary teachers are reported to be mere 5 per cent of the total teaching strength in higher education. However, a little in-depth micro picture at the state, institutional and individual levels presents clear dynamics in terms of growing scarcity of teachers and temporary teachers' phenomenon taking over the institutions of higher education. What is interesting to note is how political and economic forces operate to support this phenomenon. The temporary teachers phenomenon is full of conflicts, contests and disputations. This is creating divisions among teachers and teachers are feeling demoralized. They are forced to lead a life sans dignity. What is worse is that the teaching community may not, under the circumstances, do justice to the students inside the classrooms and contribute to a good citizenry. The consequences are indeed long term and harmful not only to the higher education but also to the nation. This is an important rationale that drives us to look into the micro picture and understand certain issues and dynamics that guide the temporary teachers phenomena in higher education.

Within the framework of the political economy of governance, an attempt is made to understand the broader market principles that affect governance through the prism of contract, efficiency and competition. The process gets fillip as the state finds it convenient to support the market principle of governance. In the political arena, the state has to manage the contradictions among various social groups and economic resources are diverted to address those short-term contradictions, leaving not enough resources for education and health. Politics and economics run into contradictions. Political compulsions, being dominant, guide the resources to be diverted through populism and politics in areas where necessarily efficiency fails to operate (for example, subsidy and waiving off the farmers' loan). The inefficiency in resource allocation then impinges upon education and health to be managed by limited resources. It is this macro dynamics that guides and supports the temporary teacher phenomenon. State imposes ban on recruitment and allows temporary teachers to grow. What is interesting to understand is the phenomenon of shortage of teachers and growing casualization which is not captured through macro-level information. However, if we understand the micro realities state, institution and individual specific, then we can easily understand how managing teachers runs into difficulty. Governance fails and affects students adversely.

The aim of the chapter is to portray the micro realities of higher education through the understanding of temporary teachers phenomenon. There are UGC regulations; however, in many states, the regulations are evaded and states may have specific regulations guiding the temporary teachers. There may be diverse temporary teachers nomenclature and contract salary. The phenomenon continues for a long period. During this period, injustice is done and teachers may have to appeal in the court of law. Judiciary alerts state governments to redress injustices and in some cases strongly orders the state government to put up with the system of growing ad hoc appointments. In spite of all these, state fails to comply. When the movement of teachers grows strong enough, the state governments attempt to create order. However, any attempt to create order further runs into trouble as state fails to manage with limited resources. Wherever teachers movements are strong, they are able to get better salary and conditions of service. Higher education in the field becomes a battlefield of claims and counterclaims, conflicts and the process of resolution of conflicts, hierarchy and ways to minimize the hierarchy. The delivery of services by teachers through scholarly accomplishments fails. What is worse, the phenomenon of temporary teachers has come to stay. Many state governments putting a ban on direct recruitment are under pressure to absorb those temporary teachers into a permanent cadre of teachers.

UGC REGULATION

The UGC used to make distinction between guest and part-time teachers and that of visiting professors for a fairly long period. Remunerations, too, used to be different in the above cases. Contract or substitute teacher meant a teacher appointed against leave vacancy.

Later on, guest teacher was the nomenclature as per UGC guidelines to mean temporary teacher.

As per the UGC regulation, 2010 (UGC 2010b) and amendments made from time to time, teachers should be appointed on contract basis only when it is absolutely necessary and when the student–teacher ratio does not satisfy the laid down norms. In any case, the number of such appointments should not exceed 10 per cent of the total number of faculty positions in a college/university. The qualifications and selection procedure for appointing them should be the same as those applicable to a regularly appointed teacher. The fixed emoluments paid to such contract teachers should not be less than the monthly gross salary of a regularly appointed assistant professor. Such appointments should not be made initially for more than one academic session, and the performance of any such entrant teacher should be reviewed for academic performance before reappointing her/him on contract basis for another session. Such appointments on contract basis may also be resorted to when absolutely necessary to fill vacancies arising due to maternity leave, child-care leave and so on. An average salary for a contract teacher, as per the Seventh UGC Pay Commission, turns out to be in the range of around ₹75,000 per month. The appointment of such contract teachers is a practice in Delhi University.

There are also UGC guidelines for the appointment of guest teachers (UGC 2010a). This is largely followed by the state governments. The salary in this case is ₹1,000 per class upto a maximum of ₹25,000 per month. In this case, only 25 classes per month are permitted. State governments usually follow guest teachers guideline modifying it in a manner that the number of classes per month can be substantially increased. The appointment of guest teachers is as rigorous as the appointment of assistant professors against regular vacancy. In different states, temporary teachers are variously called: Samvida/Athiti Shikshak in Chhattisgarh and contractual teachers, part-time teachers and guest faculties in Assam. Many state universities may not be adhering to UGC regulation (UGC 2010a), in making such appointments. The process of appointment of different category of temporary teachers is highly varied and is different from that of permanent teachers.

It is important to note that UGC regulation makes a distinction between the contract teachers and guest teachers. Why have the two types of temporary teachers—costly and cheaper variant been proposed?

MACRO PICTURE OF THE STRENGTH OF TEACHERS

As per the All India Survey of Higher Education, the total number of teachers has declined during 2015–2016 to 2017–2018 by almost 2.34 lakhs. The decline has been highest at the level of assistant professors, by 1.20 lakhs, followed by the decline in both the posts—associate professors and professors. Both taken together account for a decline by over 70,000. This decline is not compensated by the rise of temporary teachers. Rather temporary teachers also witness decline during the same period. It means that there is a decline in the absolute sense in the magnitude of all types of teachers. During the same period, the enrolment of students has gone up from 34.6 million students in 2015–2016 to 36.6 million during 2017–2018.

As per the All India Survey of Higher Education, in 2015–2016, there were 112,006 temporary teachers working in universities and colleges, which had come down to 45,148 temporary teachers in 2017–2018 (Table 13.1). Of the total 17,006 teaching posts in various UGC-funded central universities, 6,080 were lying vacant on 1 October 2016, according to official data. The rising vacancies and the slow pace of filling up those vacancies means higher casual and contract based teaching in higher education. In Delhi University alone, the number of ad hoc teachers is said to be around 4,000. There are some temporary teachers who are working for over a decade with a break in the service for a month in a year. They are known by different names such as part-time teacher, ad hoc teacher, temporary teacher, contract teacher, visiting teacher, and guest teacher. The insecurity of such teachers raises issues of human rights, on the one hand, and the issues of quality in higher education, on the other. It is indeed surprising to note that the macro picture reveals the falling number of permanent teachers as well as temporary teachers. One would have expected the rising number of temporary teachers with rising vacancies of teachers and enrolment of students. It would be interesting to look at few

Table 13.1 *Position of Teachers during 2015–2016 to 2017–2018*

	Professor	Associate Professor	Assistant Professor	Demonstrators	Temporary teachers	Total
2015–16	146021	174657	1009196	76933	112006	1518813
2016–17	114170	147629	945558	91534	66895	1365786
2017–18	110522	139443	888427	79505	66858	1284755
Decline during 2015–16 to 2017–18	35499	35214	120769	2572	45148	234058

Source: MHRD (2017, 2017, 2018).

micro realities in order to assess the vacancies and the magnitude of temporary teachers.

MAGNITUDE OF TEMPORARY TEACHERS

Government data show there are 16,600 sanctioned posts for teachers in central universities in India. Of these, 5,928 posts are vacant (Pandey, 2018). It was reported that in some central universities, particularly new ones, contract teachers at the entry level are being appointed. It is found to be difficult to get vacancies filled up at the higher levels through the direct recruitment, pension non-portability being an important factor in attracting good faculty from other universities at the level of professor. For example, in the case of Central University of Jharkhand, the sanctioned posts of professors, associate professors and assistant professors are 22, 44 and 88. However at respective levels only 8, 18 and 70 positions could be filled. Thirty-five posts of teachers were filled up through contractual appointments. Over 35 per cent of the permanent faculty is the contractual teachers (NIEPA 2018a). We can examine another example from Sikkim University.

Sikkim University was established in 2006. As the university is running in rented buildings the student intake is limited to 20 students in many departments. In the school of professional studies 13 of 45, in the school of languages 17 of 37, in the school of physical sciences 6 of 31, in the school of human sciences 6 of 19, in the school of life sciences 5 of 31 and in the school of social sciences 5 of 49 teachers are temporary. Overall 25 per cent teachers are temporary in Sikkim University (NIEPA 2018b).

Take another example from Punjab University, which is a state-funded public university. It was reported that of 1,873 sanctioned posts of teachers in the government colleges of Punjab 1,292 posts are vacant. There are 882 guest faculty and 221 part-time teachers to compensate for rising vacancies of teachers (NIEPA 2018c). In the state of Telangana with 1,651 vacancies against the 2,771 actual sanctioned positions, one can notice a gloomy picture of growing number of temporary teachers in universities. It is unclear as to the actual number of sanctioned posts and vacancies in the government degree/affiliated colleges in the state (NIEPA 2018d).

BACKGROUND

In the backdrop, it needs to be pointed out that the state government imposes ban on recruitment in various manners. In the selection committee, there may be a provision for a government nominee to be the member of the selection committee. The state government may not nominate a member and thereby halting the process of recruitment. In almost all the cases, whenever a vacancy is to be filled up, the university has to seek permission from the state government to fill up the vacancy. However, the state government may not permit the university to fill up the vacancy for a long period.

There is another problem in the filling up of the vacancy in the university departments and colleges. It relates to the preparation of rosters for following the reservation policy. In Kerala University there was the tradition of developing the rosters at the level of the department. When university took the decision to prepare the rosters by taking university as the unit, there was a huge protest and it was later withdrawn.

The confusion arose when the central government in August 2017 asked the UGC to make a department-wise roster of teacher vacancies reserved for scheduled caste and scheduled tribe candidates, instead of the current norm of having an institution-wise roster. The response of the central government was due to the Allahabad high court judgment in April 2017, which struck down a UGC circular prescribing institution-wise reservation to fill vacant faculty positions. The court held that there are departments without any SC/ST teachers. The Supreme Court upheld the high court order later, prompting the UGC to send a proposal to the HRD ministry stating that the number of reserved posts in SC/ST and other backward class categories should be done department-wise. The ministry asked the UGC to go ahead with its proposal. In the meantime, the UGC directed all the universities to hold up the process of recruitment. It is argued that preparing the roster department-wise will go against the SCs and STs and will also create problems of roster, if for example, there is one teacher department. As it was later realized that treating department as a unit will cut down the reserved posts and will go against the representation of marginalized sections of society, the government decided to bring an ordinance to restore the old system of treating university as a unit for the preparation of roster. However, in the meantime, the parliamentary committee on the SC/ST welfare took cognizance of the issue and wrote to HRD and other ministries of the harmful consequences of restoring the new practice of treating department as a unit in following the reservation policy. A 10-member interministerial committee was set up to look into the issue in March 2018 and this panel recommended that a review petition be filed in the SC to undo the UGC's order. It remains an open question why the government has not passed an ordinance and preferred to file Special Leave Petition to the Supreme Court. Any delay in the Supreme Court judgment is likely to encourage the temporary teacher phenomenon in the Indian higher education system.

It is against the above backdrop that I would like to present the temporary teachers phenomenon in selected states, universities and colleges to understand few inner dynamics.

GUEST FACULTY PHENOMENA IN TAMIL NADU

Ad hoc teacher phenomenon was initiated in Tamil Nadu in 1997 when the contract teachers in the name of guest teachers were allowed to draw consolidated ₹2,500 per month. In the next two decades, guest faculty with PhD were drawing a salary of ₹15,000 per month and the guest faculty with MPhil a salary of ₹13,000 per month and with postgraduate degree ₹10,000 per month. With a meagre salary of ₹15,000, the contract teachers were struggling for over two decades. A hope was generated when the Tamil Nadu government announced in the assembly in May 2018 that a special examination would be held to regularize the 3,544 ad hoc guest teachers who were eligible for permanent appointment. The announcement has a catch as it is said that only 37 per cent of guest lecturers are eligible for permanent position as per UGC criteria for selection. Further, many fear the special test may also disqualify many teachers. It may be noted that before 1997 the contractual teachers used to be absorbed in the permanent service after judicial intervention. The state government then changed the name of contract teacher as guest lecturer being appointed in the service only for 10 months in a year. This prevented the contract teachers to be absorbed into permanent positions in government colleges. Guest faculty in the universities of Tamil Nadu is appointed by a selection board with head of the department as the chairman. In the colleges, it is the directorate which obtains the vacancy position from the government colleges and announces the appointment of guest lecturers in the colleges. There was no recruitment of permanent teachers since 2015, adding to the phenomenon of guest teachers who may have to struggle for decades to be absorbed in the permanent positions.

The Hindu on 31 May 2018 carried a news item that is no less interesting to understand the temporary teacher phenomenon in Indian higher education. The Bharathidasan University in Tamil Nadu passed a resolution in the syndicate that 362 guest lecturers in 10 constituent colleges will be designated as assistant professors, thereby making it possible to avail the benefit of research guide. UGC regulation on PhD does not permit temporary teachers to guide the research students. What a brilliant way was chosen to nullify the UGC regulation by the change of nomenclature from guest lecturer to assistant professor.

The politics behind the phenomenon of temporary teachers may be seen through the interplay of power politics between the state and the temporary teachers. State initiates the temporary teacher phenomenon and continues with it for a long time. When the struggle of teachers reaches a critical limit, the state makes a populist announcement to absorb some of them through the conduct of test. No doubt, some guest teachers may win while others lose. This will aggravate the division among teachers. It is also important to see how the change in the nomenclature to the guest lecturer to be appointed only for 10 months is a useful way to stop entry to permanent position. The economics of the phenomenon is no less important. It saves a lot of money to the state government as the difference in the salary of permanent teacher and guest teacher is huge. It is also important that the state government has its own rules of recruitment and salary structure for the guest faculty. It does not follow UGC regulation. By not following UGC regulation it further saves ₹10,000 per month per guest faculty as UGC permits ₹25,000 per month as fixed remuneration to the guest teacher (NIEPA 2018e).

The essential component of the political economy model of governance noted above is that there is an element of power of the state that is used to weaken the teachers and divide them. A hope is always raised and by employing them on contract makes them vulnerable throughout the professional life of a teacher and force them to work hard more than what is paid to them. This allows rent seeking by the state. Further, in terms of budget, it allows state to save money, which then can be utilized for other populist schemes which help them to grab power. However, the temporary teacher phenomenon is certainly weakening the structure of higher education.

The guest teacher phenomenon continues in the state of Tamil Nadu in spite of the court directive in 2005 that the government must stop guest teacher appointment and fill up the posts through regular appointment by the Teacher Recruitment Board. In another judgment, in *M Saravankumar and Others* v. *The Secretary to Government Department of Education*, 2005 (3) MLJ 538, the court has categorically deprecated the appointment of guest lecturers for years together without filling the regular vacancies and issued directions to fill up the vacancies. The said court order notes that this is demeaning to the teachers who are treated almost as casual employees. What interests will such teachers have in the work? It notes that they are getting ₹4,000 per month, less than the peon of the government. Is this the way to treat the gurus of the youth of the modern day? Successive judgments point out the sorry state of affairs of guest teachers. In *Rattanlal* v. *State of Haryana*, AIR 1987 SC 478, the Supreme Court noted that the guest faculty appointment was a breach of Articles 14 and 16 of the Constitution. Guest teachers are the victims of arbitrary hire and fire policy. They are denied of leave benefits. The government appears to exploit the situation of unemployed youth. It is bound to have serious repercussions on educational institutions and the children studying there. Such court order presents the circumstances under which it announced in the Tamil Nadu state assembly recently the

Table 13.2 *Number of Guest Lecturers in Arts and Science Colleges*

Year	Government Colleges	Private Aided Colleges	Total
2015	462	1476	1938
2016	490	1582	2072
2017	599	1794	2393

Source: Directorate of Collegiate Education, Government of Kerala.

regularization of guest teachers through the test conducted by the Teacher Recruitment Board.

GUEST TEACHER PHENOMENON IN KERALA

The scenario in the state of Kerala with respect to guest teachers is also interesting and it is not free from problems. In Kerala, the number of guest teachers is increasing in the last three years (Table 13.2).

In Kerala, guest teachers are also called daily wage/contract teachers. The remuneration of guest lecturers was enhanced at ₹500 per teaching hour subject to the ceiling of ₹25,000 for those having UGC-prescribed qualification and ₹300 per teaching hour subject to the ceiling of ₹20,740 for those without UGC-prescribed qualification, working in government colleges in 2012 and 2015 as contained in GO (Rt) No: 1293/2018/HEdn, dated 4 July 2018 of higher education department, government of Kerala. On the basis of the above calculation, the guest lecturer will have to engage 50 lectures and 69 lectures per month for the teachers with UGC-prescribed qualification and non–UGC-prescribed qualification, respectively. As per the UGC regulation, the guest lecturer cannot be allowed to be paid more than ₹25,000 per month. The government of Kerala announced the revision in the remuneration of the daily wage/contract teachers. The revised remuneration was the result of the long-drawn battle between Association of Kerala Government College Teachers and the All Kerala Private College Teachers Association with the state government of Kerala. The remunerations are presently as follows: (a) UGC qualified hands—₹1750 per day subject to a maximum of ₹43,750 in a month on daily-wage basis. (b) Non-UGC hands—₹1600 per day subject to a maximum of ₹40,000 in a month on daily wage basis. (c) The workload, teaching hours and so on shall be in accordance with the existing norms applicable to regular teachers. In the new notification of the government, the gap between UGC-qualified hand and non-UGC-qualified hand was greatly reduced (NIEPA 2018f).

However, the temporary teacher phenomenon is not free from problems even in Kerala. The government of Kerala issued guidelines from time to time as per UGC regulations. In 2012, by a modification of the previous order Higher Education (C) Department GO. (P) No. 28/2012H.Edu, dated 25 January 2012, it directed a guest teacher to attend all the works assigned to the appointed post. It increased the workload of guest teachers from 25 classes in a month to 50 classes in a month. It allowed guest faculty to be appointed in all posts in the absence of regular faculty, on the basis of the workload for teaching the course, regardless of whether the post itself is a sanctioned post or not currently, in anticipation of sanction for the post after the deputy director of collegiate education ensures that there is sufficient workload for engaging the extra teacher as a guest. The deputy director, director of collegiate education was authorized to create a pool of qualified guest/contract faculties at regional level from which colleges can be permitted to appoint them as per requirement. Thus, the Kerala government ensured that at least all the vacant posts will be filled through the guest lecturers, if not the permanent teachers, and it enhanced the salary way above the UGC-stipulated salary of ₹25,000 per month. What is important to note is that guest lecturer was very much treated like a regular teacher, except the voting rights. More importantly, the guest teacher employed in private colleges out of the empanelled list of the deputy director of collegiate education were also entitled to the benefit of salary from the government. This is indeed a remarkable step by the government of Kerala to provide for the salary of guest teachers from the government fund in order to ensure that the teaching does not suffer in the entire state. The private colleges were brought under the control of five zonal deputy director of the department in the state.

TEMPORARY TEACHER PHENOMENON IN KASHMIR UNIVERSITY

Kashmir University covers colleges of 12 districts. There are 44 government colleges. Two sample colleges and four departments scenario with respect to teachers is given below (Table 13.3). In the two sample colleges, the contract teachers are almost 200 per cent of the permanent teachers. Pupil–teacher ratio (PTR) is very high without contract teachers. It is only because of contract teachers that PTR could be brought to a lower level. It seems that so far as colleges are concerned, with the expansion in the number of colleges and enrolment there are no new creation of post in relation to the demand for it. Over the years, vacancies increase and in the absence of permanent teachers, the college is forced to appoint temporary teachers. Such a high increase of contract teachers shows that colleges are actually running on contract teachers. Scenario in the postgraduate departments is not that bad, yet in specific departments, temporary teachers may be very high in number.

It is important to note that contract appointment of teachers in Kashmir University is guided by its own norms. As per UGC regulation, contract teachers should not exceed 10 per cent of the permanent faculty. The contract is terminated at the end of the academic session. The qualification for appointing the contractual teachers is as per UGC regulation in universities but in colleges sometimes non–NET/SET/PhD candidates are also being appointed. For contractual appointment, dean of the concerned faculty is the chairman and head of the department, two senior faculty members and the nominee of the VC are members of the selection committee. Contractual appointment is made by one of the colleges designated by government as nodal college. No interviews are conducted for contractual appointment in colleges and non–NET/PhD/SET candidates are asked to appear in a screening test. With respect to colleges, the selection of permanent teachers is made by Jammu and Kashmir Public Service Commission. The criteria for appointing contractual lecturers and teaching assistants in government degree colleges in 2018–2019 are framed by the university.

With regard to emoluments, the central universities are paying gross salary without allowances, whereas the University of Kashmir pays a consolidated amount of ₹35,000 per month to PhD with NET/

Table 13.3 Status of Teachers in Sample Colleges and Departments of Kashmir University

	No. of students	Sanctioned	Actual	Vacant	Contract teachers	PTR (without contract)	PTR (with contract)
Govt. Degree College, Shopian	4716	41	28	13	79	168	44
Government Degree College Handwara	5247	47	16	31	72	327	88
Department of Psychology	108	7	6	1	2	18	13
Department of Education	500	17	12	5	5	41	29
Department of Management	600	29	22	7	14	27	16
Department of Zoology	118	17	12	5	0	10	16

Source: NIEPA (2018g).

Table 13.4 *Different Nomenclatures and Remuneration of Temporary Teachers of J&K State*

Categories of Temporary Teachers	Remuneration	Source of Funding: Government/ Central/College
Contractual Lecturer Ph.D. with NET/SET (University of Kashmir)	35000 per Month	State Government
Contractual Lecturer Ph.D. or NET or SET (University of Kashmir)	30000 per Month	State Government
Contractual Lecturer (Higher Education Colleges)	28000 per Month	State Government
Teaching Assistant (Higher Education Colleges)	22000 per Month	State Government
Contractual Lecturer (Central University of Kashmir)	40000 per Month	Central Government
Teaching Assistants (Central University of Kashmir)	30000 per month	Central Government
Contractual Lecturer (M. Tech) NIT Srinagar	45000 per Month	Central Government
Contractual Lecturer (Ph.D.) NIT Srinagar	54000 per Month	Central Government

Source: NIEPA (2018g).

SET candidates and ₹30,000 per month to NET or SET or PhD candidates. This clearly states that emoluments are not as per UGC regulations, and there is a hierarchy of temporary teachers and their emoluments in the state (Table 13.4).

CHALLENGES OF TEMPORARY TEACHERS

Temporary teachers usually perform the duty as the full-time faculty since they have to engage two to four classes every day in view of acute scarcity of teachers. Sometimes senior and permanent teachers also take liberty in asking them to engage their classes. They are expected to perform all management-related jobs, such as admission, timetable, and examination-related work. Vulnerability of a temporary teacher can be seen when they are forced to be a co-author of the publication. They do all the hard work, still they are denied the first authorship. The head of the department/institute, instead of assigning any official work to the permanent teacher, prefers to assign the work to temporary teachers who are obliged to work due to insecurity of the job. Temporary teachers always feel that they cannot displease the authority. This goes on sometimes for years in the expectation that they will be made permanent. Discrimination and insecurity do not end here. After the conclusion of the academic session, they have to re-apply and undergo the recruitment process all over again. There is no guarantee that they will be recruited again. Even during the academic session, they can be fired any time owing to different reasons. The temporary teachers feel insecure throughout the session. As in the new academic session, the eligibility criteria can change and the experienced contractual staff is not preferred and freshers are selected for the job in some of the cases.

The differential salary with different nomenclatures is another aspect of discrimination. The salary in many cases is less than the minimum wages, and as observed in some court judgments, even a grade four employee of the central government has more security than have temporary teachers. Under these circumstances, temporary teachers suffer from low esteem. It was reported by many teachers that sometime they have to postpone many important decisions of life due to low salary and insecurity. Temporary teachers hardly avail any leave other than casual leave. They are denied earned leave, medical leave, maternity leave, or provident fund, health insurance cover or any kind of benefits.

The counting of past service while serving as contract teacher is also a matter of dispute. UGC regulation clearly says that the services of such contract teachers will be counted under the conditions stipulated in the UGC regulation. However, when such contract teachers are absorbed in the permanent job under the procedures laid down in the recruitment rules, they are denied the count of past service as contract teacher by misinterpretation of rules by the authorities. This causes hardship to the teachers as they suffer from delayed promotion and loss of financial benefits. All universities involve temporary teachers also in invigilation, evaluation, timetable making, cultural activities, and other work, except those where financial and long-term responsibilities are involved. The temporary teachers are engaged in the organization of seminars and so on. The work of guiding PhD level research is not assigned to the temporary teachers. However, they are assigned the project and dissertation guidance work at PG level. Contract teachers suffer in terms of conducting research as they are kept busy in engaging the classes and time is hardly left for research. Without research they fail to accumulate research points needed for promotion. Lastly, it is a gross injustice to deny equal pay for equal work. The temporary teachers' phenomenon is the violation of the Constitution of India.

CHALLENGES OF GOVERNANCE IN HIGHER EDUCATION

From the discussion on the phenomenon of temporary teachers in the universities and colleges in India, the role of state in the management of teaching resource was explored. It was shown how inefficiency in the management of teachers is the result of both economic and political factors. The casualty in the whole process is the quality as higher education continues to persist with poor quality of teachers who are not only paid less but also suffer from insecurity, indignity and injustices in all forms. It cannot be expected to have high quality of teaching and research with temporary teachers who undergo mental and physical harassment for a long period. With low quality of recruitment of teachers on ad hoc basis, the state feels pressure to regularize them at a later stage. The somewhat unconditional absorption of teachers then leads to the continuance of such teachers in the system, creating a trap of low-quality higher education. Challenge of governance in higher education is to come out of the trap through a central government policy and programme in partnership with the state government where a sizeable number of colleges and universities are chosen to fill up the vacancy of teachers with high-quality recruitment.

The genesis of the problem is the way in which the government adopts strategies to meet the shortage of teachers with the expansion of colleges. With the need to create posts, state governments find it easier to continue with the high vacancies for a longer period. Then after the court intervention or local pressure, they partly fill up the post with direct recruitment and partly allow the universities to recruit temporary teachers. State governments, such as Kerala, at least show promptness in the recruitment and appointment of teachers with relatively higher salary and even pay for the temporary teachers so appointed in the private colleges. In states such as J&K, the government allows the vacancies to rise and even do not create additional posts, then the onus is upon the respective government colleges to recruit temporary teachers based on the guidelines of the state government. The colleges are forced to raise fees to compensate for the salary payment to temporary teachers. We also noted the strategy in Tamil Nadu where temporary teacher phenomenon has assumed great proportion and the government is now considering absorbing them on a permanent basis.

In all the strategies, an economic compulsion is to save money by not employing permanent teachers as they become a long-run financial liability. Hence, state governments are guided by the economic motive in the continuance of the phenomenon of temporary teachers. The phenomenon suits politically to any state government as well. The reason is that populist governments are always guided by the vote politics. The populist policy already drains resources in various social welfare measures of the government. The preference to address the shortage of teachers in higher education becomes the low priority for them. The temporary teacher phenomenon is the victim of populist vote bank approach of the governments. Both economic and political arguments support the temporary teachers' phenomenon. How to come out of vote bank politics is indeed the challenge in higher education.

The important point is that governments will have to be sensitized of the importance of higher education in the national development. Unless it emerges as a priority in all policy discussions the politics and economics will compel state governments to continue the temporary teachers' phenomenon.

REFERENCES

Ministry of Human Resource Development (MHRD). 2016. *All India Survey of Higher Education 2015–16.* New Delhi: Department of Higher Education, Government of India.

Ministry of Human Resource Development (MHRD). 2017. *All India Survey of Higher Education 2016–17.* New Delhi: Department of Higher Education, Government of India.

Ministry of Human Resource Development (MHRD). 2018. *All India Survey of Higher Education 2017–18.* New Delhi: Department of Higher Education, Government of India.

National Institute of Educational Planning and Administration (NIEPA). 2018a. *Recruitment Process of Teachers and Status of Temporary Teachers in Jharkhand by Dr Ranvijay.* New Delhi: NIEPA.

National Institute of Educational Planning and Administration (NIEPA). 2018b. *Recruitment Process of Teachers and Status of Temporary Teachers in Sikkim by Dr. T. J. M. S. Raju.* New Delhi: NIEPA.

National Institute of Educational Planning and Administration (NIEPA). 2018c. *Recruitment Process of Teachers and Status of Temporary Teachers in Punjab by Prof. Dr Kirandeep Singh and Dr Jatinder Grover.* New Delhi: NIEPA.

National Institute of Educational Planning and Administration (NIEPA). 2018d. *Recruitment Process of Teachers and Status of Temporary Teachers in Telangana by Dr Ramabrahma and Dr D. Veera Babu.* NIEPA: New Delhi.

National Institute of Educational Planning and Administration (NIEPA). 2018e. *Recruitment Process of Teachers and Status of Temporary Teachers in Tamil Nadu by Dr A Subramanian.* New Delhi: NIEPA.

National Institute of Educational Planning and Administration (NIEPA). 2018f. *Recruitment Process of Teachers and Status of Temporary Teachers in Kerala by Dr K P Suresh.* New Delhi: NIEPA.

National Institute of Educational Planning and Administration (NIEPA). 2018g. *Recruitment Process of Teachers and Status of Temporary Teachers in Jammu and Kashmir by Prof. Mahmood Ahmad Khan.* New Delhi: NIEPA.

Pandey, N. 2018, 19 July. 'Govt Asks UGC to Have University Faculty Appointments Deferred Till SC Hearing on Reservations'. *Hindustan Times.*

University Grants Commission. 2010a. Revised Guidelines for the Scheme of Appointment/Honorarium of Guest/Part-Time Teachers. New Delhi: Ministry of Human Resource Development. Available at: https://www.ugc.ac.in/oldpdf/xiplanpdf/Appointment_Honorarium_Guest.pdf.

University Grants Commission. 2010b. *UGC (Minimum Qualifications for Appointment of Teachers and Other Academic Staff in Universities and Colleges and Measures for the Maintenance of Standards in Higher Education) Regulations 2010.* New Delhi: Ministry of Human Resource Development. Available at: https://www.ugc.ac.in/oldpdf/regulations/englishgazette.pdf.

Chapter 14

Leveraging Technology to Solve the Pentagon Puzzle of Higher Education in India

Pankaj Mittal

The higher education system of our country is basically confronted with a pentagon puzzle, comprising of five issues: access and equity (percentage of persons in the eligible age group having access to higher education and the disparities with reference to region, religion, caste, gender, financial status and so on), relevance (the relevance of education being imparted for employability and for inducing human values), quality (quality of education as viewed from international perspective), governance (professional management of the vast Indian higher education system) and financing (ensuring adequate funding of higher educational institutes to ensure equitable access to quality education). Since India got independence in 1947, a number of commissions and committees have been set up, which concentrate on addressing these issues. In this chapter, I discuss these issues and try to solve the pentagon puzzle by effectively leveraging technology.

Smartphones and laptops with internet connectivity are seen in most hands today. With easy access to these devices and internet at a relatively low cost, people in general and youth in particular, is spending a lot of time on just browsing the internet or engaging themselves with social media or just surfing the web. If this engagement can be gainfully used for learning, it can provide a better and more productive way of utilizing the time and resources. With Industry 4.0, time management, skilled workforce, upskilling, organizational skills and thirst for knowledge would be the most important components sought in the job market.

ENHANCING ACCESS AND EQUITY

The higher education in India has witnessed manifold increase in its institutional capacity since independence. In the past 70 years, the number of universities has increased from 20 to 957, the colleges from 500 to 43,000 and the teachers from 15,000 to nearly 15 lakhs. Consequently, the enrolment of students has increased from one lakh in 1950 to over 357 lakhs in the year 2018. The expansion in institutional capacity in terms of the number of universities/colleges and teachers has provided greater access to the students to post-secondary education. However, the gross enrolment ratio, that is, the ratio of persons enrolled in higher educational institutions (HEIs), to the total persons in the age of 18 and 23 years, is still about 25.7 per cent, whereas the enrolment ratio is about 36 per cent for countries in transition, 54.6 per cent for developed countries with a world average of 29 per cent. The situation is even worse in STEM disciplines, particularly for women in STEM where the enrolment figures are very low. As per All India Survey of Higher Education Report 2017–2018, at the undergraduate (UG) level, the highest number (36.4%) of students are enrolled in arts/humanities/social sciences courses followed by science (17.1%), engineering and technology (14.1%) and commerce (14.1%). The total number of students enrolled in arts courses is 95.06 lakh, of which 47.2 per cent are males and 52.8 per cent are females. Science is the second major stream with 48.51 lakh student, of which 51.3 per cent are males and 48.7 per cent are females. Engineering and technology is the third major stream with 40.19 lakh students enrolled. The share of male students enrolled in engineering and technology is 71.4 per cent, whereas female enrolment is 28.6 per cent. At the postgraduate (PG) level, maximum students are enrolled in social science, and management stream comes at number two. However, in engineering and technology courses, 20.07 per cent of the students are opting for PhD after their PG. It is followed by science, in which 6.9 per cent of the students are opting for PhD and in medical science 4.9 per cent of the students are opting for PhD. In social science, 2.45 per cent of students are opting for PhD after the PG course in the same field. This shows that apart from the issue of access, the issue of equity with respect to gender and other reasons also confronts the higher education system of the country. India needs to make sustained efforts to increase access to higher education (the target being 30% by 2020) apart from addressing gender disparities, wherein access is generally lower for girls as compared with the boys. It further needs to be recognized that, in addition to the fact that the enrolment rates are generally lower for the females compared to the males, the females belonging to the lower castes, and residing in rural and backward areas, suffer more acutely in accessing higher education than other females. Also, the vast difference in the enrolment for urban and rural areas substantiates the need for providing more opportunities for higher education in rural areas, that too, especially for girls.

Another factor which can be of interest is that although GER is considered as a vital parameter for the Indian higher education system, a close scrutiny will reveal that the problem is deeper. If one considers the eligible enrolment ratio (EER), that is, the ratio of number of students enrolled in higher education to the number of persons who have passed XII class in the age group of 18–23, a different scenario emerges. The EER for India is about 55–60 per cent, almost matching the developed countries. The more astonishing fact is that EER is almost the same, cutting across caste, religion, region and gender. Thus, we do not wish to target 100 per cent EER as we need skilled manpower in many areas for which higher education may not be an essential requirement. In addition, the government of India has taken many effective steps to increase the school enrolment (such as Right to Education and Sarva Shiksha Abhiyaan), leading to a higher number of school pass outs, with the consequence that even if the EER is sustained at the same level of 55–60 per cent, the number of enrolment in institutes of higher education will increase substantially.

Therefore, there is a need to shift the focus from 'creating expansion' to 'accommodating expansion'.

The capacity enhancement of higher education space to accommodate this inevitable expansion needs a multipronged approach. First, the government can create additional infrastructure by investing heavily on this sector, both for establishing new higher education institutions and for increasing the intake capacity of existing institutions. New schemes such as Higher Education Funding Agency (HEFA) and Revitalizing Infrastructure and System in Education (RISE) in the Union Budget of 2018 are positive steps in this direction (UGC 2018). However, the desired funding is not forthcoming in the required proportions and we are still far off from the target of investing 6 per cent of GDP on higher education. The second alternative could be to involve private players in the field through the route of private DUs, private state universities and private colleges. This has been resorted to, and today about 60 per cent of higher education institutions are in the private sector, but there is a concern of their adverse effect on the quality of education, if they are not regulated properly. The issue of closure of about 104 state private universities, created by a single act, in the state of Chhattisgarh by the Supreme Court of India are the classic examples of deterioration in quality by some of the private universities which were run as commercial enterprise purely with profit motive. This is at total variance with the establishments in past when education was considered as a philanthropic activity and premier institutions such as IISc, Bangalore, AMU, BITS, Pilani, BIT, Ranchi, TISS, TFRI, Mumbai, TERI and so on were established by private houses, not for profit making but with philanthropic motives. Third, we can consider careful amalgamation of conventional and distance education, while ensuring that quality is not compromised to increase the quantity. The UGC's recent regulations for open and distance learning for promoting quality distance education are a welcome step in this direction as they aim to curb non-quality distance education institutions.

Fourth, an innovative approach to enhancing access could be adopting a flexi-time approach in our higher education institutes. The need for this is based on the fact that the existing infrastructure available in a majority of the universities and colleges in the country is not fully utilized. A rough calculation will show that out of 365 days in a year, the university works for 180 actual teaching days for a maximum 6–8 hours in a day. This shows that the existing infrastructure in any university or college is only used for 15 per cent of the time and for rest of the 85 per cent of the time, the huge and extensive infrastructure consisting of vast buildings, expensive equipment and well-furnished libraries lies unutilized. If we think innovatively and make extensive use of technology, we can exactly double the infrastructure by increasing this 15 to 30 per cent by taking recourse to flexi-timings so that the infrastructure is optimally used. The experiment could be initiated in a pilot mode in a university/college where the classes can start at around 7–8 a.m. till 7–8 p.m. with the teaching to be imparted in a flexi-time mode to accommodate higher number of students and by adjusting timings of the teachers accordingly. Experiment, if it succeeds, could be slowly expanded to the other departments and then to all the universities in the country. This can help in substantially increasing the intake capacity of higher education institutions without any substantial increase in the resources required in terms of creation of infrastructure, equipment, books, and journals and so on. The only investment required would be in increasing the number of teachers, which would also address the issue of gainfully engaging the unemployed youth of the country.

Lastly, we can make extensive use of technology for providing access to quality higher education to such a mammoth young population in the remotest corners of the country. With Information and communications technology (ICT) making inroads in the education sector worldwide, the GOI launched the ambitious National Mission on Education through ICT (NMEICT) in 2009, for employing technology to provide connectivity, along with provision for multiple access devices, to institutions and learners, and for e-content generation. The major impetus to increase in access, which will also address the issue of equity would be through the recently issued University Grants Commission (Online Courses or Programmes) Regulations, 2018, which specifies that an higher educational institution may offer certificate, diploma and degree courses or programmes in full-fledged online mode subject to the condition that all such courses or programmes are duly approved by the statutory authorities or bodies of the higher educational institution and the delivery mechanism conforms to the quality standards of the online education as specified under these regulations. With an increase in access to devices such as computers, tablets, smartphones and the internet at low cost even in rural areas, technology can be used to its optimum through online education to increase the access and equity in higher education.

PROMOTING RELEVANT EDUCATION

Today, in the 21st century, the students who pursue higher education look for immediate gain in terms of employment after passing out of the higher education institutions. This calls for a dynamic curricular content, which should evolve continuously. It is felt that the education being imparted in many of our higher education institutions is not relevant to the industry. The recent CII survey estimates that 78 per cent of our engineering graduates are unemployable as our students have a little industry and hand-on experience. The curriculum is outdated, and the syllabus updation is generally resisted by teachers who do not want to update themselves on a regular and continuous basis. The industries/companies and institutions have to arrange a special induction training or finishing schools to train the graduates to make them employable. Thus, the relevance of education being imparted in terms of both content and its pedagogy is being widely debated. We need to take urgent steps to contain the situation and make the education being imparted to our students relevant for their future. The following measures could be helpful:

- Curriculum revision should be an ongoing academic activity involving all the faculty members and students. Not only will it endow academic programmes with quality but would also add to their contemporariness and relevance. Updation and revision of the curricula should be carried out in terms of (a) current knowledge, (b) national and international developments and (c) relevance of new ideas, concepts and knowledge of the concerned discipline.
- At the same time, faculty members should be encouraged to update their knowledge in their areas of specialization especially relating to their teaching assignment through books, journals and open education resource (OER) available on the internet. This can now

be done by effectively leveraging technology. A unique initiative of online professional development of in-service teachers of higher education, using Massive Open online Courses (MOOCs) platform, SWAYAM is the Annual Refresher Programme in Teaching (ARPIT) launched by the ministry of human resource development (MHRD) in November 2018. The ARPIT is a 40-hour programme with 20 hours of video content offered in a flexible format, which can be done at one's own pace and time. The programme has built-in assessment exercises and activities as part of the academic progression in the course. The UGC has also in a proactive manner decided that the successful completion of the ARPIT programme will be treated as equivalent to one refresher course for the purposes of career advancement.

- The concept of finishing schools, which is slowly gaining importance in the industrial sector (wherein the industry has to conduct special training for the graduates to make them employable) should be amalgamated with the course structure through apprenticeship programmes to ensure that the university passouts are readily employable. SHREYAS is a programme conceived in this direction for students in degree courses, primarily non-technical, with a view to introduce employable skills into their learning, promote apprenticeship as integral to education and also amalgamate employment facilitating efforts of the government into the education system so that clear pathways towards employment opportunities are available to students during and after their graduation. It is a programme basket comprising the initiatives of three central ministries, namely the MHRD, ministry of skill development and entrepreneurship and the ministry of labour and employment viz. the national apprenticeship promotion scheme (NAPS), the national career service (NCS) and introduction of BA/BSc/BCom (professional) courses in the HEIs. It will improve employability of students by introducing employment relevance into the learning process of the higher education system, forge a close functional link between education and industry/service sectors on a sustainable basis, and provide skills which are in demand to the students in a dynamic manner, help business/industry in securing good quality manpower through an online portal.

- Special efforts shall be made to improve the communication skills of the students by creating state-of-the-art language labs for the purpose. All the students of the university should be given a compulsory training on the language labs to ensure that their communication skills, especially in the language of English, improves to enable them to face the market when they go out of the university, keeping in view the fact that English is a major handicap for Indians, especially, rural students. Special personality development programmes should be organized to ensure that the students gain confidence, are able to face the society and the outside world more effectively, feel more empowered and are easily employable.

- The teachers must change the teaching pedagogy and start using the OER available on internet to teach students in a 'flipped classroom model' whereby the students read the text and see the videos recommended by teachers and available on the internet, and come to the class for discussion to improve their understanding and to clear their concepts and doubts. This will allow the students to grasp the application of the concept, rather than just memorize it by way of rote learning.

- **Curriculum interventions:** At present, students either are not allowed to think due to rote learning system of higher education prevalent in our country or are forced to use traditional methods of approaching a problem. A major shift is required in this process by introducing a major component of 'computational thinking' right from the school level till higher education (Pant, 2018). In a news item that appeared recently, 'Asia's top university makes computational thinking compulsory', Tan Eng. Chye, who became NUS' president, said that he was not afraid to rethink the university's entire approach to teaching in order to 'future-proof' its 28,000 students for a world increasingly shaped by digital technology and automation. 'Things are moving very fast in the external environment and we cannot afford to keep still,' said Professor Tan. 'The fourth industrial revolution is crucial. My colleagues know this and they understand that we must change with the times because of it. Much to the angst of some students, I have made statistics as well as computational thinking or programming compulsory for everyone, regardless of what course they do.' This new mandatory requirement means that even art and music students will be required to cover some level of computational thinking—for instance, understanding algorithms in everyday life (Pells, 2018).

Computational thinking is projected to be the 21st-century skill that is necessary for all age groups because of its applicability to the different fields. Hence learning to think computationally should not be limited to formal studies but should be accessible to learners of all age groups just like any other subject such as mathematics, humanities or sciences. Many scholars have advocated for computational thinking courses, which are catered to thinking abstractly and might be helpful in developing interest in the field of complex problem-solving.

Computational thinking is a set of cognitive skills and techniques that can be used to support problem-solving across situations and disciplines. More specifically, computational thinking entails: decomposition—breaking a (big, complicated, complex) problem into parts or steps; pattern recognition—finding and identifying patterns and trends in data; abstraction—identifying the general principles that generate these patterns; algorithm design—developing instructions for solving the problem.

Step by step, part by part, the solutions to the small problems can be brought together, and help shed light on and provide a solution to the big, complex problem. Computational thinking is useful as a problem-solving methodology, but beyond that, training in computational thinking can also help cultivate positive learning attitudes and values, such as tinkering and experimenting with solutions, debugging through finding and fixing errors, perseverance in working with difficult and open-ended problems, and confidence in dealing with ambiguity and complexity. It is extremely unfortunate that neither the educators and policy makers nor the students want to learn newer concepts that can help them future-proof their careers. They would rather agitate for concessions and guaranteed employment. But as has been so well stated in the video by CGP Grey about 'Humans need not apply', economics always wins, and humans without the right skills will have a very tough time in the future.

Computational thinking is critical for solving problems and using data effectively in modern society, but what is computational thinking anyway? Computational thinking is really a way to solve problems by specifying detailed, step-by-step solutions to those problems; collecting, representing and analysing data to support drawing conclusions or making decisions, and using a variety of techniques to improve the efficiency of our problem solutions.

PROMOTING QUALITY EDUCATION

The quality of higher education being imparted in our universities and colleges has always been a point of discussion. It is a general opinion that the quality of higher education is declining as evidenced by a number of indicators, such as reduction in the number of research publications, awards, patents, Indian universities in the world ranking and so on. The quality issue is more serious for institutes located in rural and backward areas. Urgent measures are required to enhance the quality of education being imparted in our institutes of higher education.

First, the school education, which is the baseline for higher education, should be seamlessly integrated with higher education. The quality of education at school level should get a special focus, wherein teaching perspective should shift from examination to learning, with emphasis on understanding rather than rote learning and overall holistic development of the child. To ensure holistic development of the youth at university/college level, efforts shall be made to reorient the teaching pattern with focus on all types of courses, that is, core courses (i.e. courses in the subject of specialization of the student in his/her UG/ PG programme); elective courses (i.e. courses chosen by the students as per their aptitude from other departments); supportive courses (i.e. courses in soft skills and life skills including communication and personality development) and social orientation courses (i.e. courses which provide value addition to the students' livelihood, such as courses in environmental education, human rights education, value and ethics education, societal development, peace and conflict resolution).

Second, all the students admitted in the university may be subjected to an induction semester with the first semester curriculum consisting of series of induction courses. These courses could be designed so as to substantially improve their oral and written communication

skills in English and Hindi; the development of fine arts such as paint-
ing, music, drama and so on; sports capability; leadership qualities;
life coping skills; computer and internet capabilities; foundations of
natural sciences; foundations of social sciences; understanding medical
and biological sciences; basics of health and environmental sciences;
design techniques; and so on. This exposure will help the students in
developing interdisciplinary aptitude, which will prepare them to do
well in subsequent semesters. The university may introduce summer
courses to make up for the time taken for the induction semester so
that the students can finish the courses in the prescribed time frame.

Third, at the university level, teaching should be made more effective by following a multipronged participative approach rather than
simple classroom teaching. The elements of participation may be in
the form of enquiry learning, problem-based learning, project-based
learning, teaching through case studies, discovery learning by role plays,
co-operative–collaborative learning by learning communities, class
debates, seminars, quizzes, web-based learning, home assignments and
adopting flipped classroom model and learning through MOOCs. The
model could be called as integrative teaching–learning methodology
and the universities may develop the infrastructure and faculty skills to
offer such methodologies. Different teaching pedagogies using ICT in
the form of using e-content as OER and in a flipped classroom model,
MOOCs and direct-to-home (DTH) channels can provide students
and teachers with different approaches to learning and innovation in
teaching, and optimally use the resources and time on hand. This can,
to a large extent, address the problem of providing quality education to
students in rural, remote and backward areas of the country. As a step in
the right direction, the NMEICT project, which started with e-content
production to be used as OER, has been further extended and an Indian
MOOCs platform—SWAYAM has been created on which MOOCs
are being hosted for the students studying in universities and colleges as
well as for any time learner. The MOOCs on the SWAYAM platform,
developed indigenously in India, can address the problem of faculty
shortage in universities and colleges, by providing students with the
best quality faculty from all over the country. This would also help the
students as well as teachers to update their knowledge and skill, which

would successfully bridge the gap in access to quality education and would help the nation move towards information-rich society. About 1,500 MOOCs course are already running on the SWAYAM platform with about 20 lakh enrolments.

The effective leveraging of technology can provide answers to the very many disruptions which are affecting the higher education space of India of late. Today, there are disruptions in terms of access to quality education for students who are not able to get admissions in best institutions, access to the dissemination of knowledge only by the teacher in the classroom alone within the given timings of the college/university or limited access to knowledge based on the books/references prescribed in the class by the teacher or even relating to the cost of getting quality education. Today, technology has made it possible to address these disruptions by providing any learner the opportunity to learn anytime and anywhere, that too free of cost. Today, the lessons from best teachers can be accessed online on SWAYAM, for free, thereby giving everyone an access to quality education at practically no cost. The only requirement is a computer or laptop or tablet or a smartphone with internet connectivity. For those areas where internet penetration is not very good, the access to OER is through DTH channels on the television through DTH SWAYAM Prabha. 'SWAYAM Prabha' is an initiative of MHRD for disseminating the audio-visual content developed as part of e-content and MOOCs through 32 DTH educational TV channels. These channels are broadcasting educational content in diverse disciplines throughout the day, allowing the students to choose the time of his/her convenience for watching these videos. Content telecast covers all levels of education from school education till PG education. This is particularly useful for the areas where the internet is not available or bandwidth poses a major challenge.

REGULATIONS ON MOOCs

After the development of the MOOCs course, the next issue was to give credibility to these courses in the formal system of higher education. A strong need was felt to allow credit transfer based on successful completion of these courses. For this, UGC (Credit Framework for

Online Learning Courses through SWAYAM) Regulation, 2016, were issued on 19 July 2016. The regulations clearly defined the roles of the parent institution, i.e. institution opting for MOOCs courses on SWAYAM and the host institution from which the parent institution offered the MOOCs course. The regulations stipulate that online learning courses will be made available on the SWAYAM platform and be notified every year on 1st June and 1st November. A student studying at a recognized institute anywhere in the country and having cleared the online course through SWAYAM would be awarded credits to be transferred from the host institute to the parent institute where the student is studying. Up to 20 per cent of the total courses being offered in a particular programme could be opted through MOOCs. The host institution will evaluate the students based on predefined norms and the parent institution will incorporate the marks/grade obtained by the student, in the final marks sheet. In subjects where lab experiments or practicals are involved, the parent institution will evaluate the student and incorporate these marks/grade in the overall marks/grade. A certificate regarding successful completion of the MOOCs course is issued through the host institution and sent to the parent institution. The universities have welcomed the idea and are in the process of identifying courses and getting approval from their statutory bodies which is a very encouraging sign.

ONLINE PROGRAMMES BY UNIVERSITIES

Leveraging technology further for providing access to quality higher education, UGC has recently issued the regulations for online programmes, wherein specified universities are allowed to run online programmes on specified terms and conditions. Online programmes and courses are becoming more popular over the years. Self-paced degree and certification programmes, flexible scheduling and the removal of geographic barriers are making higher education a reality for remote students, full-time professionals and others who might not otherwise be able to attend. In turn, many are choosing online programmes to improve their job and salary prospects.

In online programmes, the students can have full freedom and will be more comfortable in studying the subjects' combinations of their choices at their own pace and place and be able to pursue higher education at minimal cost along with their jobs and other activities. It can be very effectively used for upskilling the knowledge base of employees too.

PROMOTING RESEARCH

It has been seen recently that research has taken a back seat in many universities with the number of research publications reducing in both quality and quantity. India's contribution to research publications in the world has reduced from 9 per cent in the past to 2.3 per cent today. Excellence in research underpins the idea of a world-class institution since research that is recognized by peers can alone provide a fillip to the frontiers of knowledge. The quality of research determines the reputation and recognition of a university in the world.

All types of research, that is, pure basic research or theoretical research which develops new ideas or knowledge growing from the current breadth and depth of knowledge; strategic basic research which also develops new ideas but with the potential of applications being derived from such research; applied research that grows from already known principles to develop new applications and experimental research that attempts to validate known principles or develop new products and technology need to be promoted. Applied and experimental research tends to focus on technology development having industrial and commercial applications, whereas pure basic and strategic research have characteristics of public goods and have largely been subject to public provisioning. However, pure basic research and strategic research are the crucibles on which applied research or technological developments are grown. The universities shall strive to provide the ideal breeding ground for such research and ensure that the right atmosphere and talent is available for the purpose.

Adequate funding to develop both specialized physical and human infrastructure is essential to support the university's research. A separate budget head for 'research' for creating the necessary physical infrastructure at the university and also for setting up a research corpus fund shall be provided in the university budget with annual provisions.

The research funding may not be distributed to disciplines or faculties equally but the strength of a research proposal shall be the sole criterion for funding preferably on an interdisciplinary/multidisciplinary basis. In addition, the faculty shall have the liberty to apply to various funding agencies nationally and internationally. Academia shall be given full freedom in research, in terms of appointment of research personnel, use of the research project grant and the publication of results. The free spirit of enquiry and the quest for knowledge shall be the defining principles for all aspects of academic life. The universities shall make special efforts to increase the research output of the faculty. Special schemes can be launched to provide incentives to the faculty who produce quality research papers. A research advisory board can be set up to give directions to the university in various areas of front-line research.

ENSURING EFFECTIVE GOVERNANCE

The emerging challenges in the higher education sector demand for appropriate skills and competencies on the part of educational administrators to prepare the institutions to take on these challenges. Administrative machinery, which is not equipped with the necessary skills, knowledge and attitude and which is not in harmony with the needs of the progress, can retard the pace of development of a university. A flexible pattern of governance, which is responsive to the changing needs of society, global trends and knowledge, can be a powerful factor in accelerating progress. In the wake of internationalization of education, coupled with globalization and competition, the higher educational institutes need to be managed more professionally. The traditional university administration being run with 19th-century tools have to be replaced with modern management techniques with qualified, professionally trained and proactive administrators suited for the fast changing world.

It is surprising to note that India, the second-largest higher education system of the world, is managed by higher education administrators including VCs, registrars, deputy registrars, assistant registrars and other administrative staff, none of whom undergo any professional training. Even the teachers who teach in the higher education institutions do not have any formal training, in contrast to school teachers for whom training is mandatory in the form of BEd. Hence, our higher education system is being managed by administrators with no formal training on academic governance. The result is a poorly managed higher education system, which does not work to its optimal levels, and is far from being a professionally managed system. Most of the higher education institutions abroad have the concept of a 'Human Resource Management Department', which is a service department to manage the most critical resource of a university or a college, that is, 'human resource'. However, in India, it is the human resource which is given a back seat and all efforts are made to manage administration, finances and other mundane things, which have little importance as compared to professional management of human resource. For an effective management of our higher education system, we need to shift the focus from 'management of higher education' to 'professional management of higher education'.

The universities should establish a 'human resource department', which instead of being a teaching department should be a service department to take care of human resources in the university in terms of academic planning, recruitment methodologies to be adopted, including head hunting, retention strategies, and gracious exit. The human resource management department can take care of all respects of human resource right from attracting and retaining talent, staff development and training, personal and professional counselling till the gracious exit on superannuation and need-based re-employment.

A good beginning has been done by launching 'Leadership for Academicians Programme' (LEAP), by the MHRD. LEAP is a three-week flagship leadership development training programme (two weeks domestic and one week foreign training) for second-level academic functionaries in public-funded higher education institutions. The main objective is to prepare second-tier academic heads who are likely to assume leadership roles in the future. The programme would provide senior faculty with high academic credentials, the required leadership and managerial skills, including skills of problem-solving, handling stress, team building work, conflict management, developing communication skills, understanding and coping with the complexity and challenges of governance in HEIs, financial and general administration.

There is an urgent and strong need to conceive and concretize the e-governance programme and develop an ERP for the university to provide a smooth flow of information between the 'university administration' and the 'students, staff and public' so as to enhance the speed and quality of internal functioning as well as to provide a 'user-friendly' access to outsiders. The ICT-enabled tools shall be extensively used to improve the productivity, efficiency and 'customer satisfaction' with measurable results, in terms of substantial reduction in the use and movement of paper, and time taken to provide information, leading to reduced delays, cost savings as well as environmental conservation. The university should be following a participative approach to ensure effective and participative governance. This will increase faith and credibility amongst various employees of the university and between management and the employees.

FINANCING

It is said that if you want to invest for a year, invest in corn, if you want to invest for 20 years, invest in trees, and if you want to invest for life time, invest in education. Although the central and state governments are making efforts to fund higher education at its end, we are still far from the goal of 6 per cent of GDP to education advocated by the Kothari Commission in 1964 and hence the financial crunch in Indian universities/colleges is clearly evident (GOI 1966). This is more true for state universities and colleges who are at the bottom of the ladder, in terms of government funding. Apart from privatization of higher education which is making a direct inroad into the higher education system of the country, we have to think of the ways of mobilizing resources for government institutions. The universities have to make special efforts to mobilize resources, from both internal and external resources. The facilities existing in the universities have to be used to its optimum capacity for mobilizing resources.

The fee structure of the universities shall be decided keeping in mind the expenditure incurred on a course, while ensuring that most of the recurring expenditure of the course is met out of the students' fee. This has been advocated by various committees in the past, such as Punnayya Committee, Pylee Committee and Powar Committee, but raising fees in Indian universities and colleges has become a political issue, instead of an academic or financial issue, and needs delicate handling. At the same time, free ships, scholarships and educational loans can be offered to those who cannot afford the fees while ensuring that the admissions are on need-based criteria.

The Union Budget 2018–2019 has announced that the focus shall be on improving the quality of education and that ₹1 lakh crore shall be invested for strengthening the infrastructure for higher education and research, over the next four years. The new initiatives in terms of HEFA, RISE and institutions of eminence (IoE) raise some hopes for the future.

CONCLUSION

The effective use of technology can help us to solve the pentagon puzzle of higher education. The issues of access, equity, relevance and quality of higher education can be effectively addressed through quality e-content made available to the students in the form of OER to be used for sup-plementary learning or for flipped classroom model or through struc-tured MOOCs courses for credit transfer in regular degree programmes pursued by students in universities and colleges. The DTH videos being telecast through SWAYAM Prabha would address the issue of equity by reaching to students and learners in remotest corners of the country. Technology can be harnessed to provide effective governance of higher education institutes through various e-governance models which are user friendly and easy to use. Technology-enabled learning initiatives would go a long way in cutting down costs of building infrastructure in the form of brick-and-mortar classrooms, thereby addressing the problem of financing of higher education. The online content will also address the issue of faculty shortage in universities and colleges, through access to the digital content from the best faculty of the country.

Summing up, the technology-enabled learning would provide stu-dents and teachers with different approaches to teaching, learning and innovation. It will help in the capacity building of higher education institutes to handle disruptions taking place in the higher education space by optimally using the resources and time on hand. The project would also help the students and teachers to update their knowledge and skills especially for those located in rural/backward/remote areas and would help the nation move towards an information–rich society.

REFERENCES

Government of India (GOI). June 1966. *Education and National Development. Report of the Education Commission* (Kothari Commission, 1964–1966). New Delhi: Education Commission.

Ministry of Human Resource Development (MHRD). 2018. *All India Survey of Higher Education 2017–18.* New Delhi: Department of Higher Education, Government of India.

Pant, M. M. 2018. 'Computational Thinking for All'. *Townscript*, 5 May. Available at: https://www.townscript.com/e/mmp-computational-thinking-4weeks.

Pells, R. 2018, 13 March. 'Asia's Top University Makes Computational Thinking Compulsory'. *Times Higher Education.* Available at: https://www.timeshighereducation.com/news/asias-top-university-makes-computational-thinking-compulsory.

University Grants Commission (UGC). 2016. *UGC (Credit Framework for Online Learning Courses through SWAYAM) Regulation, 2016.* New Delhi: Government of India.

University Grants Commission (UGC). 2018. *Union Budget 2018–2019.* New Delhi: Government of India.

Chapter 15

Managing Student Diversity in Indian Higher Education Institutions
Achieving Academic Integration and
Social Inclusion

Nidhi S. Sabharwal

INTRODUCTION

Over the last few decades, higher education in India has seen a shift from an elite stage of development to a stage of massification. The gross enrolment ratio (GER) increased from 5.9 per cent to 25.8 per cent between 1990 and 2018 (MHRD 2018, Varghese 2015). Even though the higher education system in India is in its initial stage of massification, with an enrolment of 35.7 million students, India has the second-largest higher education system in the world. The move towards expansion has been driven by the recognition of the role of higher education in promoting participation in the knowledge economy by preparing a more educated workforce with higher education degrees and higher level skills (GOI 2000). At the same time, higher education has the potential to increase citizens' chances of inter-generational income and social mobility and therefore is considered a central instrument for achieving inclusive growth (Planning Commission 2001, 2008, Varghese et al. 2017).

Expansion of higher education in India has been accompanied by a policy focused on widening access to include students particularly from non-traditional backgrounds previously underrepresented in higher education. Affirmative action policies in the form of constitutionally mandated reservation of seats for the students from the socially excluded groups, relaxation in admission criteria and financial support have been important channels for improving the enrolment of the non-traditional learners from diverse socio-economic and academic backgrounds. The new student body includes women, first-generation students in their families to enter higher education, belonging to poor families and of 'lower' caste, from rural areas and who have studied in regional language as their medium of instruction.

In other words, in their journey to higher education institutions, these students have experienced disadvantaged life circumstances and processes that are related to factors such as poverty, gender, geographic location, belonging to a socially excluded group, no prior family background in higher education or inequitable conditions of study. Furthermore, many of the students are members of more than one disadvantaged group and experience multiple barriers which compound the effects of their disadvantage. As cohorts of students in higher education in India are diverse, so are their learning needs and challenges.

To translate opportunity of access to academic success: as measured by persistence, academic performance and degree attainment, the nature of institutional response has to take into account varying educational requirements of diverse non-traditional learners. But, increasingly, studies are indicating social class disparities in persistence rates: for example, a relatively higher proportion of dropouts from institutions of higher education are students who belong to disadvantaged social groups, including experiences of social exclusion on campuses (Sivasankaran and Raveendran, 2004, Sabharwal et al. 2014, Sabharwal and Malish 2016, Henry and Ferry, 2017). This chapter argues that many higher education institutions remain under-prepared to meet the educational needs of non-traditional learners, including cultivating a socially inclusive campus environment and have been unable to adapt adequately to their academic and social challenges. One-size-fits-all approach that may have been effective when the student composition was more homogenous is no longer applicable in the context of a diversified student body.

This chapter presents an institution-centred approach which is based on the notion that institutions have a responsibility to devise strategies of integration of students in academic and social domain. Integration in the academic spheres which is influenced by the classroom environment refers to students' academic performance and focuses on improving their abilities to meet educational demands, while integration in social spheres refers to developing social interactions and networks and involving students in out-of-class activities (Tinto 1975, 1993, 1997, 1998). To improve educational experience of diverse student body, targeted academic and non-academic support programmes will be essential, including providing adequate care to ensure that student diversity in higher education leads to social inclusion, rather than ghettoization.

A coherent framework to guide institutional actions and establish tailored strategies can be achieved only after a thorough understanding of the challenges faced by non-traditional learners from diverse social, economic and academic backgrounds. This chapter will present empirical evidence generated from a large-scale CPRHE study (Sabharwal and Malish 2016) on nature and forms of academic and social challenges faced by students from disadvantaged groups on campuses and its negative consequences on their academic performance, social interactions and levels of social inclusion. It will analyse the nature of existing institutional environment inside and outside classrooms, including dimensions related to social relations and provisions of support services that contribute to shaping the experiences of students from the disadvantaged groups. The chapter will conclude with options for interventions to achieve institutional integration of non-traditional learners in academic and social domains. The results in this chapter are based on a mixed method research study which employed a questionnaire-based survey of 3,200 students, interviews with 200 faculty members, 70 focus group discussions with students and 50 diaries of students in higher education institutions located across six states, namely, Bihar, Delhi,

Maharashtra, Kerala, Karnataka and Uttar Pradesh. In what follows the analytical approach, which includes five constructs that the institutions can be sensitive to while crafting strategies of integration of students in academic and social domains, will be first discussed.

ANALYTICAL APPROACH FOR ACHIEVING INTEGRATION IN ACADEMIC AND SOCIAL DOMAINS

Sufficiently addressing the specific concerns of non-traditional learners from diverse socio-economic groups warrants an analytical approach that focuses on the institutions to establish processes of inclusion which ameliorate the impact of disadvantages (Bensimon 2007, Ferrier and North, 2009). This approach advocates placing the responsibility of student success on the institution by ways of shifting their pedagogical practices to match the educational requirements of students from the disadvantaged social groups. This section will start with a discussion on the constructs emerging from the study that helps us understand campus experiences of students from diverse social, economic and academic backgrounds and can guide formulation of institutional integrational strategies.

The five constructs that arose from the data are demographic characteristics (socio-economic and parents' educational background) of non-traditional learners, pre-college academic background, nature of in-class and out-of-class environment, institutional culture and policy environment (see Figure 15.1). Our study shows that an interplay of demographic characteristics of non-traditional learners, pre-college academic background, institutional culture and policy environment influence the nature of in-class and out-of-class environment and the levels of integration of non-traditional learners in academic and social spheres of the institutions.

Diverse Socio-economic Characteristics of Students

The results from our study show that today higher education campuses comprise non-traditional learners from diverse socio-economic and academic backgrounds. A focus on non-traditional learners' categories is

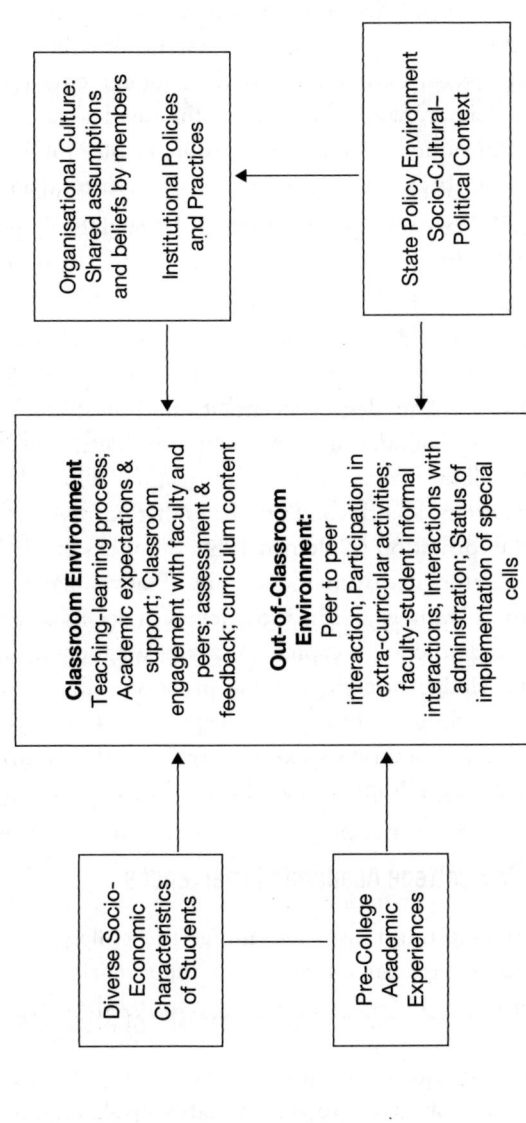

Figure 15.1 *Institutional Integration Approach: Five Constructs Influencing Students' Experiences*
Source: Prepared by the Author.

helpful in directing institutional integration efforts as these are students who have experienced disadvantaged life-processes that have resulted in inequitable conditions of study and unequal academic pathways due to which they are at risk of falling into low-performance trap and have a lower likelihood of adjusting to academic systems of college. These students are from groups underrepresented in higher education. In India, these groups encompass students from the disadvantaged social and economic backgrounds (such as the scheduled castes [SC]/scheduled tribes [ST]/other backward classed [OBCs]) from rural areas, no prior family background in higher education, non–English medium of instruction and women.

Social stratification (Clark 1973) and social reproduction theory (Bourdieu and Passerson, 1990) informs us that social status background and parent's education influence students' likelihood of gaining access to college, persistence and degree completion. For students who belong to higher castes, middle or high income students, social status background helps acquire social and cultural capital which leads to advantageous behaviours, abilities and privileges that positively impacts their human capital formation (Coleman 1988, Stephens et al. 2012). Our survey shows, students from the socially disadvantaged groups were first-generation learners and had low levels of access to avenues for formation of 'academic social capital' (Winkle-Wagner et al. 2012) which is basic knowledge of college going process, college counselling and planning (including choice of college as well as subjects to study) and academic preparation for college coursework (Tierney and Duncheon 2015, Winkle-Wagner et al. 2012).

Pre-college Academic Experiences

Socio-economic background also determines pre-college academic characteristics which have an influence on their in-classroom and out-of-class experiences. Indeed, our survey indicates that majority of students from the disadvantaged backgrounds had unequal academic experiences in primary and secondary schooling vis-à-vis their peers. These students were more likely to attend high schools with regional language as their medium of instruction, negatively influencing their abilities for the transition to English as a medium of instruction in higher education and lacked the resources that aid in college preparation. For example, majority of students from the SCs (65%), STs (57%) and OBCs (57%) reported that they studied in the government schools vis-à-vis their peers from the higher castes (44%). Similarly, majority of these students (SCs–76%, STs–77%, OBCs–78%) reported that they had studied the state syllabus in their higher secondary school. There was also substantial social group difference pertaining to pre-college marks, a proxy for the level of academic preparation in school, which also determined the choice of subjects at higher education. Moreover, experiences of students from socially excluded groups (SCs/STs/OBCs) especially are vexed in a complex interplay of their unequal social location in caste hierarchy, low economic and social capital.

Policy Environment and Institutional Culture

A conducive policy environment of equality and non-discrimination plays an important role in adapting practices for academic integration and influencing institutional culture for creation of socially inclusive campuses. Policy environment includes a mix of social, political-legal context, funding priorities, access initiatives, and information and communication of the policies of the state to the institutions. In India, the existing policy environment, at the macro level, that impacts the welfare of a diverse student body, include constitutional provisions to ensure educational opportunity; positive measures of access; policy directives to establish special institutional mechanisms to address group-specific concerns; and legal safeguards against discrimination and sexual harassment. So, for example, state affirmative action policies for students from socially excluded groups have been important channels for improving the enrolment of non-traditional learners from diverse socio-economic and academic backgrounds. Acceptance, bonding to the policy environment, and consistency of adherence to rules and guidelines are important institutional responsibilities. By engaging students systemically to include both academic and social domains, institutions have the potential to make the higher education sector, as a whole, more socially inclusive (Astin 1975, 1993, Pascarella and Terenzini 1980, Tinto 2014, Tinto and Pusser, 2006).

The institutional centred approach also leads us to look in deeper and analyse culture of the institutions (Museus et al. 2012, Tierney 1988). Institutional culture is determined by multiple factors which include not only the policy environment (as mentioned before), but also attitudes, ideologies and behaviours of participating individuals (faculty, campus administrators and students). Behaviour is based on how institutions articulate their 'norms', 'ideology', 'attitudes' and a shared understanding of assumptions which is often taken for granted by the actors themselves. The institutional culture which is a composite of dominant norms, ideologies and pattern of behaviour determine inside-classroom and out-of-class environment, and influences students' experiences and their outcomes. Our findings suggest that students from disadvantaged social groups faced an insensitive institutional culture embedded in dominant caste and patriarchal norms, stereotypes and beliefs which was shaping the values, attitudes, behaviours and interactions of faculty members, administrators and peers with the students from the disadvantaged social groups. In sections that follow, we will describe the nature of classroom and out-of-classroom environment, its impact on shaping the experiences of non-traditional learners and its negative influence on their integration in academic and social domains.

CLASSROOM ENVIRONMENT AND CHALLENGES OF STUDENTS IN ACADEMIC DOMAIN

While student socio-economic group characteristics and pre-college academic background are important factors shaping academic and social experiences of students, our findings suggest existing classroom environment which includes teaching–learning processes, nature of teacher–student interactions and prevailing attitudes of teachers were increasing academic risks of students from the disadvantaged social groups to remain in a low-performance trap.

Un-conducive Teaching–Learning Processes

Although there was a general awareness among the faculty members that their class rooms include non-traditional learners from diverse socio-economic groups with varying pre-college academic credentials, most of the faculty members were not devising mechanisms to include all students in teaching–learning processes or promoting positive in-class interactions. Traditional lecture-based method, mostly one directional, was the dominant form of transaction in the classrooms with minimal participation by students. It was not expected of students to ask questions in the classrooms and there was a limited attempt on developing assessment techniques to determine what they know, what they have learnt and what is unclear.

Along with absence of critical assessment of the competency levels of students in the classrooms, determining their learning needs and planning their class room lessons/practices accordingly was also minimal by the faculty members. Feedback on assignments and practices of learning methods such as group work which promote collective learning was also limited. Peer support on academic matters was similarly limited for the students from the disadvantaged groups. Furthermore, lack of awareness about library resources and methods of using it also posed barriers to their opportunities for academic adjustments.

Additional barriers to academic integration related to large class sizes which constrained teachers to engage with students in a focused manner, limited time in a semester system to teach the required syllabus and lower levels of abilities of students to cope up with the demands of the semester system (by way of keeping pace with the syllabus taught in the class, writing assignments, making presentations). As large class room size poses challenges for students to clarify their academic doubts during class room transactions, interaction outside teaching hours has an important role to play in academic integration. Our study shows that the practice of interacting with students outside teaching hours and providing academic support was also generally low. Majority of the students (71%) reported they rarely received academic support outside teaching hours from their teachers, with students from the disadvantaged social groups (such as the SC/ST group) more likely to feel the absence of academic support, absence of encouragement to engage in academic activities that would help them develop their learning skills and also felt ignored in the curriculum and curricular transactions which results in feeling of alienation from the classroom transactions.

Negative Attitude of Teachers and Lack of Mentoring

It was not uncommon for faculty members to look down on the academic capabilities of students from the disadvantaged social groups, especially the SCs and the STs. Many faculty members carried the prejudice against these students and commented that previously 'really motivated' students came to colleges and universities—but today due to 'reservation' (and 'not merit') and lower 'entry qualification' (low cut off marks), admission to higher education institutions is easy for some groups of students. Students also reported to being labelled as reserved category in the class. Instead of being sensitive to the rights of the students to be enrolled through the policy of reservation, often faculty members held these very students responsible for lowering the average academic 'quality' in their classrooms, and blamed the unsuccessful completion of college as a failure of students rather than the responsibility of the institution.

Regional affiliation (faculty members in Delhi blamed students from neighbouring states), students from poor background and from rural location were also considered to be the cause of overall decline of quality and loss of 'status' of their institution. There was also an absence of the notion that the support required by students in their classrooms is an entitlement and that it is the duty of the teachers to provide diverse forms of support to help their students succeed. Rather, they suggested seeking assistance outside their classrooms (through remediation programmes). The role of a teacher in integrating students in teaching–learning processes was not recognized across most institutions. We will show later that the implementation of remedial coaching is poor across the institutions under study further negatively affecting academic performance of students from the disadvantaged social groups.

Also, the role of teacher as a guide and a mentor was generally not valued across the institutions and exceptionally few faculty members were undertaking efforts to interact with students. While an institutional-level mentorship scheme existed, it was limited to one institution and most of the faculty members considered it as unimportant. The mentorship scheme was largely thus dysfunctional due to lack of interest among faculty members and lack of guidelines and coordination process at institute levels. The findings suggest that faculty members in our study were dismissive of taking the responsibility of mentorship and were rather recommending assistance of a counsellor who is 'trained' in solving issues which required advice and guidance.

Absence of Same Caste and Same Ethnicity Faculty Members

Faculty members from diverse backgrounds were few in number as our data show, which has implications on the difficulties that students from the disadvantaged social groups may face if they wish to find and interact with the same caste and same ethnicity faculty members in the hope of enjoying positive academic experiences. For example, the results from our study show that while the classrooms include students from diverse social groups (close to 60 per cent of students were from SC/ST/OBC social group), the social composition of the faculty and administrators remains largely homogenous (from higher castes). Despite the constitutional provisions of reservation in faculty positions, we find an underrepresentation of faculty members especially from the scheduled castes and scheduled tribes in higher education institutions under study. Recent data from MHRD also show that 61 per cent of the faculty in higher education belong to the upper castes (MHRD 2015).

Poor Implementation of Remediation Programmes

Implementation of remedial coaching was poor across the institutions. Faculty members' in-charge of the programme reported delay in funds and lack of teachers training to deal with academically diverse student groups to be major hurdles in the effective implementation of remedial coaching classes. Students reported lack of information from college and universities about the organization of remedial classes. Inconvenient timing of the classes was another reason given by students for not being able to access remedial coaching. On timing of the classes, students reported that due to their poor family background, many were doing part-time job after their regular classes. The perspective of being deficient rather than different and caste stigma attached to remedial coaching classes as it is perceived to be only for SC/ST posed further challenge for active participation from beneficiary groups. As a result, academic integration of students from the socially excluded groups is negatively impacted.

Consequences: Lack of Academic Integration and Falling into a Low-Performance Trap

Inequitable pre-college academic preparedness, low competency in English language, non-interactive classroom teachings, low teacher–student interactions, lack of academic support services and insensitive attitude of faculty members, including their uncaring behaviour negatively impacts engagement in learning activities and academic performance. In addition, negative stereotypes about a group's level of academic performance undermine their self-esteem, resulting in reduced confidence to engage in the teaching–learning interactions within the classrooms. The correlational analysis (Sabharwal and Malish 2018) shows difficulties faced by disadvantaged groups to engage in learning activities and low degree of integration in the academic realms in the classrooms. The correlation results show that students from the SC/ST social group found it difficult to follow class room teachings and understand the lectures and felt anxious that they were not being given attention by the teacher during question–answer sessions. Confidence level of SC and ST students was also low as compared to non-SC and ST groups as they were hesitant to ask questions, clarify their doubts in the classroom or interact with teachers impacting their active participation in classroom discussions.

Negative attitude coupled with non-interactive classroom teaching and lack of avenues for academic integration intensifies the risk of students from the disadvantaged social groups of falling in a low-performance trap. Figure 15.2 shows that these students start out with low scores at the time of joining college and are likely to perform poorer than their advantaged peers during their college years. The existing academic gap thus remains between privileged and underprivileged students given their difficulty in following classroom teaching and developing deeper understanding of the subject domains. The

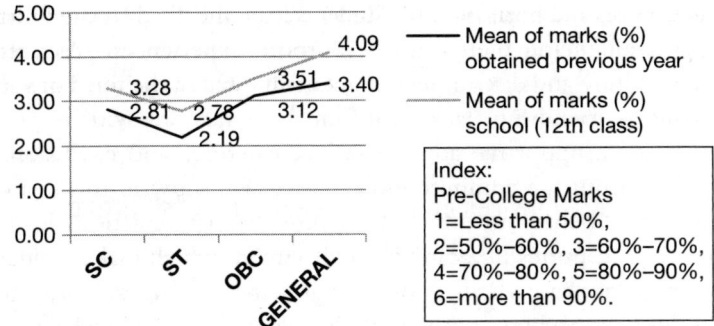

Figure 15.2 *Mean of Marks Scored across Social Groups*
Source: Sabharwal and Malish (2016).

inaccessibility and unapproachability of their teachers and peers compels disadvantaged students to rely on support from outside the college and university, indicating a fractured sense of feeling that they belong to their institution.

Academic disparities and social academic distance between students from the disadvantaged social groups and their teachers and peers have negative implications on the path to achieving inclusion in spheres outside the classroom. As we shall see in the next section, social group identity, academic differences and low performance become a source of discrimination and social exclusion for students from the disadvantaged social groups constraining their abilities to equally access or fully participate in out-of-class campus activities.

OUT-OF-CLASS ENVIRONMENT AND CHALLENGES FACING STUDENTS IN THE SOCIAL DOMAIN

Our findings suggest that students from disadvantaged social groups feel unwelcomed in their campuses, experience discrimination and an insensitive campus culture rooted in ideology of social dominance. Nature of campus culture was deeply embedded on dominant caste and gender norms, stereotypes and beliefs which were shaping the attitudes and values, behaviours and interactions of faculty members, administrators and peers with the students from the disadvantaged social groups, influencing their out-of-classroom experiences. Insensitive campus culture and discrimination get manifested in the form of social divisions in friendship, lack of informal interactions with teachers, as well as unsupportive administrative structures and exclusionary behaviour from the administration. As we will show in this section, exclusionary behaviour and lack of intergroup interactions lead to negative perceptions of a campus environment which makes students more reluctant to participate in campus activities, engage with those from different backgrounds than their own, and hinders inclusion for students from the disadvantaged social groups. A hostile campus has also been identified as a reason for non-traditional learners to develop a fractured sense of belonging, which subsequently can contribute to a reason for dropping out (Hurtado and Carter 1997, Just 1999, Swail et al. 2003, Zea et al. 1997).

Social Division in Friendship

Empirical evidence suggests that caste and gender norms existing in society are getting reproduced in campus life. Dominant values and perception of the diverse student body were being influenced by superiority of caste belonging and patriarchal norms. By their peers, students from disadvantaged groups face hostility because of affirmative action, are labelled as 'reserved category' and become a victim of micro-aggressions which takes the form of insults and caste-based jokes.

Similar to the beliefs of the faculty members, beliefs of the upper caste peers of the socially excluded groups (SC/ST/OBC) are rooted in the ideology of merit and against the idea of reservation. For example, when asked about their views on the reservation policy, the higher caste students in the student survey reported that they believed that universities frequently had to admit under qualified SCs/STs/OBCs and that reservation policy for the SCs STs was no longer needed as the lower castes social group have progressed and they do not require reservation policy. Students from the disadvantaged groups, however, felt the opposite and justified affirmative action. These sorts of debates also take place in the classroom, with students taking positions based on their own caste; teachers usually allow such polarized discussions, without highlighting concepts of social justice, equity or diversity.

Student's dominant negative perceptions towards idea of reservation, diversity and social justice separated and isolated student community into different groups based on their identities. In fact, the process of isolation and ghettoization takes its root in the initial weeks of the first year of students itself. When they recollected their experience of the initial days of college, students from the disadvantaged social groups were unable to form peer groups and were searching for students of their background in order to overcome the feeling of isolation.

Identity-based peer-group formation was dominant in all campuses, thereby impacting levels of intermingling, cooperation and social cohesion among these groups. While students from the SC and ST social groups chose not to interact with other castes due to strained interactions, insults and prevailing fear of discrimination, students from the higher castes and OBCs preferred to interact amongst themselves to maintain their social status. There were also separate hostels on the basis of caste and ethnicity along with social segregation in access to common spaces like mess halls and in participation in extra-curricular activities. Wherever disadvantaged students were active in extra-curricular activities, for example, National Service Scheme (NSS), such activities and student participation is stigmatized, with students from higher castes shunning participation in such activities.

Women in general, and women belonging to SC and ST groups in particular, are prone to gender-based stereotypes, exclusion and harassment. Lack of feeling of safety is prevalent among the women. Women in some institutions do not stay back in the campus after mid-afternoon hours due to fear for their safety and harassment from male peers and locals. It also impacts their participation in extra-curricular activities and their learning. In some colleges, male students imposed certain dress codes for women restricting their choice to wear what they like. Derogatory comments particularly towards women from the SCs and STs group also existed in some colleges to embarrass and harass them in public. Due to their multiple disadvantages, they were particularly prone on facing heightened vulnerabilities resulting in being pushed further into margins of higher education campuses.

Low Teacher–Student Informal Interactions

Our study shows that out-of-classroom teacher–student engagement is generally limited with all students, but particularly so with students from the disadvantaged social groups, who experience lower levels of informal interaction with their teachers. Two aspects affect the level of teacher–student out of classroom interactions: one, lack of awareness on the role of informal interaction with faculty on student success and, two, prejudiced views and lack of empathy which sustains the gulf in interactions. Prejudice and discrimination manifest in teacher–student informal interactions being divided on caste lines. Compared to their peers from advantaged groups, students from disadvantaged social groups experienced lower levels of interaction with their teachers outside classrooms; received little encouragement from teachers to organize events or participate in extra-curricular activities, which negatively impacted the confidence level of students and their active participation in campus activities.

Unsupportive–Inefficient Administrative Structures and Its Exclusionary Behaviour

It was found that although institutional mechanisms in the form of 'special cells' that aim to promote social inclusion and protect students from discrimination exist, many of these administrative arrangements do not function effectively. The reasons for inefficient functioning of the cells included

- Low compositional strength (in terms of number of members in the cell);
- Lack of administrative and infrastructure support received in coordination of cells (in terms of both physical infrastructure and personnel—in many places, cells were being managed by one faculty although it was a 'committee' comprised of faculty members);
- Cells were placed at lower levels in the administrative structure with limited statutory powers and access to resources;
- Non-transparent methods of appointment of the in-charge and members;

- Lack of training and guidance to manage such cells (e.g., it was reported that faculty-in-charges were not provided with adequate guidelines to run the cell and plan the activities and were functioning in a reactive manner, not preventive); and
- Lack of institutional-level planning and coordination with other cells to look after various dimensions of student welfare.

Reasons of poor implementation of such initiatives also included challenges related to apathy, prejudice and stereotypes which faculty members and administrators held that shaped their views and influenced effective functioning of these mechanisms. A distinction between 'fee paying general category' and 'sarkari damad' or 'category students' translated into differential treatment to the groups. Stipend distribution was one domain where SCs and STs experienced hostility, also suppression of information on stipends and scholarships resulted in students being unaware about their entitlements. In students' own words 'they (administration) feel that money is given from their pocket … staff member dealing with stipend distribution always get irritated by student queries.' SC and ST women students were prone to sexual harassment in the form of nonverbal gestures and 'night calls' from staff. However, fear of delay, stopping of stipend and other incentives prevented students to report harassment and complaints to college authorities.

Faculty-in-charge of equal opportunity cell and anti-sexual harassment cells admitted that students were scared to lodge a complaint. In most of the case study institutions, these cells received no complaints. As a result, they exist for 'name-sake', as expressed in the interviews with faculty members responsible of anti-sexual harassment cells across institutions. Some of those who were heading the cells had to make a conscious effort to 'balance' the activities of the cells with the 'reputation' of the institute—as 'too many complaints would curtail our publicity … it (becomes) a problem (for) the institute's reputation.' The belief that too many complaints on sexual harassment will curtail the reputation of college is indicative of internal pressures that faculty-in-charge experience while managing such an important cell. The faculty-in-charge also had to confront with their male colleagues who were mostly non-supportive to activities of the cell. Active engagement often fetched them label of 'women activist'. Thus, an overall negative institutional culture, instead of an individual, was responsible for ineffective functioning of the cells.

Low Rates of Participation in Orientation Programme and in Extra-Curricular Activities

As a result of the cumulative impact of prejudiced institutional culture (comprising caste-based interactions with their peers and teachers, unsupportive administration and non-functional institutional mechanisms of protection against discrimination), students from disadvantaged social groups were more likely to struggle with engaging in extra-curricular and other campus activities, such as orientation programmes, clubs and societies furthering their marginalization.

Rate of participation in orientation programmes, which are particularly important for the first-generation learners, low-income students, and students from disadvantaged social groups, was lower among these students as compared to their peers. This is despite the fact that the non-traditional learners were less likely to have pre-college access to avenues for college-study preparation. Low rates of participation in orientation programmes explain why the overall experience for the students from the disadvantaged social groups in initial days of college was relatively poor vis-à-vis the rest of their peers. Students found it difficult to adjust academically and socially, found the social and cultural life of campus strange and reported facing a feeling of 'fish out of water' during that period. This implies that the transition from school to higher education was difficult for the students from the disadvantaged social groups. Disadvantaged students were also more likely to be unaware of orientation programmes, welcome parties and extra-curricular activities being organized by the cells vis-à-vis non-SC/ST/OBC students. The students from SC and ST social groups highlighted lack of awareness of location of information boards; hesitancy and lack of confidence to seek information from others.

As compared to their peers from state universities and colleges, students from relatively more selective institutions (in Delhi and Karnataka) were more likely to attend an orientation programme organized by their academic departments, providing an opportunity for closer interactions with administrators and faculty members. Institutions in Bihar, Kerala and Uttar Pradesh, providing broader access to students from the disadvantaged groups, managed to organize the orientation programme for all first-year students collectively (not by department). Further, there is discipline stratification in opportunities for students for a successful transition to college. Students from institutions offering STEM subjects were more likely to access support programmes arranged by their institutions, as compared to institutions offering social sciences, arts and humanities. Within the public higher education system, therefore, there exists a situation where there is unequal access to opportunities that are focused on their smooth transition when they come to college.

Participation in extra-curricular activities across institutions was low (only 35% students) with more boys than girls and lower participation of scheduled tribes. Reasons for low participation of students in extra-curricular activities in general and specifically of students from the scheduled tribe groups and women ranged from individual and institutional factors. Individual factor was mainly related to students not having time as they were engaged in part-time jobs. Institutional factors included a limited number of extra-curricular activities being organized by their institution, lack of encouragement from teachers, informal groups being formed on the basis of social group identity such as caste, region, unsafe campus, especially for girls and stigmatization of activities where disadvantaged students were active.

In summary, our findings suggest while there is a softening effect of discrimination from its cruellest form due to strict implementation of legal measures, indirect forms of discrimination mostly exist in non-physical terrains or symbolic world of social, academic and administrative spaces. In the academic space, while physical segregation is no longer a practice, student groups get in fact, segregated in different groups based on the amount of attention and support received from teachers. Identity-based physical violence is also not reported in social spaces; however, discrimination takes the form of self-imposed segregation, derogatory remarks, humiliation, mocking and micro-aggressions experienced on a daily basis. Social distance between themselves and their peers result in an inhospitable campus environment, marginalization and isolation of students from disad-vantaged social groups. The receptivity of the administration towards disadvantaged is also poor, unsupportive and often negative. Absence of a supportive environment to overcome challenges faced by students from the disadvantaged social groups compromises their academic integration and sense of belonging to the campus community. In the section that follows, we will discuss institutional strategies to respond to academic and social challenges faced by students from traditionally underrepresented social groups.

MANAGING STUDENT DIVERSITY IN ACADEMIC AND SOCIAL DOMAINS

As more non-traditional learners from diverse socio-economic groups arrive on college campuses with varying levels of academic prepared-ness, managing diversity has two dimensions. First, managing students with diverse academic backgrounds in the classrooms by teachers; and second, managing student diversity in the social realm by the institu-tional administrators. As we have shown, since the faculty members and administrators belong to social groups different from that of the students, it is crucial that in the management of student diversity, institutional actors act with empathy (Varghese 2018) and teachers practice pedagogy of care (Meyers 2009) to provide a supportive learn-ing environment.

A multipronged strategy is required to engage students from disad-vantaged social groups in academic and social spheres. Using multiple strategies in combination is more effective than using one in isolation. For example, lack of inclusion in out-of-classroom social spaces can affect the capacity of students to integrate academically. Likewise, aca-demic under preparedness and low academic performance in classrooms can result in lack of engagement and levels of inclusion in campus activities. Moreover, obstacles that students reported were in conjunc-tion and not singly: in group discussions students across the institutions indicated that low competency in English language, poor information about student support system, low teacher–student interactions, hostility because of reservation policy and difficulty to form peer group were major obstacles for them. Therefore, it is important that institutions draw a comprehensive strategic plan that encompasses actions to foster engagement in the academic (classroom) and social (out-of-class) spaces. In this section, we will discuss strategies for improving integration of students in the academic domain and achieving social inclusion on campuses.

Strategies to Achieve Academic Integration

Academic underpreparation of the disadvantaged students for college work, in the form of low levels of proficiency in language, low pre-college scores and low academic social capital places these students at academic risk requiring concerted efforts to address their vulnerabilities. To begin with, efforts are required for smooth transition from high school to college and active targeted support is needed when they are in college. Bridge programmes involving collaboration between high school and colleges have proven to be successful for a smooth transition (Ross et al. 2012).

Provision of academic support programmes particularly in the first year as this is a 'critical year' for student life determines decision-making process of students to stay or leave the campus. Studies have shown that this is the year, especially first six weeks that determines whether the student will continue or drop out (Daubman et al.1985, Astin 1993, Tinto 1988, 2006, Trotter and Roberts 2006, Pasceralla and Terenzini 1991, Rayle and Chung 2007, Yorke and Longden 2008). It is important that language proficiency is assessed at the start of the college and continuous support is provided for language fluency in the medium of instruction followed in institutions.

Systematic and comprehensive academic support services in the form of remediation, learning laboratories and student learning centres, tutorial services and monitoring of students' progress are some established strategies that directly address academic risks of students (Tupan-Wenno et al. 2016). Learning laboratories and student learning centres are based on the concept of active and collaborative learning and is similar to the concept of learning communities. Learning community (LC) provides a network of support and this supportive community facilitates students' participation in social and academic spheres of colleges (Tinto 1997). Astin (1985) defines learning communities as 'small subgroups of students...characterized by a common sense of purpose...that can be used to build a sense of group identity, cohesiveness and uniqueness that encourage continuity and integration in diverse curricular and co-curricular experiences' (as cited in Kellog 1999). LCs also create a sense of common purpose, which enables intellectual interactions of students with their peers and teachers (Kellog 1999). In order that students are prepared for classroom discussions in advance, digital contents on subjects can also be made available by teachers.

There is a need for effective implementation of existing remediation programme in colleges and university for the benefit of disadvantaged students. Institutions where remediation programmes are in operation, need to strengthen their existing teaching–learning process. Institutions should ensure that information related to remedial and other support programmes are widely disseminated among the student population. It should also be ensured that there is no stigma attached to attending these programmes. Institutions can also organize special classes for improving general competency levels of students which could include various academic skills such as comprehension, presentation and writing. In addition, providing training for teachers to deal with academically diverse student groups is of paramount importance.

By practising pedagogy of care which includes positive teacher–student interactions, encouraging interactions in lectures, being more engaged, investing time in knowing and understanding their students, providing individual appointments and providing high levels of support, faculty members can have a positive influence on cognitive and non-cognitive adjustments of diverse student population. Faculty mentoring and peer mentoring mechanisms can be put in place to provide regular support for students. Literature on student success has established that teachers' commitment and concern towards students' welfare and positive and continuous feedback process have a significant impact on intellectual outcomes, students' social development, self-worth, students' confidence and culture of the institutions in general (Endo and Harpel 1982, Astin 1993, Thompson 2001, Cotten and Wilson, 2006,

Kuh 1995, Cole 2007, Meyers 2009, Larsen 2015). Tinto and Pusser (2006) have argued that 'students are more likely to persist when they find themselves in settings that are committed to their success, hold high expectations for their learning, provide needed academic and social support, and frequent feedback about their performance, and actively involve them with other students and faculty in learning' (p.4).

Findings from our study further suggest that there exists a positive relationship between the social background of the teacher and academic experiences of students from the socially disadvantaged groups. Positive correlation coefficients seen for both SC and ST students indicate that these students felt that teachers from their own background gave them more attention and provided them academic support than other teachers. Feeling of not being welcomed and tensions related to social background can also sometimes create barriers for the students from the disadvantaged groups to interact with faculty outside of the class-room and subsequently influence their educational experience (Allen 1992, Davis 1991, Hurtado 1994). To create an engaging academic environment for students for the disadvantaged social groups, composition of faculty members need to be represented with a wide array of backgrounds.

Strategies to Achieve Inclusion in Social Domains

Institutional arrangements in the form of student support services can mediate experiences of students and address challenges related to marginalization, isolation and ghettoization. Existing literature establishes that institutional strategies such as participation in orientation to college programmes and in extra-curricular activities play a positive role in promoting outcomes related to learning (e.g. critical thinking), forming mixed-peer groups and developing a sense of belonging to the campus community (Moore et al. 2004, Pascarella and Terenzini 2005).

Participation in orientation programmes was seen to positively impact transition to college and the extent of inclusion in social dimensions. Orientation programmes are particularly important for the first-generation learners, low-income students and students from the disadvantaged social groups, as these groups are less likely to have pre-college access to avenues that would prepare them for college. Our research shows a positive relationship between participation in orientation programme and students experience in initial days social adjustment to the college environment. Attendance in orientation programme had a positive relationship with the experience of feeling welcomed and finding the new place interesting.

For establishing process of inclusion, it is important that efforts of the administration are directed towards providing equity of support and help. Improving access to information on orientation programmes, orienting students to academic, social and physical geographies of the campus, improving rates of participation and creating awareness on its benefits among the students from the disadvantaged students are important ways of ensuring that students feel that they are included. Organization and promoting participation in orientation programmes to acquaint students with general codes of conducts (on anti-ragging rules and other codes of conduct) will also indicate an attempt on behalf of the campus administrators to create an environment conducive for diversity.

Participation in extra-curricular activities also had a positive impact on the extent of social inclusion of students in the campuses. The correlational analysis from our study shows that those students who were a member of an extra-curricular activity were generally more positive about their college. That is, they found their college interesting, had access to leadership roles and were able to share their personal feelings with others, while those who were not a member of extra-curricular activities were cautious to interact with students from other castes. To address the concerns and needs of target groups, it is important that special cells providing such student support services are more functional and effective.

To create a culture of respect, empathy and care, a more serious effort from the part of institutions is required that promotes non-cognitive and social life of student body. Informal interactions with faculty members which can take the form of being an adviser or informally engage with students to discuss personal issues are particularly important for student well-being, especially in the wake of large number of first-generation learners with lower levels of college preparation. It is widely accepted in the educational literature that the teacher has an important role to play as a guide and mentor.

Across peers, well planned and inclusive extra-curricular activities need to be introduced to promote intergroup interaction. Similar approach can also be used in classroom transactions. Instead of individual academic activities, culture of group assignments and collective learning may be promoted. Deliberate programmatic efforts, through diversity workshops and intergroup dialogues inside class and on campus, can provide an understanding about the diverse others and cultivate skills for accepting of diversity in general. Institutions play a role in fostering learning about diverse others and dialogues across differences which in turn has an effect on the campus culture. Such efforts also enhance students' and teachers' capacity to be sensitive towards diversity and promote civic learning (Thorat and Sabharwal 2013).

CONCLUDING OBSERVATIONS

The development of higher education system from an elite stage to a stage of massification, alongside concerns about equity in higher education, has led to changes in the composition of student population. As this chapter has demonstrated, massification of the sector has heralded the entry of students who had traditionally been underrepresented in higher education. Higher education institutions, which in the past served a more homogeneous elite student body, today have expanded access to students from diverse social, economic and academic backgrounds.

While this is a very positive development, a major concern that is brought to the fore is the way in which higher education institutions are managing the challenges faced by a diverse student body both inside and outside classrooms. This chapter showed that many institutions of higher education remain under-prepared in adapting to meet the educational needs of diverse learners and cultivating a socially inclusive campus environment. It was argued that institutions have not been able to adequately account for the challenges faced by students from the disadvantaged social groups, and that the institutional capacity to manage this diversity is rather weak.

The major academic challenges faced by students from disadvantaged social groups include being at risk of falling into a low-performance trap and remaining less integrated academically in the classrooms. Accommodating a more diverse student population creates new tensions in higher education institutions as while the point of entry has been 'relaxed', indicators of academic success at the point of exit call for significant academic support. Students from diverse social groups who have varying pre-college academic experiences and levels of college-preparedness in order to persist and successfully graduate from college require additional learning inputs than the rest to bridge their academic gap. This academic gap is a manifestation of the consequences of cumulative disadvantages that they face. In addition, biases, stereotype threats and uncaring behaviour of their teachers undermine their self-esteem, resulting in reduced confidence to engage in the teaching–learning interactions within the classrooms. There are government initiatives for academic support, for example, remedial coaching, but these are isolated interventions and its implementation is also weak.

Also, not feeling included in social realm emerges as a major challenge in relation to the integration of non-traditional students within higher education institutions. Varying pre-college academic experiences and stigma attached to their social group result in their marginalization in campuses and identity-based peer-group formation, leading to a sense of isolation and ghettoization. These factors affect the ability of students to participate in extracurricular activities and to realize their full potential. The challenges get accentuated because the institutional mechanisms which support and protect the interest of students from socially excluded groups, such as equal opportunity cells are weak and ineffective. As a result of insensitive and unresponsive institutional culture which also reproduces dominant norms and ideologies, mechanisms of managing experiences in academic and social spheres are mostly ineffective and students remain unsupported. A substantial change in this scenario can be brought about if interventions for academic integration are made in the classrooms, through supportive teaching–learning strategies and pedagogies. Similarly, strengthening of student support services is equally important to establish processes for social inclusion of students from the disadvantaged backgrounds, along with ensuring that respect for diversity becomes a central value while designing institutional mechanisms that aim to achieve student success in higher education.

REFERENCES

Allen, W. R. 1992. The Color of Success: African-American College Student Outcomes at Predominantly White and Historically Black Public Colleges and Universities. *Harvard Educational Review* 62(1): 26–44.

Astin, A. W. 1975. *Preventing Students from Dropping Out*. San Francisco, CA: Jossey-Bass.

Astin, A. W. 1985. *Achieving Educational Excellence: A Critical Assessment of Priorities and Practices in Higher Education*. San Francisco, CA: Jossey-Bass.

Astin, A. W. 1993. *What Matters in College? Four Critical Years Revisited* (Vol. 1). San Francisco, CA: Jossey-Bass.

Bensimon, E. M. 2007. 'The Underestimated Significance of Practitioner Knowledge in the Scholarship of Student Success'. *Review of Higher Education* 30(4): 441–469.

Bourdieu, P., and J. C. Passeron. 1990. *Reproduction in Education, Society and Culture* (Vol. 4). Thousand Oaks, CA: SAGE Publications.

Clark, B. 1973. 'Development of Sociology of Higher Education'. *Sociology of Education* 46(1): 2–14.

Cole, D. 2007. 'Do Interracial Interactions Matter? An Examination of Student–Faculty Contact and Intellectual Self-concept'. *The Journal of Higher Education* 78(3): 249–281.

Coleman, J. S. 1988. 'Social Capital in the Creation of Human Capital'. *American Journal of Sociology* 94: S95–S120.

Cotten, S. R., and B. Wilson. 2006. Student–Faculty Interactions: Dynamics and Determinants. *Higher Education* 51(4): 487–519.

Daubman, K. A., V. G. Williams, D. H. Johnson, and F. Crump. 1985. 'Time of Withdrawal and Academic Performance: Implications for Withdrawal Policies'. *Journal of College Student Personnel* 26(6): 518–523.

Davis, R. B. 1991. 'Social Support Networks and Undergraduate Student Academic-Success-Related Outcomes: A Comparison of Black Students on Black and White Campuses'. In *College in Black and White: African American Students in Predominantly White and in Historically Black Public Universities*, edited by W. R. Allen, E. G. Epps, and N. Z. Haniff, 147–153. Albany, New York: State University Press of New York.

Endo, J., and R. Harpel. 1982. 'The Effect of Student–Faculty Interaction on Students' Educational Outcomes'. *Research in Higher Education* 16(2): 115–138.

Ferrier, F., and S. North. 2009. 'Social Inclusion in VET and Higher Education'. Melbourne, VIC: Paper presented at a CEET/Faculty of Education Seminar, Monash University.

Henry, O., and M. Ferry. 2017. 'When Cracking the JEE Is Not Enough'. *South Asia Multidisciplinary Academic Journal* 15: 1–28.

Hurtado, S. 1994. 'The Institutional Climate for Talented Latino Students'. *Research in Higher Education* 35(1): 539–569.

Hurtado, S., and D. F. Carter. 1997. 'Effects of College Transition and Perceptions of the Campus Racial Climate on Latino College Students' Sense of Belonging'. *Sociology of Education* 70(4): 324–345.

Kuh, G. 1995. 'The Other Curriculum: Out-of-class Experiences Associated with Student Learning and Personal Development'. *Journal of Higher Education* 66(2): 123–155.

Larsen, A. S. 2015. 'Who Cares? Developing a Pedagogy of Caring in Higher Education'. All Graduate Theses and Dissertations, 4287.

Meyers, S. A. 2009. 'Do Your Students Care Whether You Care About Them?' *College Teaching* 57(4): 205–210.

Ministry of Human Resource Development (MHRD). 2015. *All India Survey of Higher Education 2014–15*. New Delhi: Department of Higher Education, Government of India.

Ministry of Human Resource Development (MHRD). 2017. *All India Survey of Higher Education 2016–17*. New Delhi: Department of Higher Education, Government of India.

Moore, J. L. III, L. A. Flowers, L. A. Guion, Y. Zang, and D. L. Staten. 2004. 'Improving the Experiences of Non-persistent African American Males in Engineering Programs: Implications for Success'. *National Association of Student Affairs Professionals Journal* 7: 105–120.

Museus, S. D., and U. M. Jayakumar, eds. 2012. *Creating Campus Cultures: Fostering Success among the Racially Diverse Student Populations*. New York: Routledge.

Pascarella, E., and P. Terenzini. 1980. 'Predicting Freshman Persistence and Voluntary Dropout Decisions from a Theoretical Model'. *Journal of Higher Education* 51: 60–75.

Pascarella, E. T., & Terenzini, P. T. (2005). How College Affects Students: A Third Decade of Research. Volume 2. Jossey-Bass, An Imprint of Wiley.

Planning Commission. 2001. *National Human Development Report 2001*. New Delhi: Government of India.

Planning Commission. 2008. *Inclusive Growth*. Vol. 1. New Delhi: Government of India.

Rayle, A. D., and K. Y. Chung. 2007. Revisiting First-year College Students' Mattering: Social Support, Academic Stress and the Mattering Experience. *Journal of College Student Retention: Research, Theory & Practice* 9(1): 21–37.

Ross, T., K. Grace, R. Amy, K. R. Angelina, Z. Jijun, K. Paul, and M. Eileen. 2012. 'Higher Education: Gaps in Access and Persistence Study.' Statistical Analysis Report, National Center for Education Statistics, US Department of Education.

Sabharwal, N. S., and C. M. Malish. 2016. Diversity and Discrimination in Higher Education: A Study of Institutions in Selected States of India, CPRHE Research Report. New Delhi: CPRHE, NIEPA.

Sabharwal, N. S., and C. M. Malish. 2018. *Diversity and Discrimination in Higher Education: A Study of Institutions in Selected States of India, CPRHE Research Papers 10*. New Delhi: Centre for Policy Research in Higher Education, National Institute of Educational Planning and Administration.

Sabharwal, N. S., S. K. Thorat, T. Balasubramanyam, and D. Diwakar. 2014. 'Diversity, Academic Performance, and Discrimination: A Case Study of a Higher Educational Institution'. IIDS Working Paper no. 4, vol. 8, Indian Institute of Dalit Studies.

Sivasankaran, C. J., and P. K. Ravindran. 2004. 'An Investigation into the Problem of Wastage in the Engineering Colleges in Kerala. Evaluation. Report Submitted to Kerala Research Programme on Local Development, Centre for Development Studies, Thiruvananthapuram, Kerala.

Stephens, N. M., S. Fryberg, and H. R. Markus. 2012. 'It's Your Choice: How the Middleclass Model of Independence Disadvantages Working-class Americans'. In *Facing Social Class: How Societal Rank Influences Interaction*, edited by S. T. Fiske and H. R. Markus, 87–106. New York: Russell SAGE Foundation.

Swail, W. S., K. E. Redd, and L. W. Perna. 2003. *Retaining Minority Students in Higher Education: A Framework for Success*. ASHE-ERIC Higher Education Report. Jossey-Bass Higher and Adult Education Series. 30(2): 1–187.

Thompson, M. 2001. 'Informal Student–Faculty Interaction: Its Relationship to Educational Gains in Science and Mathematics among Community College Students'. *Community College Review* 29(1): 35–57.

Thorat, S. K., and N. Sabharwal. 2013. *Need for Policy Reforms in Higher Education: Education for Civic Learning, Democratic Engagement and Social Change. Policy Brief, No. 14*. New Delhi: Indian Institute of Dalit Studies.

Tierney, W. G. 1988. 'Organizational Culture in Higher Education: Defining the Essentials'. *The Journal of Higher Education* 59(1): 2–21.

Tierney, W.G., and J. C. Duncheon (eds.). (2015): The Problem of College Readiness. State University of New York Press, Albany.

Tinto, V. 1975. 'Dropout from Higher Education: A Theoretical Synthesis of Recent Research'. *Review of Educational Research* 45(1): 89–125.

Tinto, V. 1993. *Leaving College: Rethinking the Causes and Cures of Student Attrition*. 2nd ed. Chicago and London: The University of Chicago Press.

Tinto, V. 1997. 'Classrooms as Communities: Exploring the Educational Character of Student Persistence'. *The Journal of Higher Education* 68(6): 599–623.

Tinto, V. 1998. 'Colleges as Communities: Taking Research on Student Persistence Seriously'. *The Review of Higher Education* 21(2): 167–177.

Tinto, V. 2006. 'Research and Practice of Student Retention: What Next?' *Journal of College Student Retention: Research, Theory & Practice* 8(1): 1–19.

Tinto, V., and B. Pusser. 2006. *Moving from Theory to Action: Building a Model of Institutional Action for Student Success*. Washington, DC: National Postsecondary Education Cooperative, Department of Education.

Tinto, V. 2014. 'Tinto's South Africa Lectures'. *Journal of Students Affair in Africa* 2(2): 5–28.

Trotter, E., and C. A. Roberts. 2006. 'Enhancing the Early Student Experience'. *Higher Education Research and Development* 25(4): 371–386.

Tupan-Wenno, M., A. F. Camilleri, M. Fröhlich, and S. King. 2016. *Effective Approaches to Enhancing the Social Dimension of Higher Education*. Malta: Knowledge Innovation Centre.

Varghese, N.V. 2015. *Challenges of Massification of Higher Education in India, CPRHE Research Papers 1*. New Delhi: Centre for Policy Research in Higher Education, National Institute of Educational Planning and Administration.

Varghese, N.V. 2018. 'Criticality, Empathy and Welfare in Educational Discourses'. *Contemporary Education Dialogue* 15(2): 1–21.

Varghese, N.V., N. S. Sabharwal, and C. M. Malish, eds. 2017. *India Higher Education Report 2016: Equity*. New Delhi: SAGE Publication.

Winkle-Wagner, R., P. J. Bowman, and E. P. S. John. 2012. *Expanding Postsecondary Opportunity for Underrepresented Students: Theory and Practice of Academic Capital Formation*. New York: AMS Press.

Yorke, M., and B. Longden. 2008. *The First-year Experience of Higher Education in the UK*. York: The Higher Education Academy.

Zea, M. C., C. A. Reisen, C. Beil, and R. D. Caplan. 1997. 'Predicting Intention to Remain in College among Ethnic Minority and Nonminority Students'. *The Journal of Social Psychology* 137(2): 149–160.

About the Editors and Contributors

EDITORS

N.V. Varghese is Vice Chancellor, National Institute of Educational Planning and Administration and also the founding director of the Centre for Policy Research in Higher Education at National Institute of Educational Planning and Administration (NIEPA). Formerly, he was the Head, Governance and Management of Education, International Institute of Educational Planning (IIEP/UNESCO), Paris.

Garima Malik is Assistant Professor at the Centre for Policy Research in Higher Education at the NIEPA. Previously, she was an Assistant Professor of Economics at University of Delhi. She was a fellow at the Indian Council for Research on International Economic Relations and worked as an economist with Tata Services Limited and Pricewaterhouse Coopers.

CONTRIBUTORS

M. Anandakrishnan is former Chairman, Indian Institute of Technology Kanpur, and formerly he was the Vice-Chairman, Tamil Nadu State Council for Higher Education and Vice Chancellor of Anna University, Chennai.

Narayanan Annalakshmi is Professor in the Department of Psychology, Bharathiar University, Coimbatore, Tamil Nadu. She was a scientist in the Defence Research and Development Organization, Ministry of Defence, Government of India.

Rajalakshmi Bhavana is Associate Professor at Department of Education Technology, Bharathiar University, Coimbatore, Tamil Nadu.

Sudhanshu Bhushan is Professor and Head of the Department of Higher and Professional Education at NIEPA. Previously, he served as the Additional Director, SIEMAT, Patna.

Supriya Chaudhuri is Professor Emeritus, Department of English, and has served as Coordinator, Centre of Advanced Study, Head, Department of English, and Director, School of Languages and Linguistics. She is also Faculty Coordinator, Project E–QUAL, Jadavpur University, and member, Joint Working Group in Critical Thinking and Knowledge Systems.

Bhuvana Esther is Assistant Professor and Head, Department of Public Administration, Government Arts College, Coimbatore, Tamil Nadu.

Rajen Harshe is Visiting Professor in the Department of International Relations, South Asian University, New Delhi. He is also former Vice Chancellor, Allahabad University.

Kuldeep Mathur was Professor at the Centre for Political Studies and Academic Director at the Centre for the Study of Law and Governance, Jawaharlal Nehru University, New Delhi. Previously, he was Director of the NIEPA.

Pankaj Mittal is Secretary General, Association of Indian Universities. She was formerly Additional Secretary in University Grants Commission (UGC), New Delhi. Previously, she was the first Vice Chancellor of Bhagat Phool Singh Mahila Vishwavidyalaya, Haryana.

Mohd Muzammil was Professor of Economics in Lucknow University and former Vice Chancellor of Dr Bhim Rao Ambedkar University, Agra. Earlier he had also served as Vice Chancellor of Mahatma Jyotiba Phule Rohilkhand University, Bareilly.

Furqan Qamar is currently Professor, Centre for Management Studies, Jamia Millia Islamia. He was Secretary General, Association of Indian Universities (AIU); former Vice Chancellor, Central University of Himachal Pradesh and University of Rajasthan; and former Adviser (Education), Planning Commission.

I. Ramabrahmam is currently Vice Chancellor, Central University of Odisha. He was formerly Professor, Department of Political Science, School of Social Sciences, University of Hyderabad.

Rakesh Raman is Professor, Department of Economics, Banaras Hindu University.

G. D. Sharma is currently CEO at the Society for Education and Economic Development, and is a former Professor, NIEPA.

Nidhi S. Sabharwal is Associate Professor at the Centre for Policy Research in Higher Education at the NIEPA. Previously, she served as the Director of the Indian Institute of Dalit Studies.

G. Umamaheswararao is Research Scholar, Department of Political Science, School of Social Sciences, University of Hyderabad.

Index

academic autonomy, 15
Academic Council, 162
activities of the student union (AUSU), 209
Advanced Technology Cell (ATC), 239
affiliated colleges
  academic management
    university vs autonomous colleges, 137
  admission process, 120
  autonomous colleges, 124–125
  concept, 133, 135
  concept of autonomy
    government and government-aided colleges, 149
    private self financing college, 149
  conducting of examination, 121
  Constitution, 112
  degree awarding, 150
  evolution, 111
  freedom to innovate and change, 140
    new courses, 141
    system of evaluation, 142
  good governance, 117–118
  governance mechanism, 116
  growth, 114
  growth and development
    autonomous by states, distribution, 143
  growth of autonomous colleges, 145
  implementation progress and problems, 136–137
  method of transaction, 138
  monitoring blueprint, 126–127
  new management structure, negotiation, 139
  policy intervention, 150
  potential for excellence, 123–124
  recruitment of faculty member, 139
  RUSA, 125
  single and multi-faculty colleges, 135
  size, 115
  studies, 134
  teachers association and unions, 140
  teaching and learning
    evaluation, 140
    quality, 122
  university, difference, 143
affiliation colleges
  types, 113–114
Agricultural and Veterinary Education, 51
All India Council for Technical Education (AICTE), 55, 63
All India Survey of Higher Education, 280
All India Survey of Higher Education (AISHE), 222
  Report 2017–18, 297
Allahabad University Students Union (AUSU), 205
Amendment to the Constitution of India, 42nd, 71
Association of Indian Universities (AIU), 52, 53, 55, 210

autonomy
committees and commissions,
158–161

Bar Council of India (BCI), 55
Bharathiar University
academic autonomy, 261
accountability, 256
communication, 260
equity/fairness, 259
participation of faculty, 259
policy effectiveness, 262
quality and excellence
data collection, 251
database and methodology, 248
departments, sampling, 250
governance & management
processes, 254–255
institutional autonomy and
decision-making process,
252–253
instruments used, 251
mixed method approach, 249
quantitative data, 252
students, sampling, 250
teachers, sampling, 250
tools and challenges, 255–256
response to claims, 258
TANSCHE, 261
transparency, 257

Career Advancement Scheme (CAS),
167
Central Advisory Board of Education
(CABE), 54
Central Council of Homeopathy
(CCH), 56
Central Council of Indian Medicine
(CCIM), 56
Centrally Sponsored Scheme (CSS),
72
Centre for Policy Research in Higher
Education (CPRHE), 161
study, 317

Civil Services Examinations (CSE),
204
classroom environment and challenges, 322
academic disparities, 327
correlational analysis, 326
faculty members, absenteeism, 325
negative attitude, 326
teachers and lack of mentoring,
324
remedial coaching, implementation, 325
un-conducive teaching-learning
processes, 322
college management system, 118–120
Commissions and Committees, 65
Common Entrance Tests (CETs), 75
corporate governance, 6
Council of Architecture (CoA), 56

degree of autonomy, 13
Dental Council of India (DCI), 56
depoliticise universities, 213
Distance Education Bureau (DEB), 56
Distance Education Council (DEC),
56, 64
Dr Malcolm M. Adisheshiah
initiative, 134

e-Pathshala, 223
eligible enrolment ratio (EER), 298
Enhancing Quality Assurance
Management and
Benchmarking Strategies
in Indian Universities
(EQUAM-BI), 241
excessive or ineffective regulation, 61

Global Initiative for Academic
Networks (GIAN) pro-
grammes, 239
global ranking agencies, 62
Gnanam committee report, 14
governance, 1

governance structures
institutional level, 12
system level, 10–12
governance
higher education in India
accountability, 7
challenges, 293
collegial model, 7
fundamental shift, 5
globalization processes, 5
intra-institutional relations, 3
locus of decision, 7
NPM, framework, 5
privatization, 5
state controlled model, 4
state led model, 4
structures, evolution, 8–10
new conceptualization, 28
structures in universities, 2
government arts college
autonomy, 265
best practices, 266
constant expansion, 267
equity/fairness, 264
participation/shared governance, 264
policy effectiveness, 265
responsiveness, 263
top-down communication, 264
transparency, 263
Gross Enrolment Ratio (GER), 223
guest faculty phenomena
Kerala, 287–288
Tamil Nadu, 284–287

Higher Education and Empowerment
Regulatory Agency
(HEERA), 63, 229
Higher Education Commission of
India, 36
Higher Education Council of India
(HECI) Bill, 229
Higher Education Financing Agency
(HEFA), 16, 59, 229, 299

higher education governance
role, 153
forces of globalization, 155
support for education, 155
higher education in India, 297
academic freedom and autonomy, 96
accountability
dimensions, 92–93
goals, 97
measures, 88
system, difficulties, 93
accreditation and quality assurance, 58
NAAC, 58
NBA, 59
NIRF, 59
affiliating universities, 45
AIU, 55
autonomy and accountability,
global trends, 104
BIC, 55
capacity enhancement, 299
CCH, 56
CCIM, 56
centrally funded institutions, 100
CoA, 56
colleges, 46
curriculum interventions, 303
DCI, 56
DEB, 56
DEC, 56
Deemed Universities, 101
degree of autonomy, 91
effective and useful accountability, 95
effective governance, 310–312
enrolment, 48
expansion, 316
fee regulatory committees, 60
financing, 312
governance
pattern, 100
governing boards, role, 98

HEFA, 59
ICAR, 57
INC, 57
innovative approach, 299
institutions, 44
legal and regulatory framework,
    47–53
measures, 301
MHRD, 54
    AICTE, 55
MIC, 57
MOOCs course, 307
nature of interference, 101–104
NCTE, 57
PCI, 57
policy implications, 68–69
policy messages and road map
    academics, 271
    accountability, 274
    administrative procedures, 272
    shared governance, 273
    transparency, 273
political influence, 97
primary accountabilities, 94
quality and excellence, challenges,
    268–271
quality education, promotion,
    305–307
RCI, 57
regulatory bodies, 53
regulatory framework, critique,
    60–68
role of governing bodies, 89–90
SCHE, 59
self-accountability, 95
Stand Alone Institutes (SAIs), 47
state funded institutions, 101
SWAYAM platform, 308
system, 112
trends and expansion, 89
typology of institutions, 90–91
UGC, 58
university governance, 98
    nature, 98

VCI, 58
higher education institutions, 15
Higher Education System, 176
higher educational institutions (HEI),
    50, 174
    governance & management system,
        175, 176
    accountability, 191
    effective & efficient, 190–191
    first phase, 177
    first tier, 182–186
    internal autonomy, 187–189
    methodology, 181
    participatory/shared leadership,
        187
    sample institutions, 182
    second phase, 178
    second tier, 186
    third phase, 179
    transparency, 189
transition phase, 192
    accountability, 195–196
    delivery, 196–197
    shared governance/autonomy,
        192–195
    vice chancellors (VCs), 180

Independent Regulatory Authority in
    Higher Education (IRAHE),
    63
India Higher Education Report 2019
    (IHER), 16
    governance & management system,
        17–18
    macro issues of governance, 17
    quality management, 18
Indian Agricultural Research Institute
    in Delhi, 33
Indian Council for Agriculture
    Research (ICAR), 51, 57
Indian Institute of Science in
    Bangalore, 33
Indian Nursing Council (INC),
    57

institutional autonomy to decide
curriculum, academic programmes,
& teaching method, 165
finances and administration, 167
issues related to quality assurance,
165
staff employment issues, 166
students-related issues, 165
institutional governance
autonomy, 155–158
models, 6
institutional integration approach, 319
institutional quality
concept, 224
restructuring process, 224
data, 235
drive for quality and excellence,
240
ESG, principles, 232
excellence in Indian HEIs,
231–234
funding, 228–231
GIAN programmes, 239
ground reality, 230
India, regulating and assessing,
225–228
innovation, 242
NAAC, 233
state universities, problems, 238
times higher education (THE), 236
provisions, 237
weightages, 232
integration in academic and social
domains
non-traditional learners, 318
policy environment of equality and
non-discrimination, 321
pre-college academic experiences,
320
socio-economic and academic
backgrounds, 318
Internal Quality Assurance Cell
(IQAC), 128, 241

International Network for Quality
Assurance Agencies
in Higher Education
(INQAAHE), 225

Jammu & Kashmir University
temporary teacher phenomenon,
289–291

Kothari Commission, 91
report of 1966, 14

Lord Macaulay's Education Minute,
37
Magna Charta Universitatum, 224

Management Information System
(MIS), 72
managing quality and excellence, 221
Medical Council of India (MCI), 11,
57
Memorandum of Understanding
(MoU), 207
Ministry of Human Resource
Development (MHRD), 11,
34, 54, 66, 72, 205
Motilal Nehru Medical College
(MLNC), 205

National Assessment and
Accreditation Council
(NAAC), 58, 203
National Board of Accreditation
(NBA), 59
National Commission for Higher
Education and Research
(NCHER), 63
bill, 230
National Commission Teachers, 135
National Council of Higher
Education, 135
National Council of Teacher
Education (NCTE), 57, 64

National Institutions Ranking
Framework (NIRF), 16, 59
National Knowledge Commission
(NKC), 63, 125, 222
National Mission on Education
through ICT (NMEICT),
300
National Policy on Education (NPE)
1986, 71, 134
neo-liberalism theory, 27
New Public Management (NPM), 5
approach, 179
non-teaching staff, 213–214
Non-University Institutions (NUIs),
47

online programs by universities, 308
promotions, 309
out-of class environment and challenges, 327
inefficient functioning, 330–332
low rates of participation, 332–334
low teacher-student informal interactions, 330
social division in friendship,
328–329

Pharmacy Council of India (PCI), 57
Policy Planning Committee (PPC),
169
Programme of Action (POA), 71
1992, 134
public private partnerships (PPP), 29
Centre for Civil Society, 31
Public Private Partnerships (PPP)
challenges, 31
public private partnerships (PPP)
Commissions and committees, 37
Committee, 32
entrepreneurs, 35
government and private sector,
29
government role, 31

higher education, 30
Higher Education Commission of
India, 36
higher education
level, 33
policies for privatization, 38
institutions, 34
institutions and researchers, 31
international donor agencies, 32
Lord Macaulay's Education
Minute, 37
organizational perspective, 39
privatization, neo-liberal solutions,
40
re-evaluation, 40
regulatory agencies, 40
University Grants Commission
(UGC), 36
wide appeal, 30
public universities, 61
Quality in Higher Education,
224

quality of education, 176

Rashtriya Uchchatar Shiksha Abhiyan
(RUSA), 68, 72, 125
Regional Higher Education Officers
(RHEOs), 128
Regulation Relating to the Funding
and Financing of Higher
Education, 59
regulatory body, 66
Rehabilitation Council of India
(RCI), 57
Revitalizing Infrastructure and System
in Education (RISE), 299

Sikkim University, 282
social stratification and social reproduction theory, 320
State Assessment and Accreditation
Council (SAAC), 128

State Councils of Higher Education
(SCHE), 59, 67, 72
activities, 84–85
advisory functions, 83
budget plans, 82
curriculum development, 82
directorate of collegiate education
in states, role, 73–74
financial management, 83
legal framework, 72
MHRD, 72
MIS, 72
powers and functions, 78
private higher educational regulatory commission/act, powers
and functions, 75
private university/educational
institutions, 75
regulation committee, composition, 75
structure and composition, 77–78
State Higher Education Councils
(SHECs), 12
State Public financing, 62
state-university relationship, 161–163
strength of teachers, 280
student diversity in academic and
social domains, 334
institutional arrangements,
335–337
strategies, 335–337
students unions, 212
Swaroop Rani Nehru Hospital
(SRNH), 205

temporary teachers
challenges, 291–293
magnitude, 282
Times Higher Education (THE), 225,
237

universities and colleges in India
system, 131
universities in India, 50
University Education Commission, 87
university governance, 2
university governing boards, 104
University Grants Commission
(UGC), 15, 51, 58, 60, 283
regulation, 278–280
university level institutions (ULIs), 47
University of Allahabad (UoA), 200
academic council (AC), 204
apprenticeship, 204
AUSU politics, 210
centrals (CUs) character, 203
committee report, 211
elections, 209
executive council (EC), 205
faculty members, 208
pecuniary gains and privileges, 204
problems, 202
recruited administrative officers,
216
student indiscipline, 208
University of Hyderabad (UoH), 203
university
defined, 201
Veterinary Council of India (VCI), 58